The
Two-Lane
Gourmet

The
Two-Lane
Gourmet

Fine Wine Trails, Superb Inns, and
Exceptional Dining Through California,
Oregon, and Washington

Tom Snyder

Foreword by Frank J. Prial

St. Martin's Griffin ✿ New York

In using this guide, please be assured that no fees were solicited
or accepted by either author or publisher for any listings
or recommendations appearing herein.

www.stmartins.com

Book design by Michelle McMillian

Excerpt from *The Grail: A Year Ambling & Shambling Through an Oregon Vineyard in Pursuit of
the Best Pinot Noir Wine in the Whole Wild World* by Brian Doyle. Copyright © 2006 by Brian
Doyle. Reprinted with the permission of Oregon State University Press.

Library of Congress Cataloging-in-Publication Data

Snyder, Tom, 1934–
  Two-lane gourmet : fine wine trails, superb inns, and exceptional dining through California, Oregon, and Washington / Tom Snyder ; foreword by Frank J. Prial.—1st ed.
    p. cm.
  ISBN-13: 978-0-312-36471-7 (alk. paper)
  ISBN-10: 0-312-36471-7 (alk. paper)
    1. Wineries—Pacific States—Guidebooks.   2. Vineyards—Pacific States—Guidebooks.
3. Hotels—Pacific States—Guidebooks.   4. Taverns (Inns)—Pacific States—Guidebooks.
5. Restaurants—Pacific States—Guidebooks.   6. Scenic byways—Pacific States—Guidebooks.
7. Villages—Pacific States—Guidebooks.   8. Automobile travel—Pacific States—Guidebooks.
9. Pacific States—Tours.   I. Title.

TP557.S57 2007
917.904'34—dc22   2007022691

First Edition: October 2007

10 9 8 7 6 5 4 3 2 1

*For all the vintners, winemakers,
innkeepers, hoteliers, restaurateurs,
and chefs who spent patient hours sharing
their crafts, dreams, and passions.
Some became my teachers;
many are now my friends.*

Contents and Trail Guide

Central California Coast 36

Oxnard Area 36

Santa Barbara Area 38

Santa Ynez Area 40

Santa Maria Area 48

Acknowledgments

Special thanks go to Daniela Rapp, my editor at St. Martin's Press, for her continuing wisdom and unwavering support, and to California project manager Melissa Biliardi for her knowledge of viticulture. Each invested this work with generosity from the outset, providing winetasting expertise as well as guidance. Initial planning by Stephany Boettner was indispensable when, with a short lead time, it was still necessary to circumvent holidays, special events, and a difficult harvest that came on the installment plan.

Further thanks go to those who kept me focused and on the road: Jonni Biaggini; Phil Bilodeau; Shannon Brooks; Gail Camposagrado; Honore Comfort; Michael Davidson; Dawn Endean; John Enquist; Shannon Flynn; Christine Forsyth; Terri Gieg; Tom Glidden; Jennifer Gould; Koleen Hamblin; Tana Bader Inglima; Stacie Jacob; Kellie James; Laura Kath; Gina Keough; Lota LaMontagne; Elizabeth Martin-Calder; Michelle McMillian; Rhonda Motil; Regan O'Leary; Mary Pat Parker; Tyffani Peters; Sue Price; Sabrina Soares Roberts; Frances Sayers; Kimberly Scargle; Craig Schmidt; Cathy Seghesio; Scott Steinlowski; Richard Stenger; Kristina Streeter; Kerrie Walters; Christopher Weir; Carrie Wilkinson; Carly Williams; Carolyn Woodall; Lonnie Wright; and Sherrye Wyatt.

Support from the Phantom Tasters, who visited wineries to provide confirmation and comment, was invaluable. I am grateful as well to a host of roadside brothers who, whenever they discovered that I was a tour-book writer who'd got himself hopelessly lost, were kind enough not to laugh. . . .

Foreword

BY FRANK J. PRIAL

Forty years or so ago, when I first explored the wine roads of the West, they were, essentially, all back roads. St. Helena, in the Napa Valley, was a country town, and everyone strolling Main Street knew everyone else. Sonoma, just over the Mayacamas Range, was the same. The shops were the shops of any American farm town; they catered to no-nonsense folk who made their living from the soil. The restaurants were practical places where men in bib overalls who had never heard of a double espresso discussed weather reports and grumbled about the new little wineries popping up all over the place. They called the new people "them damned boutiquers."

Wine grapes were a major crop, as they had been all along, and a lot of wine was made—workaday jug wine, mostly, meant for wine-drinking immigrants and their progeny in the big cities of the East. A lot of it was still shipped off—in jugs—to be bottled close to where it would be drunk.

Tourists, not many, were beginning to drift up to the valley and they were generally well treated, even if the locals couldn't imagine what they found so interesting about fermenting grape juice. None of them, the winemakers or those first hardy wine-drinking visitors, could have imagined in those innocent days how quickly that idyllic pastoral world would change.

Now, on a typical summer weekend day, the traffic through the Napa Valley on Route 29 and on the Silverado Trail to the east slows to a crawl, parking lots at the better-known wineries overflow, and visitors often must wait in line for a chance to taste a few wines. Shops that once sold farm supplies now hawk T-shirts and corkscrews, and the restaurants are both expensive and overbooked. What's more, these phenomena are hardly limited to Napa and Sonoma. Calistoga and Healdsburg have become—I hate the word—trendy, as has most of the South Central Coast, the Monterey Peninsula, the Russian River Valley, and just about anywhere wine is made in California. Innocently, the crowds gather and sadly the old wine world fades from view.

Ah, but here, like some western hero of old, comes Tom Snyder, aptly named "The Two-Lane Gourmet," to rescue us from the Disneyfication of the wine world. On our behalf, he has tooled a Jaguar over some 2,100 miles of roads less traveled, finding hidden little wineries, delightful eateries, and bed-and-breakfast hideaways run by the kind of warm and welcoming people who recall the California I fell in love with those many years ago. What's more, for true devotees of the unbeaten path, he has done the same for Oregon and Washington State.

Consider if you will, the wineries he offers us along the Corralitos Wine Trail in the Santa Cruz Mountains. The wineries, Tom advises, "welcome guests, though tour and tastings are by appointment only. Farm vineyards are a quiet treat, with time to savor and reflect." How long has it been since you last had time to savor and reflect? On anything.

I'm not much for tasting notes; they tend to change, mine anyway, from day to day, even from hour to hour. The wines I like today may well bore me tomorrow. I like his travel notes—the sky, the sea, the open road—and, I'll admit it, his vivid word pictures of the meals he relished in some of those country inns.

Damn, I wish I'd had Tom's book when I first wandered through the wine country. On the other hand, there's no reason not to use it now. Never did those two-lane roads sound more appealing. Somewhere he calls it retro-touring. I'll forgive him that. I can't be upset with any guy who compares a great Cabernet with the sound of a smooth-running radial airplane engine.

Wanderlust and Wine

This book celebrates curvy backcountry roads, charming inns, inviting wineries, and intimate dining. If that sounds sensual, it is. Robert Louis Stevenson, both a writer and wanderer, thought of wine as bottled poetry. And Homer, the classical Greek road writer, called wine "honey for the heart." A thirteenth-century Venetian mosaic depicts Noah among the vines with a cup of wine. Both Noah and the vines look happy.

Yet there is more to it—more than can be written, spoken, or painted. Two-lane highways lead us as much to mystery as toward the next bend. An inn is more than shelter, and a chef's gift for touching our senses can shimmer in the candlelight, with wine as a centerpiece.

For wine has a spiritual nature. Over the millennia, as humankind joined in sacraments, broke bread together, and found joy in one another's company, wine was often at hand. Vineyards still express wonder and a special sense of being—perhaps magic as well.

Brian Doyle (see Connections) writes of the vineyard as an erotic rendezvous: "the vines fertilizing each other madly when no one is looking, the little tiny bras, the little tiny cigarettes, the recriminations at dawn." [p. 9]

It's downright glorious. So, *The Two-Lane Gourmet* is your touring guide for romantic, lighthearted adventures, wines, and meals. This book is for anyone who wants to know about delightful and often undiscovered places to sleep, eat, and prowl about—with an eye to bringing home a tall tale or two and special vintages over which to share them.

Wine, good food, and conversation are at the center of this tour of winemaking regions through the Pacific Coast states. Along the way, you'll come to know remarkable inkeepers, along with chefs and winemakers eager to share interesting pairings of food and drink. Yet their comments are always offered as guidance—a way to expand possibilities—not as rules. The days of limiting red wines to red meat, with white wines consigned to fish or fowl, are over.

What's more, your own palate is unique, and your mouth is coated with personal enzymes. How your pleasures unfold are far more important than convention. Angela Bennett of Silvan Ridge Winery puts this friendlier view in plain words. "Our wines smell good," she says. "They taste good. They're well-balanced and attractively priced."

Still, it bears special mention that this book is by necessity a Whitman's Sampler drawn from some two thousand wineries in California, Oregon, and Washington, where new vineyards are popping up at a rate of five or six per week in each state. Those same wineries also attract excellent inns and restaurants—all to your benefit. The purpose of this book is to help you establish a base camp in each area. After that, explore further, making the adventure your own. In short, *The Two-Lane Gourmet* seeks out the unique "finds"—special places that can lead you on toward the romance of your own discoveries. And keep in mind that winter months—the doldrums of February come to mind—are often a fine time to visit a winery and sip before the fire.

Journeys end where and when they wish. Part of the joy is opening ourselves to new experience and letting the journey be what it will. So, the first thing to recognize is that all wine-and-cuisine trails are imaginary. Our trail links wine regions in California, Oregon, and Washington to form a grand tour of some 2,103 point-to-point miles, plus another 800 miles of local driving and occasional backtracking. The route is made up of two-lane roads with connecting highways. Interstate travel, like an inoculation, is sometimes necessary.

Note: The Two-Lane Gourmet *is arranged from south to north and any region can be visited in three days or less. To aid you, each area is listed in geographical order in the Contents and Trail Guide section at the front of this book. Within each area, inns are usually listed first, with wineries and any special attractions next, followed by restaurants.*

Throughout, you'll be your own gourmet. Let's spend a moment with that idea. The term *gourmet* suggests an individual with a selective palate and some knowledge of food and wine. What is often missed in any definition is that gourmets are intensely curious people—they don't usually follow people who seek comfort in rules. That's the other aim of this book: to whet your curiosity as well as your appetites. Explore and enjoy!

WINETASTING 101

Let me first confess my own foolish past. When going out for dinner or a glass of wine, I usually ordered the house red. If there was a wine list at the restaurant, it was about the last thing I wanted to see, since I didn't recognize most of the names and they were often hard to read in dim light anyway.

After a time I stumbled onto Cabernet Sauvignon, learned to pronounce it, and made that my wine of choice. I stuck with it like a mantra. It was, after all, a quantum leap from the Lancers and Blue Nun of early school days. But ordering it every time was also like buying cars that were always the same color.

Such was the state in which my friend Melissa, who happened to be in the wine industry, found me. She was kind but firm about the value and pleasures of winetasting.

"It'll be fun," she said.

"But I like only Cabernet."

"Of course you do. That's why your palate will profit from a little variety."

"But—"

"What time on Sunday would be good for you?"

So, off we went the next weekend. Of course, I'd never been winetasting before and had no idea how it was supposed to go. What would I do or say? At our first stop, a glance informed me that most tasters were swirling whatever wine had just been poured for them.

"That's to aerate the wine a bit," Melissa said. "It brings up the flavors."

Aha . . . another tasting-room mystery revealed. Maybe this could be fun after all.

By the time we were sampling the red wines, my confidence resurfaced. We were riding straight into Cabernet country. So, I lifted my glass to swirl. In a twinkling, a dollop of wine slopped out—with more than a little glee, I suspect.

"No, no," Melissa whispered. "You're a beginner. Just leave the base of your glass flat on the countertop. Swirl it that way. And next time . . . don't wear white."

My odyssey through wine country was under way. Since then, I've learned that after a few sips to get acquainted, it's not necessary to finish whatever is left in the glass. Tasting rooms have dump buckets on the bar top, a convenient bit of crockery, so you can dispose of remainders. Or you can spit. Either is a good idea if several wineries are to be visited.

If you've been on outings to taste wine or are skilled in dealing with wine lists, you may want to skip over this next part. Otherwise, join me for a few tips:

Most tastings progress from lighter white wines through more robust reds. Some differences will be remarkable right from the start; others will be subtle. You'll also notice that the traditional shapes of the bottles reflect their contents. Cabernet bottles have full, rounded shoulders— these are the linebackers of wine. Pinots and Chardonnays display a svelte, sloping form. Rieslings and Gewürztraminers feature upright Teutonic shapes. Some say that these different forms have to do with how well a wine ages in the bottle, but that's less convincing than the strength of tradition. I doubt that it matters one way or the other to a robust Cabernet. But as a winetaster, I'd certainly care if the wine came in a bottle that looked like it should be wearing a tennis outfit.

Make a habit of swirling each wine in the glass before sipping. This action helps open up the complex flavors after years of captivity.

Sniffing may not reveal much to you at first, but as a wine is swirled, its scent will change. Keep at it and differences in each wine's aroma or *nose* will become familiar as well. The senses of smell and taste are closely intertwined physiologically and in brain pathways. Soon, you'll come to know red wines and recognize the nuances of whites. Be prepared to let a freshly uncorked red wine rest for a bit, and once in the glass, swirl it several times before sipping. Reds will need more exposure to oxygen to soften the tannins, improving both aroma and taste. These wines reward patience by opening up after a bit. Whites are less fussy, which makes them nice for lunch but less engaging over an evening's conversation.

Listen to the tasting-room staff. Many are well trained and offer a wealth of knowledge. They may seem to be speaking in tongues at first, but stick with it and read the tasting notes provided. Matters will soon become clearer. Some wine aficionados even take copious notes to acquaint themselves further with the qualities of each wine and vintage.

Like taste, the idea of wine is different for everyone. If you have a memory for baseball stats, you may even become an avid notetaker. Otherwise, don't be intimidated by the scribbling and comparisons of others, just enjoy. You can even draw hearts and flowers if you're with someone sweet. No one will care; they're into their own notes.

Feel free to coin your personal terms of wine appreciation. It's impossible to express sensations through mere language anyway. In that regard, wine may be less like food and more like perfume or music, with melodic harmonies standing out over supporting bass lines. Wine enthusiasts often find hints of blackberry, chocolate, leather, dust bunnies, or gasoline in just about everything. At least they say so. One wine writer reported that a wine had hints of cat pee. Of course, the question is: how did he recognize the taste? If you encounter a wine that smells like urine or plywood, my advice is to move on.

A number of vintners producing premium wines do not have tasting rooms, but rely on distributors, the restaurant trade, and local outlets. But the tasting room remains king and great vintages sell out in a hurry, so don't miss a wine that calls to you by waiting to buy at home. You'll be better at finding wines you truly enjoy during a tasting—not to mention the thrill of shared discovery. Winemakers often take their turns working a tasting room, and when someone exclaims over one of their wines, you can bet there are happy people on both sides of the counter.

Each winery is making an investment in you as a taster. Check for a placard on the counter or ask if the tasting room charges a fee. A few in Northern California charge $25 or more, but many tasting rooms still require no fee. Even if a winery asks for a fee of $5 or so, the advantage will still be yours—no sampling is offered by supermarkets.

One lesson from winetasting applies directly to restaurants: glassware. Stemware placed at the table may not reflect the kind of wine you order. Smaller glasses might not do much harm to white wines, but a big red Pinot or Cabernet deserves a large Burgundy glass, regardless of the amount of wine poured. It's okay to insist on it.

Planning to cover more than a couple of wineries between meals? It's an excellent idea to have a designated driver. And take as much care driving into a winery as exiting. In short, take responsibility for yourself but keep a close eye on the other guy.

The wine industry is well aware of the snob quotient that developed back in the '90s. Discussing wine in a statistical, mechanical way became a new arena for folks who liked to display their knowledge. So, we all need some defense— some shape-shifting method of survival when wine threatens to become a competitive subject. And I can recommend nothing finer than Frank J. Prial's piece entitled "Short Course in Wine Tactics," from *Decantations* (see Connections). His advice has saved me from floundering more than once. Here's a sample to bolster your spirits if someone burdens you with nonessential information:

Then there is the word bramble. *Do you know what a bramble is? It's a bush, right? Do you know what a bramble tastes like? Of course not—who eats bushes? Nevertheless, that's what you're going to say if the wine is red: "It has a real bramble taste; yes sir, a real bramble taste." Don't worry. It appears on a dozen different California wine labels, and it's a safe bet those guys don't know what it means either. For sure, your host doesn't. [p. 13]*

--- *Travel Tip* ---

Before turning the ignition key, be sure to check out the Web sites of each destination winery, inn, or restaurant. Business hours, phone numbers, and street names change with frequency—not to mention highway construction that can eliminate a whole section of road. Most digital mapping sources on the Web are notoriously inaccurate when it comes to the back roads of wine country. Instead, use directions or maps obtained from the Web site of estates, inns, and restaurants you plan to visit—they have a vested interest in bringing you there safely and with ease. *The Two-Lane Gourmet* provides Web site addresses for virtually all of the properties covered.
Local phone numbers are also listed. Many properties list 800 numbers as well, but experience has shown that these numbers are often useless for wireless phones when you are on the road.

Whenever possible, obtain copies of maps provided by local winegrower associations and visitor centers. These may not be to scale, but give a great overview of the locations of member wineries. Check with state wine boards or commissions for information on the various regions as well. Discover your own favorites, but trust me on this: know before you go. None of this will ruin a feeling of spontaneity in wine country. As Charles Kuralt once remarked, "On back roads you can never have too many maps or too much fuel."

HANDY WINE TERMS

Here are some terms it's helpful to know around tasting rooms. If you find these interesting, you'll love Tom Stevenson's splendid work, *The New Sotheby's Wine Encyclopedia* (see Connections).

Acidity: Emphasizes complex flavors in a wine and balances the sugars present. Some is necessary to retain life in a wine and prevent it from tasting flat. Too much acidity ruins a wine's *finish* and can be felt in the throat. Too little acidity makes food-and-wine pairings difficult.

Aging: Back in the day, retaining a wine in barrels or keeping it in bottles for decades was popular and thought to improve the product. And in fact, a good wine may age well in bottles for a century or more—a major attraction for wine collectors interested in profit. Today, however, wines are allowed to spend less time in oak barrels (where they may absorb excess *tannins* from the wood) or bottles. This practice also reflects the drink-it-now nature of the current wine market. Such wines are said to be more "approachable," and consistent with data showing that 90 percent of wine sold in the United States is consumed within a few days.

Appellation: A region with similar soil conditions and climate for wine-grape growing, recognized in the United States as an American Viticultural Area (AVA). Washington was once a single AVA. Now, Walla Walla, the Tri-Cities area, and banks of the Columbia Gorge, for example, all comprise different appellations and microappellations. The Napa region of California was the first to insist that labeling be consistent with a wine's AVA origin. Oregon and Washington are also establishing stringent rules regarding AVA claims for wine.

Barrels: Most wineries use oak barrels from French or American coopers; many use a combination of the two. These are used to store—or in some cases, ferment—wine before bottling. Barrels may be reused, though each winery has its own preferences on whether (or how many times) a barrel may be reused. Doing so can reduce both cost and tannins taken up by the next fill of wine. At a cost of $850 or more apiece, plus a substantial effect on the quality of a wine, barrel choices are a serious matter.

Biodynamics: A logical—some would say imperative—step beyond organic certification. This system is based on the view of a farm or vineyard as a living organism, with a unique character and a cycle of natural processes that are balanced and independent of mined or manufactured chemicals. The goal is to be both low-impact and self-sustaining.

Blend: Few wines are derived from only one grape variety. Instead, wine with a strong presence like Cabernet Sauvignon may be mellowed a bit by adding perhaps 5 percent Merlot. Creative winemakers are experimenting with blends such as Cabernet Sauvignon, Cabernet Franc, Malbec, and Zinfandel to produce layered complexities in excellent blended wines.

Bottle Shock: Wine is a live thing in many respects. The fermentation process by which the addition of yeast transforms grape juice into wine is followed by a period of aging, typically in oak barrels, during which the wine develops its complex flavors, and then usually in bottles (some winery-restaurants serve directly from the barrel). Pumping the contents of a barrel into more than 200 individual bottles stresses the wine and often disassociates those flavors, requiring storage from six months to a year or more for the wine to settle down—even though it might have been ready to drink straight from the barrel. Sometimes, a wine remains green and no amount of aging will improve its qualities. But that's not bottle shock; it's simply a wine that is insufficient. Forever young, one might say.

Brix: The measure of the amount of sugar in grapes, used to determine the optimum time for harvest. Potential alcohol level in a wine is estimated by multiplying the Brix value by 0.55. So, a result of 26° Brix would theoretically produce an alcohol content of 14.3 percent for a wine. Higher amounts of alcohol act as a solvent and the wine can be poorer for it.

Cap: In a fermenting tank, grapes release carbon dioxide, which floats the grape skins to the top. This forms a cap holding both flavors and colors. To maintain contact with the juice, wineries punch the cap back down. This is done by hand or by pulsing air bubbles to saturate the cap. Harsher methods can break up the skins and seeds, introducing excessive tannins into the juice.

Capsule: Covering applied over the top of a wine bottle. Once made of lead, these are now a plastic or a harmless foil that can be folded by the waitstaff at a restaurant into a fine little saddle for the newly removed cork—all part of the romance.

Chilling: White wines are typically chilled, but reds are usually served at or just below room temperature. This practice is fine, except in the heat of summer, when chilling a red is not only permissible, but encouraged in the advertising of some vintners.

Cork: Traditional stopper used to bottle wine, supplied primarily by Portugal and Spain. Punched from strips of bark from the cork oak tree—which is not killed by the harvest process—corks vary in quality and are a problem for winemakers. They can pick up a mold—not the kind that may appear under the *capsule* and is harmless—that taints the wine inside a bottle. When that occurs, even among the top labels, the wine is said to be "corked" and is in total ruin. It smells like mildewed books or a wet dog. Because handcrafters of fine wine are often lower in the ranks of cork buyers, inferior corkage can be a problem. Plastic corks have become a temporary answer for volume producers, but screw caps are making strong inroads—with significant advantages. In a world where nearly 1.5 billion bottles per year are spoiled by cork taint, this issue is not likely to go away.

Crush: Predominantly a California or West Coast term for wine-grape harvest or *vintage*.

Cuvée—(coo-vay): French term meaning "from the vat." In the Champagne region of France, a cuvée is a fine blend of sparkling varietals. In still wines, the term may convey some distinct blend, perhaps from several vineyards. In general, the term suggests prestigious food or drink.

Estate Bottled: Words used on a label to indicate that the contents are from a single *appellation* and that all production and bottling have been under the control of the selling vineyard. Wineries often buy and sell grapes to one another for blending purposes, so this is not an empty term.

Gravity-Flow Processing: Assists in a gentle, minimalist handling of the fruit, from crush through barreling, by use of gravity-feed from one process to the next, without the use of pumps. Largely a Pacific Northwest approach, it is a calculated response to the delicate thin-skinned nature of Pinot Noir grapes. Often found in Oregon, this system is spreading as new wineries are built. Derided by some, it nevertheless makes artistic and financial sense where possible.

Green: Except for Verde wines that are supposed to be green, the term is usually pejorative and means that a wine is too young to drink. When shopping for wine, it's a good idea to avoid vintages that are close to the present year—especially in Cabernets. These typically require more time in the bottle.

Finish: A wine's aftertaste should linger in the mouth and especially at the back of the tongue. It is a quality of fine wines. A good finish can even surprise you by intensifying some time later. More than once, I've been back out on the road, only to have the finish of the last wine kick in. The best recourse is to go back to the winery and buy as much as you can.

Ice Wine: Pressed from late-harvest grapes frozen on the vine by the first frost. These grapes, hard as marbles, must be picked before midmorning, lest the water thaw before pressing. The resulting wine is a delicate, aromatic balance of sweetness, high in acidity: a lovely dessert wine.

Label: Year of harvest, winery, and often specific vineyards and blends appear on the labels, front or back, along with alcoholic content, which should be around 13 to 14 percent. Some Zinfandels run higher, but high alcoholic content can harm an otherwise good wine. Today's labels are often things of beauty in themselves. Just as wine is being brought together with food, so is label art becoming more popular as an expression of a wine and its maker's philosophy.

Lees: Sediment of grapes and yeast—harmless guck—that will settle out from wine as it is aged. Depending on a winery's practices, this may be filtered out. It's nothing to worry about. Some wine collectors pay thousands for a bottle of wine that will have more than a little sediment.

L.I.V.E.: A European approach offering certification as a Low Input Viticulture and Enology operation. The program encourages vineyards to maintain a natural balance, yet allows growers to respond to a critical situation without losing certification for several years, as they would under an organic program. Some growers see L.I.V.E. as a middle way; others view it as transitional.

Oaky: A double-edged term that refers to the subtaste (and aroma) of oak taken on by a wine after being stored in an oak barrel. If the barrel time is too long in young wood and the flavor becomes too forward, the term is negative. However, in a big Chardonnay, for example, the term may be part of a positive description of the wine's character.

Oenology: Often spelled today as *enology,* this term refers to the study of wine and winemaking. The traditional spelling is used here to remind us of the word's heritage, for if it is pronounced quickly as o-enology, the word's classic Latin root *vino* (where *v* is pronounced as a *w*) is revealed. It reminds us of the rich connection between humankind and wine.

Organic: Sustainable practices in winegrowing that involve the use of no pesticides or herbicides in the vineyards. Organic or *Biodynamic* practices carry both more expense and greater risk and require annual certification. Most vineyard managers can manage invasive plant life, but a year of unexpected pestilence can be crippling; it takes time to come up with a nonchemical solution and a year's harvest may be lost. One alternative, as the industry moves toward more widespread adoption of organic farming, is the *L.I.V.E. program*.

Pairings: Food-and-wine pairings are to some a kitchen art; this is most true at home. Restaurants typically suggest a wine to go with a particular order, or one that will best serve the table. Yet when the restaurant is affiliated with a winery, or you are gazing at a special bottle of wine at home, choice moves in the opposite direction. Author Leslie Sbrocco's book, *The Simple and Savvy Wine Guide: Buying, Pairing, and Sharing for All* makes a fine countertop mentor. (See Connections.)

Phylloxera: An infestation caused by a subterranean louse that attacks the roots of grapevines, moving from one vine to the next like a viticultural herpes—it even looks like leafy cold sores. Native to the United States, it appeared in Europe during French experiments with American varieties around 1860. More than six million acres of vines were destroyed in France alone and it has subsequently reappeared in the Pacific Northwest. French winegrowers tried drowning the lice or spraying them, but only grafting their vines onto American rootstocks offered a permanent solution. Gallic pride was further injured when the grafts produced better wines than before. Infestation, however, remains a threat both here and abroad.

Reserve: This term has little legal standing, but has been traditionally associated with the finest a winery can produce. Larger vintners may print the term indiscriminately on labels. Smaller wineries still use the term in earnest, however. A tasting-room trial will let you know if it's true. Handcrafted wines labeled Reserve should quickly reveal their true merits.

Sustainable Practices: Along with organic farming, sustainable practices embrace natural solutions to pests, fungi, and nutrition. Once the province of a few greenies, sustainable practices are now found in vineyards throughout California and the Pacific Northwest. Is it difficult and expensive? Yes. Still, if past experience with herbicides and pesticides are any indication, sustainability is not just a goal, but a necessity.

Table Wine: A concise labeling term used to denote a wine of less than 14 percent, but more than 7 percent alcohol content by volume. When the jug-wine fad on the West Coast faded, Table Wine became recognized as cheap and of poor quality. Recently, vintners have begun to revive this entry in the marketplace under a variety of names. Table Wine need not be dismissed out of hand; it can be as good as, or better than, a single-vineyard varietal.

Tannins: Part of the taste of big reds like Cabernet Sauvignon, tannins are compounds found in both grape skins and barrel oak. Most tannins drop out in aging as part of a wine's natural sediment. When they do not, acidic sensations can arrest the wine's taste and quality. Despite time in the barrel or bottle, it may never wake up.

Terroir—(tair-wahr): A French word referring only to soil and location, the term now includes climate as it influences the land of a specific appellation or vineyard. Terroir is the sum of what lends an identifiable character to a particular varietal. And it is what provides a sense of place—a feeling of unique connection through the wine being tasted to the land itself.

Varietal: A wine named for the grape from which it is made, rather than its origin in a European district like Bordeaux or Champagne. By law—as enforced by the Alcohol and Tobacco Tax and Trade Bureau (stemming from the Bureau of Prohibition in the Eliot Ness days)—any wine so labeled must be composed of at least 75 percent of the grape varietal printed on the label.

Vintage: The year in which grapes used in a particular wine were harvested. This is the date appearing on wine labels and has nothing to do with the year in which the wine was bottled. Note that *The Two-Lane Gourmet* makes no mention of vintage when describing various wines. That's because weather affects each year's harvest differently. Further, if a terrific vintage is discovered, it may be sold out before you learn of the winery. Or the next vintage may not equal the last. So, to avoid disappointment, lines of wine—samples of a winery's core wines—are presented.

SELF-PRONOUNCING GUIDE
TO POPULAR WINES

Wonderful wines are produced worldwide, but we'll focus on popular West Coast varietals.

Cabernet Franc—(cab-er-nay frohnk): Produced from a noble grape (which means its wines are likely to be good no matter where the vines are planted) that originated in the Bordeaux region of France. It's the daddy of Cabernet Sauvignon, yet derives from thinner-skinned grapes with lower acidity and a softer touch on the palate.

Cabernet Sauvignon—(cab-er-nay sov-ing-yaunh): One of the most popular of the noble reds, with deep color, notable tannins, and overtones of oak. A tough-skinned grape, it withstands disease and late rains. Aging brings its edginess into balance with powerful flavors, and blending with wines such as Cabernet Franc and Malbec can make this wine ready to drink without much aging.

Chardonnay—(chard-o-nay): A full-bodied yet delicate white wine that does not take blending all that well and is sensitive to time in the barrel, especially if of new oak. Some wineries are now offering a no-oak rendition of this wine, which can bring its true character forward. Often described as buttery, especially in California, it can be much brighter and complex from vineyards farther north.

Claret—(clar-et): Renamed by the British, this term refers to Bordeaux red wine, much prized until its quality was lost in bulk production for volume sales. It is now in modest revival in the Pacific Northwest as a red blend with both character and aromatic harmony.

Gewürztraminer—(gah-vertz-tra-meener): Much prized by students and underpaid faculty members in the 1970s and '80s, when European imports of good wines with low prices flooded the market. Not strictly of German descent, this white wine was originally produced in the Italian Alps and retains the spicy flavors and aroma that first attracted American vintners.

Malbec—(mal-beck): Often used as a blend wine for Clarets and red Cabernets, this is a soft, yet bright wine close to Merlot in its finish. Outstanding Malbecs are now being produced in Eastern Washington, where its traditional overtones of plum are well developed.

Meritage—(rhymes with either *heritage* or *mirage,* depending on the tasting room): A red or white premium blend in which none of the wines included reach the requirement of 75 percent or more single *varietal*. Once considered little more than Table Wine, the trend toward blending by top wineries has carried this wine-form to a higher level: an excellent wine in its own right and often carrying a *vintage* label.

Merlot—(mair-lo): One of the first French varietals to become popular in the United States as soon as Americans learned to pronounce its name, this lush wine rivaled Chardonnay as the big seller of the 1980s and '90s. Further, where other varietals might yield two or more tons per acre, Merlot vines can produce up to six tons. Overexposed, it fell into decline and is only now making a comeback, despite taking some serious hits in the motion picture *Sideways*. A very good Merlot often has a taste of chocolate layered in with those of fruit and light oak. If you are interested in training your perception of subtle tastes like these, sip a good Merlot, have a bite of dark chocolate, then sip again. You may be surprised at what pops up in the flavor.

Muscat—(mus-cat): Not to be confused with treacly bottom-shelf Muscatel, this wine has come to be appreciated in the United States only over the past few years. It is primarily a dessert wine, though it may vary from sweet to relatively dry. Prized by inventive chefs who enjoy working with sorbets, a bit of Muscat can be just the thing, with its peach flavor and perfume.

Petite Sirah—(pay-teet seer-ah): A fairly new but exciting grape, this varietal was developed prior to the 1960s in France and appeared on the U.S. West Coast about a decade later. Even its spelling is subject to friendly debate. Petite Sirah is often used in blending, but has a growing band of followers along the West Coast who prize the wine's richness.

Pinot Gris—(peeno-gree): Along with Pinot Blanc, this is a white mutant of Pinot Noir. Oregon is a prime producer and positions the wine as an alternative to Chardonnay. The wine is being developed to age well and has a light richness that is gaining favor.

Pinot Noir—(peeno-nwah): A late-blooming red wine on the U.S. market, Pinot Noir vines require optimum conditions and care to flourish and the northern area of Oregon's Willamette

Valley appears to have just those conditions. This is an admirable wine, remarkable in its complex flavors and aroma, with little bother from the tannins that can sometimes be too forward in Cabernet Sauvignon and related Bordeaux wines.

Riesling—(reez-ling): This true German white wine was introduced to the Pacific Northwest in the late 1800s by immigrants. Its grape has the capacity for an exceptionally wide range, from crisp and dry to complex and full-bodied. Pacific Northwest vintners began learning how to handle fussy Riesling grapes in the 1970s and have been producing outstanding wines ever since, rivaling the California appellations.

Sangiovese—(sahn-jee-o-vay-zeh): Italian wines arguably have the longest tenure in viticulture, yet few of their wines have rivaled French varietals in the United States. Poor-quality bottles of Chianti, recognized primarily as candleholders, undoubtedly contributed to that sad state of affairs. Now, West Coast vintners are working to bring Tuscan definition to Sangiovese, with elegant flavors and a smooth finish.

Syrah—(Seer-ah) Often used for blending purposes in Rhône-style wines, including those from Chateauneuf du Pape, this grape probably originated in ancient Persia. Today, many wine-makers are producing a stand-alone version. But that chapter is still beginning and Syrahs can run the gamut from watery to edgy. The ideal is both spicy and fruity, but with a complex character rather like a rich Merlot.

Viognier—(vee-ohn-yay): A shy white wine that was once confined largely to the Rhône Valley in France. Not planted until the mid-1980s in the United States, this varietal is now grown from California's Temecula Valley to Northern Oregon and Washington. A classic white wine often overlooked, it offers an alternative to both Chardonnay and Riesling.

Zinfandel—(zin-fan-dell): A red wine of Croatian descent that has been often been mishandled and mislabeled. It is elastic enough to pass for a white wine and a White Zinfandel craze appeared on the West Coast in the 1980s, rivaling the love affair of Californians with Chardonnay. Sometimes it is the province of winemakers interested in pushing up alcohol content without ruining the wine. Stay tuned on this one.

——— *Happy Couples* ———

Pairing wine with food can sometimes be a daunting prospect. Three useful tips are: **(1) follow the source**—dark, earthy foods such as mushrooms will be happiest with deep, earthy Pinot Noirs or well-structured Zinfandels; **(2) follow the sauce**—red sauces are more important than the meat or pasta they cover, white sauces are more influential than the fowl or meat they accompany. Red sauces or Cajun flavors play well with powerful Tuscan-style red wines or a Pinot Gris that announces itself right from the first pour; **(3) follow value**—pair good wines with good ingredients. If you're choosing a fine white wine with some stature and want to pair it with a salad niçoise, use extra-virgin olive oil, a white-wine vinegar, and a classy tuna, like Papa George Gourmet Albacore, which is not only rich tasting, but far richer than most in omega-3, plus it's dolphin-free and available in a kosher variety. Visit **www.papageorgetuna.com** for more ideas.

FROM THE ETRUSCANS TO TWO BUCK CHUCK

Wine illuminates the gentler side of life. Unlike beer, which hoots for a Saturday winner, wine is the subtext of amiable conversation and romance. Served at a luncheon for two by the sea or during a candlelit dinner, wine helps capture the moment while holding a careworn world at bay. Seldom are wine drinkers loud or morose; the grape seems to have a salutary effect our hearts recognize.

Fossil vines dating back some sixty million years offer early evidence of grapes, with documented winemaking turning up about five thousand years ago in Mesopotamia, Persia, and Egypt. Yet it was the Etruscans who first made a joy—and business—of viticulture. Around 600 B.C.E., when Rome was little more than a city-state, Etruscans were well established along the western region of the Italian peninsula in what is now Tuscany: a lovely, arid region well suited to wine grapes.

Vineyards love soil that might otherwise be fobbed off as pasture: located for the most part on sloping land, with chalky or granular composition, excellent drainage, and some volcanic ash in the mix. The Etruscans knew that the idea is to get the vines to dig in a little, and to produce rather than merely grow.

Etruscan influences may still be seen in Tuscan villas. These were originally manor house fortresses, with the occasional tower and small window openings suited to defense, built atop vineyard hills. The Etruscans also passed written language on to Rome. And that may have set the tone for both cultures. The Etruscans got into making and exporting wine, while the Romans exported written law—and themselves. (See Rick Steves' DVD in Connections.)

The overriding problem at the time was that no one had a

decent bottling system. Pottery jugs with narrow necks and flared tops served well as containers and could be artfully decorated, but spoilage was a problem. Most vintners of the day settled for stuffing oil-soaked rags into the opening, which guarded in part against spilling but provided no seal to speak of. As slave galleys plodded through Old World seas, the wine often turned to vinegar, not a high-profit item. As a result, wine remained a stay-at-home drink for centuries.

By 300 C.E., the Romans were having limited success with corked ceramic bottles (amphora) designed by the Greeks, in which a heavy layer of olive oil—often more than half the container's contents—was floated on top of the wine as a sealant. Still, you can imagine how that would taste after having been bounced around a bit in a storm, or hauled to market on a wooden cart. The Romans called it wine, but it should have been sold as a vinaigrette salad dressing.

Enter the French. They were good at storing wine in barrels, though that made the wine hard to transport. So in the seventeenth century, Louis XIV moved to standardize bottles and Dom Perignon took it from there. A Benedictine monk, Perignon was fooling around with sparkling wines that might attract both praise and silver to the church. He tried everything to seal his bottles, but the wine either went flat or blew up. The solution came from two traveling monks who had well-corked bottles with them. Dom Perignon realized what the expansive nature of cork could do for sparkling wine. Champagne has since launched far more than a thousand ships, not to mention weddings, anniversaries, and send-offs of every variety.

Meanwhile in the New World, early colonists were trying to make something of the wild grapes found in this country. But most had a gamy quality that didn't translate well into wine. It wasn't until German and French immigrants brought varietal rootstocks with them that some vines began producing true wine grapes. To the west, winegrowers were putting down roots in Senecu, New Mexico, in 1629. Tribal uprisings put an end to later missions, but not to the mission grape, which produced a sweet wine that kept well. That grape later turned up in Southern California, harvested under the guidance of Father Junipero Serra, who needed a sacramental wine along with funds for expansion. Mission plantings remained under cultivation until the 1980s.

If Southern California was later bypassed in favor of wine-growing colonies to the north, it would nevertheless set the tone for West Coast viticulture for more than a century. Almost none of those who became winegrowers in the region had any background in agriculture. They were following a dream. That trend continues today.

It worked pretty well, too. Napa and Sonoma developed as strong viticulture areas and there were other plantings around the United States when Prohibition became the law of the land in 1919. Overnight, America went officially dry, though alcohol consumption itself increased by an order of magnitude. And throughout Prohibition's fourteen years, vintners—being far more visible than bootleggers—struggled. Within a year, overall vineyard output dropped by half. Sacramental wine producers held on for a while, as did juice producers, but the wine industry was in shambles.

Loopholes were discovered, however. California doubled its vineyard acreage when the price for grapes jumped ten times to fill consumer orders for "fruit juice" to be made in the garage. Yet even that boom went bust. Worse, the plantings that had replaced good varietals were inferior. Even when output was up, the product made poor wine and served better as jelly for the nation's peanut butter sandwiches.

Even by 1960, recovery was feeble—only a few hundred acres of Cabernet Sauvignon, Pinot Noir, Riesling, and Chardonnay remained in California, a state with close to a half-million acres of vines. Pricing, distribution, and taxation went from erratic to nonsensical, as each state was allowed to do whatever it wished about wine and spirits. And despite the passing of nearly fifty years, thorny issues over what can be shipped across state lines are still not resolved.

Still, winemakers are a resilient lot and wine drinkers are patient. Indeed, if bread and cheese had suffered such a fate, we all would have starved to death by now. Yet after all these years, the squinted eye of prohibitionism still regards us with its glassy stare.

The aim of controlling what others do is a notion that dies hard, if ever. But it did not dampen the passion of West Coast vintners. Napa Valley roared back into production, with Sonoma not far behind. In Southern California, Leonard and Brooks Firestone tapped into the right combination of soil and climate to establish a vineyard in 1972. That was unheard of in northern Santa Barbara County, but it worked. The idea spread across the entire Santa Ynez Valley and traveled right on up U.S. 101 to dusty Paso Robles. Where virtually no vineyards existed a decade or so ago, the area now boasts—at last count—well over a hundred wineries. In the Pacific Northwest, prices for tiny but promising plots went ballistic after vineyards planted during the early 1970s started producing superb wines. Since then, West Coast winemakers have been winning international awards—many in head-to-head competitions on foreign soil. As recoveries go, this one is practically a Broadway show.

Has the industry suffered setbacks? You bet. A few years ago, weather conspired with (or against) California vintners to produce a wine glut of major proportions. Not only were barrels of premium wine going for a song, but the perceptions of consumers were being altered by the introduction of the Charles Shaw label, rights to which had been purchased by shoot-from-the-hip Bronco Wine. When introduced to a huge consumer market by the Trader Joe's chain at just $1.99—not a bad wine for the price—the Charles Shaw label was dubbed Two Buck Chuck and sold by the carload. Trader Joe's was moving one million cases each month, and nonprofit organizations rented Penske trucks to haul off as much of the stuff as possible for fund-raisers.

But the central issue was that consumers who had been buying premium wines began to wonder if they were worth the cost for Sunday night pizza. If Chuck was a thin wine, it was at least on the dry side. Some time passed until the Slow Food movement and vintners were able to persuade consumers to take another look at how foods enhanced by wine become more flavorful—and which foods don't pair well with a wine at all. If a fast-food burger doesn't care, they remind us, chances are the wine won't either.

All this had a notable effect on the industry, especially in the Pacific Northwest, where wineries have been locked in a thirty-year struggle to gain recognition for world-class products. Many wineries now use the word *value* right alongside traditional V words, such as *vintage* and *varietal*. And for small-lot producers wishing to build enduring relationships with wine buyers, the pairing of value with quality yields dividends in sales and loyalty.

The world has also turned a few clicks over the last three decades. Younger consumers, whose first experiences are varietals, rather than the syrupy wines of their parents' time, are far more interested in winemaking and food pairings today. West Coast vintners look to these young aficionados as a generation able to appreciate finer wines—and to raise the bar.

Southern California

California is, and may always be, astonishing. Hollywood's movies became the storytelling medium of our time. Sun-drenched beaches drew millions to a dream lifestyle reflecting California's celluloid self-image. The state is also a land of possibility—a place that transformed casual into laid-back, with everything from embroidered jeans with the knees cut out to thongwear.

A nexus of energy seems to reside in California. Yet even that can grow tiresome, which may account for well-entrenched professionals who suddenly throw off the harness to go in search of something less emotionally nomadic, something closer to the land.

Except during harvest, life moves at a slower pace in wine country, though a few acres of that rural feeling can cost millions. Still, the state's viticulture brought America to the world stage of wine, confusing Italy and annoying France. California's successes also gave ideas to Australia and New Zealand, both of which are major players. Not to mention Latin America and one day, perhaps, Iceland. One never knows.

Yet part of what is so appealing about life in the vineyards has nothing to do with competition. Instead, it is the collegial feeling to be found among winegrowers, along with their sense of personal responsibility for the land. Few, if any, industries show daily evidence of such cooperation as winegrowers offer one another. In short, it's about getting better together.

All this has led to happier days for wine lovers. Now, everyman has a seat at the table. A glass or bottle of very good wine no longer doubles the cost of a meal. For the wine industry, it wasn't easy. California is rich in military technology and corporate farming, but huge government subsidies are not awarded to winemaking, though it might be a good idea—if only as a preventive measure. In any case, winegrowing started in opposite ends of the state and traveled toward the middle. Southern California was first, with the Franciscans leading the way. Father Junipero Serra is said to have planted his first vineyard in 1769. But wine grapes were being harvested in the Southwest as early as the 1580s. As many of those clerics and settlers moved westward, they may have been first to plant in California.

For all our enthusiasm over the success of West Coast wines, it is still important to remember that, historically, the gold standard for how wines are measured has been French. Regardless of a bumpy road, the French industry and our own are intertwined. Without centuries of experience in the Burgundy, Bordeaux, and Rhône regions in France—plus the number of West Coast winemakers who trained there—we would have few, if any, of our big Cabernets, elegant Syrahs, and delicate Pinots. No single nation has done more to blend wine, food, art, and conversation than France. We have grown up with the fruits of *le culture général*. If a bit of competitive foolishness was also involved, let us acknowledge our debt to the French and, in the Hollywood tradition, cut to the celebration.

Note: *As a reminder, this guide is a sampler—an opportunity to visit unique inns, wineries, and restaurants. Be sure to explore beyond that. Local wine trails will take you along glorious backcountry roads, with knockout views around every bend. So, enjoy. Return to enjoy again. And take a designated driver with you—or take it easy.*

TEMECULA AREA

Inn at Churon Winery → Leonesse Cellars → Wilson Creek
Winery & Vineyards → Mount Palomar Winery → Baily
Vineyard & Winery → Carol's Restaurant

A third of the way from San Diego to Los Angeles along I-15 is one of the fastest-growing areas in Southern California. Not long ago, Temecula was a small agrarian town. Now it's a bustling resort area with eighteen wineries or more within minutes of one another. If you want golf or a spa and shopping as part of your winetasting experience, this is indeed a place to sample a bit of everything. A map of the wineries is available from Temecula Valley Winegrowers Association. Visit www.temeculawines.org or phone (951) 699-6586. The Temecula Valley Convention and Visitors Bureau also offers a detailed planning guide on their well-designed Web site. Visit www.temeculacvb.com or phone (888) 363-2852.

A few minutes east of I-15, along Rancho California Road, are a number of top wineries, some with luxurious inns, and a few with excellent restaurants. So let's begin by settling in. Sited atop its vineyards, **Inn at Churon Winery** features a French château look at 33233 Rancho California Road. Visit www.innatchuronwinery.com or phone (951) 694-9070. Accommodations are superb, with inviting fireplaces and spa-style tubs, if you can pull yourself away from the view. An unhurried breakfast is served in the dining room, or by request, on your patio. A tasting room is part of the inn, where guests may join an evening wine reception, and if you're relatively new to winetasting, the reception will help your palate get its bearings. You can't go wrong with any of the whites, and the tasting-room staff will guide you along. These are wines with full aromas and fruity richness. Their Viognier, coming into favor these days, is a standout. Churon's reds are excellent as well. Be sure not to miss their Syrah. Light on the palate, yet rich and jammy, with undercurrents of oak. Just the thing for sipping by a fireplace.

With two or more days to spend, you'll be able to visit all the tasting rooms that interest you in the Temecula area. For one day, or to set your palate for later discoveries, begin out on De Portola Road and work your way back, especially if it's a weekend and other visitors are headed in the opposite direction. An easy route is south along Anza Road. At the junction with De Portola Road, turn east (left) and continue a few minutes to **Leonesse Cellars** on the south side at 38311 De Portola Road. Visit www.leonesse cellars.com or phone (951) 302-7601. Here, you'll find that rare combination of warmth and handcrafted wines in a châteaulike setting. It's a reminder that awards are deserved by tasting-room staff as well as by the wine. Take a tour and settle in to sample the delightful and unusual range of wines from Leonesse. If you're a white-wine buff, yet curious about the darker side, home in on the White Merlot. It's a delicate wine, done in a Rosé style, but complex and rich in its fruity qualities, with a full-mouth finish. The Leonesse Merlot is superb: very smooth, with a balance of fruit and spice, and an elegant, long-lasting finish. For Cabernet

Sauvignon lovers, Leonesse has an outstanding offering. Barrel-aged for more than two years, this big red opens quickly and is light on its feet. The blend reduces any hint of edginess, leaving a memorable drink-or-keep wine. Attractive pricing. Don't leave for home without some.

Continue east on De Portola Road and turn west (left) on Glenoaks Road to the T-intersection with Rancho California Road, and turn southwest (left). **Wilson Creek Winery & Vineyards** will be on the north side of the road, just after the turn, at 35960 Rancho California Road. Visit www.wilsoncreek winery.com or phone (951) 699-9463. This is a traditional family-run estate winery. It's fun, too—almost a college campus atmosphere. And if you haven't visited the idea of wine-as-dessert in a while, or if you're a card-carrying chocolate freak as I am, plan to stay a spell. First, for you white-wine fanciers, sample the White Cabernet. Produced from red Cabernet grapes, this wine can surprise you. Smooth and fruity, with the depth of a red, it has deeper aromas than its color would suggest, plus a grand finish. If you're ready for something new at a holiday buffet, this one could be just what you've been looking for. As for reds, you can just knock yourself out. Aside from inaugural Reserve Cabernets, Wilson Creek's Syrah is excellent, and their Estate Syrah is both big and lovely. If you're a Cabernet Sauvignon fancier, this wine may cause you to reconsider. It is full-flavored, with fruit, spice, and a smoky oak undercurrent that seems just right.

Here is an attention-getter for chocolatismos. Picture a two-ounce chocolate cup filled with Decadencia, a rich Chocolate Port. After you've downed half, it's refilled with Wilson Creek's Almond Champagne. Finish that, and an additional side of Almond Champagne appears. Now, consume the chocolate shot glass that started it all. . . .

Whether today or tomorrow, **Mount Palomar Winery** is next at 33820 Rancho California Road. Visit www.mountpalomar .com or phone (951) 676-5047. Ask about the history of this winery's founder, John H. Poole, a true pioneer. California natives will remember when KBIG-AM broadcast live from the dance floor of the Great White Steamship, which carried a world-record twenty-five million passengers to Catalina Island and back in its fifty years. Well, before establishing this vineyard in 1969, John set up that radio station, which danced its way into the hearts of a generation of Southern Californians.

Though the history here is free, Mount Palomar also has a fine deli that will help you keep your shiny side up. And the wines here are recognized as top-notch. Their Chardonnay is rich, but drier and less buttery than many. Oak is subdued, allowing crisp fruit flavors to flourish, leading to an unusually long finish. Which leads us straight to Mount Palomar's outstanding Riesling. If you like a drier Chardonnay, their Riesling will hold your interest. Still delicate, this wine has heady aromas and a superb finish. In red wines, the Castelletto Sangiovese is outstanding, as is the Cabernet Sauvignon. But don't miss the Meritage. This wine has a long, classic history stemming from Bordeaux blends, and Mount Palomar has done well in extending that legacy. If Cabernet Sauvignon is a little too athletic for you, this wine offers the same oak-and-tannin base, but in a very smooth, velvety blend that will pair well— and hold its own—with almost any food from broils to spicy dishes.

Just a bit farther west is **Baily Vineyard & Winery,** just around the corner at 33440 La Serena Way. Visit www.baily winery.com or phone (951) 676-9463. This is a top-tier winery with the well-recognized **Carol's Restaurant** on the premises.

Award-winning wines and an outstanding menu combine to bring Southern California travelers here time and again.

To cross Los Angeles from Temecula Valley and reach Highway 1 on the coast, take northbound I-15. At the Highway 91 interchange—to avoid driving too far inland—take westbound 91. A portion of this state route is a toll road, and worth it. Continue on Highway 91 for the opportunity to take northbound I-5. Continue to the exit for I-10 westbound toward Santa Monica. I-10 will narrow down near the beach, where you'll pass through a tunnel and be northbound on Highway 1 in Malibu. Continue on Highway 1. In light to moderate traffic, crossing Los Angeles will take two hours or more. Everyone wishes it could be easier. It just isn't.

Central California Coast

Central California's coast and valleys begin, more or less officially, on the Oxnard Plain and continue to an indeterminate point near Monterey Bay. A social geographer remarked that Northern California begins where the largest cash crop is neither produce nor wine, but a substance. That said, let's focus on wineries, inns, and restaurants northwest of Los Angeles.

OXNARD AREA

Herzog Wine Cellars → Tierra Sur Restaurant

Oxnard, with its strawberry fields and beaches, has never been a wine destination. That may change with the opening of **Herzog Wine Cellars,** which has been producing prizewinning premium wines since the nineteenth century, and is now focusing on Special Reserve and artisan wines. Visit www.herzogwinecellars.com or phone (805) 983-1560. From Highway 1, take the Rice Avenue exit north. From U.S. 101, exit south on Del Norte Boulevard to a right to 3201 Camino Del Sol. Although this is a techie-style neighborhood, Herzog's architecture is welcoming, and once inside the open spaces soar and flow toward the winetasting bar. Interested in what an interior designer can do with confluent right angles? Take a long look at the intricacy of form in the wall-filling display of Herzog wines. The effect is mesmerizing, and to a wine lover, encouraging as well.

Herzog's Special Reserve Merlot and Cabernet Sauvignon, both from Alexander Valley, are excellent and represent a fine distinction between two handpicked, polished reds. An undercurrent of oak and tannins support the higher berry flavors, and both finish smoothly. Herzog's Special Reserve Syrah from Edna Valley is even more enterprising. Syrahs can sometimes be a little weak in the knees, but this wine is delightful: strong fruit over a base of undeniable breadth. Drinkable now or later, Herzog's Syrah will stand up to a wide variety of foods and spices. Read on to see how.

Tierra Sur Restaurant is located on the Herzog premises and represents a singular achievement in adapting Mediterranean cuisine to Baja-influenced menu items. The result is a spice-focused interpretation of West Coast favorites such as lamb with salsa. Never heavy, this combination requires a light hand and a clear goal. Chef Todd Aarons provides both. And the Syrah? Delicate as it is, this wine will embrace the spicy overtones in either grilled meat or fish. A prix fixe meal with wine pairings is also available and well served. *Salud!*

SANTA BARBARA AREA

Santa Barbara Winery → Wine Cask
→ bouchon santa barbara

Most of Santa Barbara County's wine culture exists in valleys to the north. Yet with this city's Spanish-surfing-Mediterranean blend of style and substance, Santa Barbara caresses the imagination like no other. My days here, living up on Alameda Padre Serra, were sweet beyond compare, so we might pause for a little winetasting. And if the sense of this place reaches out to you, fine restaurants are close at hand.

On the beach side of the freeway, at 202 Anacapa Street on the corner of Yanonali Street, is the tasting room for **Santa Barbara Winery,** located here since the early 1960s. Visit www.sbwinery.com or phone (805) 963-3633. This urban winery is a paradigm for oceanside Santa Barbara—off-the-shoulder, yet still off-the-wall. Tasting-room staffers display an easy, classy knowledge; the laughter is frequent but never off-key. And with the front door often left open, you can smell the Pacific. Oh, yes, they also have wine. Their Chardonnays and Sauvignon Blancs are full and rich, with little except your personal enzymes to make a choice. Reds are a somewhat different matter. These present an increase in complexity and balance, with firm tannins, that can make your eyes wander. Compare the Joughin Vineyard Negrette and Joughin Primitivo to taste different characteristics from the same vineyard. As light-hearted tasting goes, this is an attractive tasting room with great potential.

Locals and visitors alike dote on the **Wine Cask** restaurant in El Paseo at 813 Anacapa Street. Visit www.winecask .com or phone (805) 966-9463. Some places lose their flair, not El Paseo. It is truly a courtyard passageway, so secluded that it's been hip from the outset. And Wine Cask's dining area is what most French bistros would be, if they could, with high ceilings, muted lighting, and enough space between tables to contain the privacy of your own conversation. Add more than forty wines available by the glass, plus an atlas-sized wine list, and cuisine that is as worldly as it is local. Vegetarian request? Just let them know in advance and enjoy the surprise.

bouchon santa barbara at 9 W. Victoria Street serves up California cuisine as if it had a French passport. Visit www.bouchonsantabarbara.com or phone (805) 730-1160. Salads and appetizers are excellent and the entrées are celebrations in themselves. Try the house-made ravioli as a prelude to a seafood dish. Presentation is grand and the menu is structured around local growers and specialty shops like C'est Cheese.

From Santa Barbara, consider two routes north. For a warm day (or evening), there's nothing quite like the drive up coastal U.S. 101. About ten minutes beyond the tunnel, at the Highway 246 junction, turn east toward Solvang and continue into the Santa Ynez area. Or on cooler days, exit the freeway in Santa Barbara onto Highway 154 for the San Marcos Pass. This smooth, curvy two-lane, with grassy tablas and oak-shrouded arroyos, sweeps past Lake Cachuma toward Santa Ynez, Los Olivos, and Solvang: wine destinations of fame and merit.

SANTA YNEZ AREA

The Ballard Inn & Restaurant → Fess Parker's Wine Country Inn & Spa → Santa Ynez Inn → Artiste Impressionist Winery & Tasting Studio → Sunstone Vineyards and Winery → Lucas & Lewellen Tasting Room → Daniel Gehrs Wines → Richard Longoria Wines → Los Olivos Café & Wine Merchant → Fess Parker's Wine Country Inn Restaurant

This cozy valley region evolved from a Santa Barbara hideaway to an area with few peers in the production of handcrafted wines. The fruit here is favored by sloped terroir, with ancient riverbed drainage, plus morning sea mists that give way to high midday temperatures. Viticulture spread throughout the area in the early 1970s as local vintners like Pierre Lafond and Brooks Firestone began to produce interesting wines. For excellent printed guides to the region, visit www.syvva.com or phone (805) 686-0053. As a rule of thumb, great inns tend to follow great estate vineyards. The Santa Ynez Valley has a plentiful share of both.

The Ballard Inn & Restaurant at 2436 Baseline Avenue is a top inn by any measure—a superb bed-and-breakfast, with friendly, yet meticulous service. Visit www.ballardinn.com or phone (805) 688-7770. The inn's superb restaurant, choreographed by chef-owner Budi Kazali brings a flair for Pan-Pacific dishes to each night's offerings. Menus change regularly but keep an eye out for shellfish dumplings that are a wonder in lobster broth with shiitake mushrooms. The dining-room staff is well versed in wine-food pairings and able to suggest combinations from mild to wild. All in perfect taste, of course. In a secluded area, between Los Olivos and Santa Ynez, the Ballard Inn offers a shady veranda during the day and neighborly streets to walk after dinner. This place, with its lovely accommodations and fine dining, is truly an inn for all seasons.

In Los Olivos, **Fess Parker's Wine Country Inn & Spa** at 2860 Grand Avenue is one of a kind. Visit www.fessparker.com or phone (805) 688-7788. Furnishings and service infuse the inn with a fashionable quality that reflects the affable owner's personal grace and sense of style. This is a place for amiable conversation—an artform that Fess himself seems to have invented—and for relaxation. Not to mention wedding parties and soirées with a western touch. The inn and spa bring it all together in a country-gentleman fashion. A full breakfast is included, and as a guest of the inn, you'll enjoy a complimentary bottle of wine and time to consider life in its fullness.

Santa Ynez Inn at 3627 Sagunto Street in Santa Ynez has few peers and is located within steps of several tasting rooms. Visit www.santaynezinn.com for an online preview or phone (805) 688-5588. The inn's exterior is pure California Country in design. Yet by degrees from the lobby and adjacent library, the inn engages you with fireplace-lit rooms and suites that are worthy of English or French royals. As with true elegance, it's understated, of course. But every detail, from furnishings to light control is inviting and intuitive. Let your imagination roam and this inn is surely one place it will settle. Evening desserts and winetasting are complimentary, and a delicious gourmet breakfast prepared by chef Johanna Trujillo is included. From meaty to vegetarian, she has a light touch. Take in the special moments this inn offers and relish the tree-shaded grounds and the solitude this valley has always conveyed.

To discover how the Impressionistic qualities of art and winemaking produce a remarkable blend—and tasting-room experience—be sure to make time for **Artiste Impressionist Winery & Tasting Studio** at 3569 Sagunto Street, just a few steps west of Santa Ynez Inn. Visit www.artiste.com or phone (805) 686-2626. Vintner Bion Price and his partners have created an unforgettable studio for wine and art lovers. In the foyer is the tasting bar, surrounded by ceiling-high displays of prints by the artists whose works appear on Artiste's labels. To the rear of the tasting room are instructional areas where students of art and winemaking can pursue their crafts. Yet none of this is more striking than the wines themselves. All are blends and light on their feet. First Dance is a hearty but sensuous amalgam of Neo-Burgundy, Pinot, and Syrah. Impromptu picks up the tempo, and Perfecto relaxes a bit, with its Rhône style: full on the palate, with a posh, lingering finish. Rustique carries a label from an original painted in wine on paper by resident artist Christina LoCascio. Everything about this wine is elegant and surprising—even in a current-year vintage.

I asked Bion how he managed to create Rustique.

"I think that wine has a slight advantage over the others in its bottle age. . . ."

"Of course, but a predominant Merlot, blended with Cabernet Sauvignon, Cabernet Franc, Grenache, and Viognier? Those are a lot of plates to have in the air all at once."

Bion grinned. "Who would have guessed those varietals worked together? I didn't, until we tried it."

Artiste reminds us that in tasting, there is always art.

After tasting and viewing at Artiste, it's a pleasant drive south to sister winery **Sunstone Vineyards and Winery** at

125 Refugio Road. Visit www.sunstonewinery.com or phone
(805) 688-9463. From tree-shaded parking, a curving path will
guide you past rich plantings of lavender and rosemary toward a
tasting room of warmth and welcome. A Rice family enterprise,
everyone contributes here. Linda Rice is a designer. Notice the
river rocks lining the doorway, each handpicked and placed by
Linda. Her builder-husband, Fred Rice, handled overall construction. Let your eyes linger over the details, for they embody
both the quality and organic nature of this winery. Built in a
Provençal style, the structure is in no way pretentious. Instead,
it also projects the engaging nature of a hacienda from early
Californio days when splendor rose from simplicity and regard
for the land.

As for the wines, they are prizewinners initially created by
consulting winemaker Daniel Gehrs, a name synonymous with
innovative, handcrafted premium wines of exceptional character. Three organically grown wines of note are Rapsodie du
Soleil, an excellent Syrah blend; Sunstone's award-winning Reserve Syrah, with deep color, aroma, flavors, and an elegant finish; and Eros, an estate blend of complexity and balance, with a
superb finish.

From Sunstone, return north and turn left (west) on Highway 246 into Solvang for the **Lucas & Lewellen Tasting
Room** at 1645 Copenhagen Drive. Visit www.llwine.com or
phone (805) 686-9336. Housed in a renovated shop, this tasting
room invites relaxation and a bit of rumination. This is due in
part to the combined vision of retired judge Royce Lewellen,
who knows this valley and its people, and master vintner Louis
Lucas, who has sold wine grapes to a dozen or more premium
California wineries. The gift shop is well stocked with items you

won't find everywhere. Part of that is because Royce admires craftsmanship in every form—especially in winegrowing. Royce once remarked that he'd been a judge for twenty years, making decisions every day. "But these winegrowers are making decisions every five seconds." He could have included winemakers as well; one of which is Daniel Gehrs, whom we'll meet in a moment. But to put the winery's tasting room's wines in perspective, wine writer Michael O'Shea once paraphrased humorist Will Rogers by saying, "I never met a Lucas & Lewellen wine I didn't like." No arguments there, for the Lucas & Lewellen wines are splendid: smooth, velvety, and filled with character. Their Chardonnay is a triple-gold winner and sells for just more than twenty bucks. If you are drawn to value-priced prizewinners, don't pass this one by. Of course, red wines are quick to win my heart and Lucas & Lewellen offers a line of beauties. Their Syrah reveals the paradoxical nature of truth: it is both lively and composed. Its viscosity is high enough to make perfect windows against the side of your glass and the wine opens quickly into deep, rich fruit flavors, with earthy bass notes underlining harmonies of spice. Altogether grand to drink now, it should age gracefully as well. A special treat, which like Malbec is usually reserved for blending, is the Petite Verdot. Not easy to find in the marketplace, this wine from Lucas & Lewellen is remarkable in its fullness and delicacy. Dark and velvety, this is a remarkable wine—far more complex and robust than one would expect—yet with a smooth don't-let-me-go finish. Then, just when it appears impossible for Lucas & Lewellen to top themselves, along comes their Cote del Sol Cabernet Sauvignon—full-bodied and rich, this wine needed a light touch of Syrah to round off the edges and remind us what we first liked about red wines. Tannins and underlying oak textures are present but well controlled, allowing the wine's jammy quality to come through across the full palate and fade away into a holy-smokes finish. This wine rang up double-gold and best-of-class awards. Which is to say that I may be easy, but never indiscriminate. Enjoy.

Over in Los Olivos, **Daniel Gehrs Wines** is located in historic Heather Cottage at 2939 Grand Avenue. Visit www .dgwines.com or phone (805) 693-9686. Daniel acknowledges that his interest in winemaking in the Santa Ynez area was a bit premature. The action was still up north. But with support from his wife Robin—who went back to teaching as needed to keep their own winery dream alive—Daniel kept the family enterprise moving forward. He rescued abandoned properties, became winemaker at Zaca Mesa, and spurred development of award-winning wines from other family estates, including Lucas & Lewellen and Sunstone. The Daniel Gehrs tasting room is managed by daughter Jennifer Gehrs, as the winery continues its focus on producing high-quality wines with moderate pricing. Jennifer is also winemaker, bottler, and label designer for her own Vixen line of wines. I asked Jennifer about her path and passion in viticulture.

"If I were to put any stock in 'fate,' I would have to say that was what led me here. Yes, I grew up in the wine industry. But it was never suggested that I pursue this as a career. It simply landed in my lap at age twenty-one, and I've been enjoying it ever since. I would have been foolish not to take advantage of contacts with growers at some of the best vineyards in Santa Barbara County, and my dad's help as a consultant. Six years and six vintages later, my interest has blossomed into a passion. I don't know where this path will lead, only that I will continue to follow it until the road ends . . . wherever that may be."

Under the Vixen label, with its foxy Art Nouveau design, Jennnifer's wines are lighthearted and inviting. Her Viognier is bright, crisp, and filled with complex aromas and flavors of spice and blossoms. It is also quite full on the palate, not unlike this region's buttery Chardonnays, but with an air of mystery complemented by a long finish. The Vixen Cabernet Franc is smooth, velvety, and playful, with a musical quality to fit its story. This wine fills the palate in a subtle fashion, leading to a languourous finish—a wine for either conversation or quiet reflection.

A few steps away, the tasting room for **Richard Longoria Wines** is at 2935 Grand Avenue in Los Olivos. Visit www .longoriawine.com or phone (805) 688-0305. Richard Longoria was well into his development of a full range of superb wines when he was taken by the aromas and flavors of Cabernet Franc and produced a few lots. But as once was true, even of stalwart Chardonnay, wine buyers were skeptical. Cabernet Franc was known as a good wine for blending but not as a stand-alone. Rick was determined to change that viewpoint and has done so, with the help of an inspired artist series of labels for his Cabernet Franc: Blues Cuvée. Taking a lead position in winemaking is difficult enough. Blending art, music, and wine adds to the complexity.

"As one of the first winemakers to come to the Santa Ynez Valley in 1976, I developed a pioneering spirit about our area's possibilities for winegrowing," Rick says. "I've been driven to discover what grape varietals grow well here, and do my best to produce wines that help define what the highest potential is for our region. Longoria Wines will always be a laboratory for this pursuit and exploration." Longoria's wines demonstrate it.

Los Olivos Café & Wine Merchant is just down the street

at 2889 Grand Avenue and is one of the mainstays of this village, almost a culinary general store for the town. Originally, the place was a restaurant only, but owners Sam and Shawnda Mamorstein recognized an opportunity when an adjoining shop went vacant. He knocked out a major part of the intervening wall and filled the shop with more than three hundred wines to complement the café's unique California-style Mediterranean cuisine. Visit www.losolivoscafe.com or phone (805) 688-7265. The café's luncheon, afternoon light, and dinner menus are so extensive that you'll have an opportunity to pair food with your choice of wines, rather than the other way around. Petite dishes are also available. Even designated drivers are not left out. Try the cranberry-ginger cooler or rosemary lemonade with your meal. Wine lovers will find any number of dishes to enhance a tempting Viognier or Riesling, from paella or hand-rolled spinach gnocchi to a Greek pizza. A well-turned or hearty red will find companionship with everything from exquisite roasted veggie dishes to Kobe beef specialties. Take advantage of the small split-plate fee and order a delectable combination. And be sure to check out the wines from Bernat, Sam's own label. Reservations are a good idea year-round, and you'll want to be seated early—the better people-watching tables are out front. Los Olivos Café is a place to dine with enthusiasm, sip excellent wines, enjoy a conversation, and watch California's passing parade.

Fess Parker's Wine Country Inn Restaurant is just a bit farther along and across the street, at 2860 Grand Avenue. Visit www.fessparker.com/restaurant.htm or phone (805) 688-7788. In the dining room, as with the inn itself, furnishings are a mix of class and country. Laura Kath and Doug Margerum joined Fess Parker and me for dinner one evening. In his seamless way, Fess shared stories about his life and what this inn means to him. Food, paired with selected wines, enriched the conversation. Chef Troy Tolbert stopped by to suggest an entrée of grilled Hawaiian swordfish, spiny lobster with roasted gold beet creamy rice, and persimmon vinaigrette. It won several votes along with Doug's Margerum M5 wine. My vegetarian choice was crispy sun-dried tomato polenta, grilled portabella mushrooms, and wilted spinach. A Margerum Columbia Valley Pinot Gris seemed just right, and was.

By dessert, conversation drifted to how we all came to be here, at this time. As it happens, I once worked with the late Tom Blackburn, who wrote the lyrics for the "Ballad of Davy Crockett," and I'd been carrying a long-undelivered message from him. Fess smiled about that in the gentle, open way he has.

"Tom Blackburn was one of my closest friends," he said, "and it was a really good song. What many of those who remember the show don't realize is that *Davy Crockett* lasted only a short time, while *Daniel Boone* went on for years."

We traded another tale or two, ordered nearly every chocolate item we could, and said good night. The town closes up early and in walking a block or so to my inn, starlight uncommon to the coast shone down to round out a perfect evening with dear people.

SANTA MARIA AREA

The Historic Santa Maria Inn → Firestone Vineyard → Curtis Winery → Fess Parker Winery & Vineyard → Zaca Mesa Winery → Rancho Sisquoc Winery → Cottonwood Canyon Vineyard & Winery → Costa de Oro Winery → The Wine Cottage Bistro

For wine-country maps and information, visit www.santa maria.com or phone (805) 925-2403. The Santa Maria Valley is a distinct and fast-growing part of Santa Barbara County but maps of wine country are sometimes narrow in coverage. Be sure to have Santa Maria's own guide at hand.

For lodging, **The Historic Santa Maria Inn,** 801 South Broadway, is in a class by itself. Visit www.santamariainn.com or phone (805) 928-7777. Opened in 1917, this oasis has offered first-class accommodations to travelers and movie stars— including Clark Gable, who made the inn a regular stopover on his treks north from Hollywood. With the rise of first-class vineyards in this area, the Santa Maria Inn has maintained its graciousness and fine dining. Also featured is a below-ground wine cellar and bar for those who appreciate sipping while touched by a sense of history.

For a lovely tour through Santa Maria's wine country, continue west on Highway 154 from the Santa Ynez area, and turn right (north) on Zaca Station Road, just a few yards short of the U.S. 101 entrance. If you miss the turn, don't worry. Just cross over the bridge and make a *cautious* U-turn to make it back to Zaca Station Road.

Firestone Vineyard is first along the Foxen Canyon Wine Trail at 5000 Zaca Station Road. Visit www.firestonewine.com or phone (805) 688-3940. Firestone Vineyard was first planted in 1972, and it has changed the face of this region.

I asked Brooks Firestone to reminisce a bit.

"After twelve years at Firestone Tire and Rubber Company, I felt my tour was over. We also wanted to move into the country, where there was more room and a good place for kids. My father found this ranch. Nothing much was being done with it, and I started studying the possibilities."

"What did you discover?"

"It seemed clear to me that wine is a commodity and that just growing grapes left the whole marketing end open. So, we went to work on the idea of a winery. In this area, that was a fairly new idea at the time and it took awhile to move it along."

But founders Brooks and Kate Firestone did move it along. Son Adam was adept at both winemaking and management, so the family vineyard estate is now under third-generation direction. The Firestone Vineyard tasting room also set a new standard for the area. With a soaring roofline and open interior, the centerpiece tasting bar fills quickly on weekends. Firestone has a reputation for crisp California wines with an earthy quality. Tasters often notice it first in white wines: the Chardonnay is as bright as it is buttery, and where Sauvignon Blanc can sometimes be a little bland, Firestone's will stand up to grilled shellfish or a spicy lamb dish. The Reserve Merlot is smooth, yet has admirable complexity, and Firestone's Syrah is rich, ripe, and filled with spice. For a top-end taste, be sure to try the Bordeaux-style blend of The Ambassador. Oak flavors are light but sufficiently present as a bass note, highlighting deep fruit and spices, overtones of chocolate, and a long, delectable finish. Firestone Vineyard is a historic starting point for a classic California wine trail. Enjoy your time here.

Curtis Winery is within walking distance, a quarter mile farther north, at 5249 Foxen Canyon Road. Visit www.curtiswinery.com or phone (805) 686-8999. Although Firestone Vineyard and Curtis Winery are related—tasting-room fees are interchangeable—the two are remarkable in their differences. Where Firestone soars, Curtis lifts like an ocean mist. Their vineyard is dedicated to Rhône-style wines, and the tasting room carries an ephemeral Moorish-Mediterranean-Modern quality that suggests homeyness steeped in mystery. Even Curtis Winery labels are deep-hued in their celebration of the land and its bounty. The Viognier is a lovely white wine, though not so well known as Chardonnay in this region. Fruity and barrel-aged, with a mouth-filling texture and up-front fruitiness that brings both citrus and lilac to mind. Curtis Vineyard Syrah is to red-wine fans what their Viognier is to white fanciers: a paradox. Curtis Crossroads Syrah is deep in aroma, dense yet lithe, and never imposes itself on wine-and-food pairings. The Crossroad, a Syrah Noir, goes a step further in blending Syrah with Grenache. An oak-shaded arroyo for the fruit and gentle wine-making make this a complex but not overbearing wine that surprises many winetasters. Let one of them be you.

Fess Parker Winery & Vineyard at 6200 Foxen Canyon Road is among the busier of the tasting rooms in this area, yet manages to convey a feeling of returning to the old homestead. It's a rambling place, with low-angled rooflines and verandas that mirror the surrounding hills—and plenty of space to swing your arms. Visit www.fessparker.com/html/winery.html or phone (805) 688-1545. The winery and vineyards have been a long-term family venture. I wondered about that and asked Ashley Parker Snider.

"Not long ago, I had dinner with your dad, Ashley, and it strikes me that each person in your family is a strong individual. How did all that work out when developing vineyards and a winery from scratch?"

"I feel fortunate to work with my brother, husband, dad, and mom. Truthfully, it can be a little stressful at times. But we started out in this business with little knowledge and have grown together as a family and as vintners. We made mistakes along the way, but have learned so much, not just about the business but ourselves as well."

"You seem passionate about both your family and creating award-winning wines."

"It's gratifying to develop into a winery considered to be one of the top producers from the Santa Barbara area."

"And you stay away from trends?"

"Yes. We made the decision to stick to our varietals and our convictions, by playing to family strengths and the land. Santa Barbara County is special as a viticultural region to be sure. . . . It's also very easy on the eyes!"

It is that, and Fess Parker wines are indeed award-winners, well matched to the region and its terroir. Two winning whites are the Santa Barbara County Viognier and Ashley's Vineyard Chardonnay. The Viognier, largely from neutral barrels, offers fragrant aromas of fruit and spices. If you're not yet familiar with Viognier, this wine will present the crispness of a Riesling, coupled with a softer white. Delicate but not shy, this wine will work well with spicy foods without losing its table manners. The Ashley's Vineyard Chardonnay represents a California classic, only more so. With fruit-forward aroma and a buttery texture, you might expect this wine to be rounded and well-balanced. Yet it also has a crisp quality coupled with a nuttiness and slight oak undertones, with a long finish, that make it perfect for a stand-alone or a wine to pair with white meats or soft cheeses like Brie or Camembert. Fess Parker's Santa Barbara County Syrah is attention-getting right out of the bottle. Robust, dark, and somewhat northern in nature, it can open quickly or be a cherished keeper. If you've been looking for an able-bodied Syrah, this one may get your attention, as can their Santa Barbara County Pinot Noir. Pinot grapes are indeed delicate things—ask any wine-grower in Oregon—and require special care in California's softer climate. Yet the aroma and complex flavors of this wine are a testament to the attention of vineyard management and wine-making at Fess Parker. The wine is substantial and balanced, without giving up its delicacy—straight from the wine frontier, with a handful of wildflowers.

Zaca Mesa Winery at 6905 Foxen Canyon Road is a wonderful place to sample wines and picnic. Walk back down into the grove of shady oaks from the out-back parking area and everything appears expansive. In the tasting-room courtyard, giant chess pieces are set up on contrasting tiles. Make an opening gambit on your way in, and by the time you've finished your tasting, several players will have advanced the game. The tasting room and bar are spacious with no sense of crowding on a busy day. Visit www.zacamesa.com or phone (805) 688-9339.

Zaca Mesa has a strong reputation and wines are well presented. Their Estate Bottled Viognier is superb, overdelivering on its attractive price. Rich and dry, this wine will pair well with fish or fowl, while holding its own with Asian spices. The Z Cuvée is a blend with Grenache and Syrah on a foundation of Mourvèdre. Well-aged, this is a bold but smooth red that will do well with red-sauce pastas, grilled meats, and dishes rich with herbs. Zaca Mesa's Syrah is an outstanding example of how well this varietal can be crafted. It has an exceptionally deep color, with complex fruit aroma and flavors, and a long spicy-oak finish. The wine will cellar well and is bold enough to stand up to almost anything from the grill.

Rancho Sisquoc Winery at 6600 Foxen Canyon Road is a place that seems to spring from earlier times. It's not hard to imagine silver-saddled Californios from more than a century ago drifting in for a taste and a good vintage or two for the trail.

Winery manager Mary Holt smiles. "We work hard here to

make guests feel at home. Our tasting room is comfortable and inviting and we want to keep it that way."

I mention that Rancho Sisquoc is a favorite of two-lane travelers new to winetasting.

"We treat a guest who knows nothing about wine just as we treat the connoisseur. It helps to remember that at one time we were all among those who were learning," Mary says. "So, we open our doors and spend time letting guests get to know our wines."

And their wines are lovely: bold, yet smooth, and well-balanced. For reds, a good starting place is Sisquoc River Red. Sounds like an ordinary Table Wine, but it isn't. Not by a long shot. For oak fans, this wine leaps from the bottle and opens quickly with rich oak-tempered aromas and fruit. Not pushy, but full-mouthed, with a first-class finish. Rancho Sisquoc's Cabernet Sauvignon is classic: full and rich, with fruit and coffee flavors. It is not shy but neither is it too assertive, and unlike some Cabernets, opens quickly on being uncorked—a terrific wine. But there's more waiting in the wings. The Cellar Select Meritage (see the Self-Pronouncing Guide to Popular Wines) is marvelous. This wine may be more complex than the Cabernet red. It is somewhat reluctant to leave the bottle at first. But once it opens, Rancho Sisquoc Meritage is remarkable. Full in aroma and flavor, this wine could satisfy those who like both Pinot Noir and Cabernet Sauvignon. Lustrous and bright, it also shows a depth admirable in any blend. Looking for something that's both athletic and alluring? This Meritage may answer your call. Visit www.ranchosisquoc.com or phone (805) 934-4332.

If you were to imagine a place in farm country where a friend lived and made excellent wine, **Cottonwood Canyon**

Vineyard & Winery at 3940 Dominion Road would pretty well fit that image. Proprietor-winemaker Norman Beko produces small lots of premium wines that can dazzle, and the place is as friendly as a shady front porch on a summer afternoon.

"Our aim is to share our experience and environment as much as our wines," Norm says. "Our guests spend, on average, an hour and a half tasting and discovering food-wine pairings."

Like many estate wineries, Cottonwood Canyon is in transition. Visitors will soon find a restaurant and luxury bed-and-breakfast accommodations to enrich their experience of wines known for long-term aging and attention to detail from handpicking to corkage. Cottonwood Canyon's Barrel Select Chardonnay is a vision unto itself: pristine and bright, it displays a fruit-forward aroma and flavors that are full, yet not so buttery that the essence is lost—much more like a northern Chardonnay, with undeniable elegance and a grand finish. Consider pairing this white with anything from herbed dishes to Gulf Coast grills—this wine can dance to Asian or Cajun flavors. Cottonwood Canyon's Santa Maria Valley Pinot Noir extends from a lovely nose into mouth-filling fruit flavors that benefit from a few moments to open up. This is a well-developed Pinot Noir with soft tannins and a long earth-tone finish, approachable yet worthy of cellaring. It may well be, though, that the Sharon's Vineyard Pinot Noir from Cottonwood Canyon is the belle of the ball. Opening almost immediately, this is a wine you could serve on the *Orient Express* between stops, and still keep bottles of it for a decade. It is elegant, conversational, and given to an enduring finish that both surprises and satisfies. When winemakers speak of wine with a sense of place, this Pinot Noir has it.

"What are you really up to here at Cottonwood, Norm?" I asked.

"We create distinctively different, age-worthy wines," he answered.

No doubt. Visit www.cottonwoodcanyon.com or phone (805) 937-8463.

Continue north on Dominion Road and bend left onto Foxen Road, which becomes E. Betteravia Road. From there, it's easiest to take U.S. 101 northbound for 1 mile and exit at Stowell Road. **Costa de Oro Winery,** located just over the freeway to the east, is easily reached via the Stowell Road exit. Look for the tasting room and farm market on the west side at 1331 S. Nicholson Avenue, a few yards short of the stop sign. Visit www.costadeorowinery.com or phone (805) 922-1468.

Whether you follow this enchanting little wine loop north or south, include Costa de Oro. The tasting room design includes delightful features—be sure to notice the bar top—that Ken or Teresa Burke will be glad to point out. This winery may always be in transition. It evolved from a vegetable-growing hobby that became a major agricultural operation and found land suitable for wine grapes and little else—good fortune for us all. Once a roadside stand, this tasting room is still a good place to load up on fresh produce for a healthy picnic. And the wines are grand, accumulating high scores and show awards. Costa de Oro's Estate Chardonnay absolutely sparkles on being uncorked. Breathy and eager, with layered citrus, it can be paired with a surprising range of dishes. Costa de Oro's Sauvignon Blanc is a pirouette of unexpected flavors. Bright as well as elegant, this Blanc has the acidity to pair well with dishes from grilled shellfish to light Asian spices. The Colson Canyon Syrah is complex, yet inviting, with splendid aromas and layered flavors that extend into a long, lovely finish. But we are climbing

Jacob's ladder here. The Estate Gold Coast Pinot Noir is more than an excellent wine. Not really Central California, yet not Oregon, this wine is in a league of its own. Like many reds, it's good to give it a little time to relax after time in the bottle. Ah, but when it does, the aroma and fruit flavors wave off that extra touch of brightness that some Pinot Noirs present. This is an accommodating wine with a firm bass line and just the right harmonies at the top end—delicate aromas, exceptionally well-balanced flavors, and a decadent finish. Make no mistake; this is a wine to leave home for.

The Santa Maria Valley has often been a bit short on inspired restaurants. **The Wine Cottage Bistro** is a grand exception. Located at 285 S. Broadway in Orcutt, just south of Santa Maria along Broadway / Highway 135, turn left (west) on Clark Avenue and make another left on Old Town Orcutt's Broadway. You may also exit westbound on Clark Avenue from U.S. 101. The Wine Cottage Bistro will be on the right a block or so down. This little area may yet be to Santa Maria what SoHo is to New York. It's where the action is—with great food and an excellent wine selection. Visit www.winecottagebistro.com or phone (805) 934-4546. Rebecca Jacobs and Aimee Sigala dreamed up this marvelous place, their families jumped in. Together, they've made it all work, with charm, warmth, and a mutual understanding of how food-and-wine pairings must evolve to suit both season and uncommon releases. Both carnivores and veggivores will be delighted by the range of selections. Spanish flavors are present in some dishes, but enrich rather than intrude. Pair the wild boar short ribs—cooked more than four hours with lovely spices—with Ambullneo Bulldog Reserve, a decadent and sometimes brooding wine that remains balanced and sophisticated. The combination of spiced meat and earthy wine is truly mind-bending. Or try the brick-fired Spanish flatbread paired with A Silver Horse Big Easy: a blend of Tempranillo, Grenache, Cabernet Sauvignon, and a touch of Syrah. All wonderful, of course, but the molten lava cake for dessert is still inbound! Pair its luscious bubbling chocolate center with a Three Saints Cabernet Sauvignon from Happy Canyon and melt away into the universe. . . .

LOS ALAMOS AREA

Skyview Motel → Café Quackenbush in the Art Brut Gallery → Bedford Thompson Winery & Tasting Room

If you're roaming the Santa Maria Valley for a day or more, include a visit to Los Alamos. The town is one of those places that manages to reinvent itself as necessary. When the stagecoach route died, the town teamed up with a narrow-gauge railway and built a depot—it's now the Depot Antique Mall and Wine Pub, with about as much stuff as can be packed in. But things went sour for the narrow-gauge line when Southern Pacific Railway bypassed the town with its larger operation. Yet by the mid-1930s, automobiles were in and Los Alamos was right on U.S. 101. Business flourished until today's highway planners again bypassed the town. So, the place is reinventing itself once more. The **Skyview Motel,** above the highway at 9150 Highway 101 maintains its rustic ambiance—and its 360-degree view—while updating all the interiors. When I visited, the parking area looked like that of a Volvo-BMW dealership. Check it out at www.theskyviewmotel.com or phone (805) 344-3770. The place has been a landmark for U.S. 101 travelers, and with on-going restoration, will likely be so for years to come.

Down in town, you'll find two special places to eat, browse, and taste. Chef Jesper Johansson serves what should be called breakfast cuisine at **Café Quackenbush in the Art Brut Gallery** at 458 Bell Street. Visit www.generalstoreca.com or phone (805) 344-5181. Light, marvelous dishes that won't make your boots feel heavy, plus designer lunches that can get you through the day. Ask for a table on the gallery side and browse the collection while waiting for your fare.

Just a few steps down the street is the **Bedford Thompson Winery & Tasting Room** at 448 Bell Street. Visit www.bedfordthompsonwinery.com or phone (805) 344-2107. Founder and winemaker Stephan Bedford does more than highlight his own wines. He's a fountain of information on winemaking and a spellbinder, for Stephan is also a playwright and actor. You wanna know wine? He can do an improv on the state of winemaking that will both inform and entertain. Don't miss the curtain . . .

SAN LUIS OBISPO AREA

Salisbury Vineyards Tasting Room and Gallery → TASTE → Apple Farm Inn & Restaurant → Tolosa Winery → Piedra Creek Winery → Claiborne & Churchill Vintners → Kynsi Winery → Wolff Vineyards → Saucelito Canyon Vineyard → Ortman Family Vineyards → Baileyana-*tangent* Wineries → Café Roma

A glance at California's overall shape suggests an arm, with San Luis Obispo as the crook of its elbow—physically and culturally.

To the south are the beaches and postcard views. Above, the focus shifts to coastal valleys, with some of the most rapidly developing wine regions in the world. Fine inns and spas populate the region as well, so take some time here.

For a century, countless travelers along the earlier stagecoach route and U.S. 101 have gazed up at the schoolhouse on a hillside bluff, not far north of Pismo Beach. It seemed perfectly sited as a link from the past to the future, so it was saddening to see this landmark fall into disrepair in the 1960s. But where we highway regulars saw a dying schoolhouse, John Salisbury saw a tasting room. Renovation took years to complete, but for the family—and for travelers—it was worth the wait. Whatever your academic regrets, you'll love going to this school. **Salisbury Vineyards Tasting Room and Gallery** is located on the west side of U.S. 101, between Avila Beach Road and San Luis Bay Drive. Either exit will lead you to the schoolhouse at 6985 Ontario Road. Visit www.salisbury vineyards.com or phone (805) 595-9463. Salisbury wines seem suited to their terroir, yet are as distinctive as the tasting room. Their Pinot Naturale is layered, complex, and as Impressionistic as its label. Is it a Pinot Gris? A Chardonnay in disguise? Perhaps both, yet neither. Aroma and flavors are both bright and rich, with light bass notes, and the finish is slender and lingering. Salisbury's Syrah is superb. In a wine world where Syrah is sometimes misunderstood, this one is dark, dense, and mysterious, with persuasive tones of earth and smoke, plus a come-back-to-me finish. The Pinot Noir from Salisbury is just lovely—with an artful label reflective of this gallery-style tasting room. As you drive north along our mile wine trail, you'll find other renditions like this—different from those in the Central Coast—yet not with the Salisbury touch. Richer than it is bright, more amiable than athletic, this Pinot displays complexity and textures that this tender varietal can produce. Classes are over for now, but stick around for after-school activities.

Continuing on to San Luis Obispo—the first of many college towns on this grand tour, so pedestrians rule—head straight for **TASTE,** a unique tasting room supported by the San Luis Obispo Vintners and Growers Association, at 1003 Osos Street. Visit www.slowine.com or phone (805) 269-8278. Take the Osos Street exit southeast to Monterey Street. The tasting room is right on the corner. Maps for the city and nearby wineries are also available, plus a new method for sampling wines from throughout this ascending wine region. Management and staff of TASTE are knowledgeable about wine, and more to the point, they know the territory. Their tips on exceptional wines with unfamiliar labels make a visit well worthwhile.

The **Apple Farm Inn & Restaurant** at 2015 Monterey Street, just off the freeway, began as a small but memorable restaurant along U.S. 101. Back when a gallon of gasoline was only twenty cents, automobiles were also much slower over twisting highway grades. If you were headed north from L.A., mealtimes and overnights coincided nicely with towns like San Luis Obispo and Paso Robles. Since its 1976 opening as a restaurant, Apple Farm has grown to be a full-service inn. It has a quiet, secluded feeling, with rooms opening onto a garden court. This is a fine place to stay while exploring San Luis Obispo wineries. Visit www.applefarm.com or phone (805) 544-2040.

Tolosa Winery at 4910 Edna Road / Highway 227 is first on the Edna Valley loop and maintains a strong commitment to naturally expressed flavors in their estate-bottled wines. Visit www.tolosawinery.com or phone (805) 782-0500. Tolosa also produces two versions of their excellent Chardonnay: a traditional oak-barreled version and a no-oak interpretation. Make no mistake; these are both fine examples of Chardonnay from this region. Yet when tasted in tandem, first oak, then no-oak, the effect of a year in barrel versus tank can be surprising. The oak-barreled Chardonnay is full, rich, and on the buttery side, with a solid personality. No-oak is lighter, brighter, with a transparency in both aroma and flavor, plus a finer range of pairings: grilled fish or spicy risotto dishes, Spanish tapas or earthy fruit. No-oak Chardonnay enhances each in an unexpected way that must be experienced. Tolosa's Estate Pinot Noir has captured attention since its introduction. Tolosa's Central Coast Pinot Noir is their new kid on the block. Bottle-friendly, this wine holds deep color and aroma and opens almost immediately, filling the palate and offering a long finish. Tolosa correctly terms it a feminine wine, though she displays broad shoulders to match her grace and she can go the distance.

Piedra Creek Winery at 6425 Mira Cielo Drive, just east of Highway 227. Visit www.slowine.com/memberwineries.fsp and be sure to phone (805) 541-1281 to arrange a tasting or to be sure of new hours. This is one of California's emerging producers of premier handcrafted wines—very small, and a most worthwhile stop. To sample Romeo Zeuch's wines is to link arms in a dance across the centuries with Etruscan, French, and California winemakers. More than most, each wine from Piedra Creek carries a timeless signature. Their Pinot Noir has aromas and fruit flavors not usually found south of Oregon. And Romeo's Zinfandel is both robust and luscious, with tiptoe balance and an ability to age well. But Piedra Creek's San Floriano captures the essence of winemaking. A blend of estate-grown

Lagrein, with support from Merlot and Petite Sirah, and a touch of Dolcetto, this wine is marvelous in its richness. It opens fully in only a few minutes, with a flood of complex aromas and flavors. It will pair well with everything Italian, most meats, and almost anything vegetarian. And it makes lovely Romanesque windows in the glass.

Claiborne & Churchill Vintners at 2649 Carpenter Canyon Road / Highway 227. Visit www.claibornechurchill.com or phone (805) 544-4066. A charming place to visit and taste wines has been created here by Claiborne Thompson and Fredericka Churchill Thompson. Step inside their straw-bale winery building, where plastered walls are as thick as those of old California adobe structures—at a fraction of the weight—where neither heat nor air-conditioning is needed. The enterprise is another example of vintners who left the dark (in this case, academia) to find light in winemaking. Even so, they left a paper trail. You might ask Clay about the Runestone label.

But what was the tipping point for Clay and Fredericka?

"I'd already discovered a 1978 Edna Valley Chardonnay on a shelf back east," Clay says. "So we stopped in San Luis Obispo. Everything lined up, as with a midlife crisis. I talked myself into a job at a winery and here we are, happy in making our own wine."

Claiborne & Churchill focuses on dry Alsatian wines: Gewürztraminer and Riesling, along with Pinot Gris, and a few cases of Pinot Noir. These last two—which invite side-by-side tastings for sense of place—are the Twin Creeks and Edna Valley Pinot Noirs. The Twin Creeks is full and bold, without being aggressive, deep in color, and mouth-filling, while the Edna Valley is more subtle in the way its intensity is expressed, with fruit flavors and a sense of deep-rooted earthiness from the vines.

Now to their award-draped Central Coast Dry Gewürztraminer: Drawn from whole-cluster pressings, this wine is complex and balanced, with flavors that float over the palate to produce an enduring and endearing finish. I could only wish for two variations of it to taste. This is a splendid wine, true to its German heritage, yet uniquely expressive. I poured it for dinner with a friend who is a master of blending flavors like curry and saffron with vegetables, lamb, or seafood. And the truth is, edgy wines are often needed to stand up to the test of her cuisine. Yet the Gewürztraminer from Claiborne & Churchill infused its own aromas and distinctive flavors to produce a lively pairing—and a lengthy conversation about dessert.

Just minutes south, depart Highway 227 to the east for **Kynsi Winery** at 2212 Corbett Canyon Road. Visit www.kynsi.com or phone (805) 544-8461. Look for the classic Mack truck still earning its daily keep, as does the barn owl that lives on the property and appears on the label. Owls help control vineyard rodents, which are themselves nocturnal. The charming tasting room and winery are located in a renovated dairy barn from a half-century ago. High coved ceilings and the original cold room door leading to the wine vault contribute to the tasting room's unique character. When on a wine quest, it's easy to forget that vineyards are part of agriculture. This winery is a reminder. The wines here are as fresh and timeless as the setting. Owners and winemakers Don and Gwen Othman focus on high-quality, low-yield Pinot Noir, Syrah, Pinot Blanc, Chardonnay, and Zinfandel. Kynsi's wines are balanced, with depth, complexity, and a timeless sense of place.

At Tiffany Ranch Road, turn left (east) and left (north) again at the T-intersection for **Wolff Vineyards** at 6238 Orcutt Road. Visit www.wolffvineyards.com or phone (805) 781-0448. The

winery, tasting room, and picnic area are on a peaceful hilltop—
you can see visitors unwind as they settle in, and owner-
winemaker Jean-Pierre Wolff obligingly signs bottles for special
occasions. Jean-Pierre's award-winning Syrah and Petite Sirah
offer an opportunity to compare these two similarly named but
different wines under the same winemaker's hand. Both are big
and luscious, with controlled tannins, and extraordinary finishes.
See what you can find in each. If not sold out, be sure to sample
the Teroldego as well. Quite different from wines produced in
northwestern Italy, this deep-colored, fruit-filled wine dances
from the bottle with great body and low acidity. All these wines
are balanced, complex, and inviting.

At Biddle Ranch Road turn left (west) for **Saucelito
Canyon Vineyard,** just around the corner at 3080 Biddle
Ranch Road. Visit www.saucelitocanyon.com or phone (805)
543-2111. Bill and Nancy Greenough rescued a prairie-grass
vineyard dating from the late 1800s. Even today, much of the
planted acreage remains dry-farmed, but Zinfandel vines are
hardy, producing remarkable wines under the Greenoughs' care.
And this line is splendid. Examine the label first, its dusky sunset and broad-hewn mountains will preview the wines. Saucelito
Canyon's Estate Zinfandel is deep and rich with aroma and flavor. The Zinfandel Reserve is even more concentrated in flavor,
from sip to finish, with chocolate-blueberry overtones. This is a
big, complex wine. Try a bite of dark chocolate with it to bring
up that range of flavors—and to prepare you for the Zinfandel
Late Harvest, from whole-berry fermentation. For many, this
wine will be dessert enough, but paired with an assortment of
fruit, nuts, and cheese or dark chocolate, the Late Harvest will
sing for you.

You'll find **Ortman Family Vineyards** co-located with

Saucelito, and the shared tasting room is charming—filled with stories and photographs from more than a century ago. Visit www.ortmanvineyards.com or phone (805) 473-9463. The Ortman story is rich with history, from Chuck Ortman's earlier days in Napa Valley during the 1960s to evidence of his vision you'll find in your market or wineshop. In making a move to Edna Valley, of which he expected great things, Chuck was recognized as Mr. Chardonnay by the press, and shortly after launching his Charles Ortman label in 1979, the wine's quality attracted an irresistible offer from wine giant Beringer. Shortly thereafter, the label was changed to Meridian—now shipping a million cases a year based on Chuck's original philosophy of winemaking. With his son Scott, Chuck has now returned to the Ortman tradition of hands-on winemaking. The Ortman Family Chardonnay grabs your attention from the first sip and doesn't let go, with delightful aromas leading you right down the fruit-garden path, to a long finish that may leave you breathless. The wine's handcrafted textures also carry over into the winery's Pinot Noir. Even the labels share an embossed, deckle-edged reminder that these wines stem from the same view of wine vision. But where the Chardonnay is a dancer, the Pinot Noir is a gymnast: graceful, sure of its footing, and still able to surprise. Pair either of these with fish or fowl and you won't go wrong. The Pinot Noir is a patient wine, though, and will ask the same of you. Give it time to recover from the bottle before sipping your reward.

Continuing north on Orcutt Road, watch for sister wineries **Baileyana** and *tangent* in a renovated 1909 schoolhouse at 5828 Orcutt Road. Visit www.baileyana.com or phone (805) 269-8200. This estate was an early pioneer of Burgundian-style wines in this area. Founder Catherine Niven recognized the long growing season in the Edna Valley, plus a unique combination of volcanic ash, alluvial soils, and loam. Together, these cried out for old-world winegrowing. Estate vineyards are at the foot of a volcanic cone, part of a chain reaching beyond the coastline into the ocean. The volcanic sense of place comes through—as just a whisper—in the Edna Valley Syrah from Baileyana. This is a robust but well-mannered Syrah exhibiting both structure and complexity in its fruit, plus a long, elegant finish. Award-winning Pinot Noirs, and a marvelous Cuvée are the result. The *tangent* label is devoted to premium white wines produced without oak barrels or lactic fermentation, allowing the wine's central character to shine through. The Ecclestone is bright, with crisp fruit, and most of all, a lovely transparency of flavor and finish. In the tasting room, hands-on detailing is everywhere. Baileyana and *tangent* present one of the most charming gift shops to be found along the Central Coast in wineries—a wonderful place to browse while sampling elegant wines.

San Luis Obispo is a college town, so there is no lack of hip restaurants. But for an unforgettable dining experience, head down Osos Street toward the classic California railroad station for **Café Roma** at 1020 Railroad Avenue. Visit www.caferomaslo .com or phone (805) 541-6800. Reservations are suggested, for this delightful restaurant is a favorite with locals as well as travelers. Owner Marco Rizzo has created, on an accessible property, a taste and feeling of Tuscany—maybe more. Dinner is like having your own catered affair. The waitstaff is well versed in food-wine pairings, and when seated at a table you'll notice that everything is just so. I watched a younger staff member resetting a table under the guidance of a gracious man along in his years. Nothing was criticized, only corrected. Café Roma offers a list of excellent wines by the glass or bottle, moderately priced, as are menu items. Consider Per Bacco's award-winning Pinot Grigio with the linguini pasta and fresh clams, or pair the wonderful squash-stuffed ravioli with Melville's lively Syrah. Enjoy, as Marco moves like a gentle Italian breeze from table to table, never intruding, yet missing nothing. However distracted they may be, diners still realize the worth of taking a meal in Marco's care at Café Roma.

PASO ROBLES AREA

Paso Robles Inn → Villa Toscana → Martin & Weyrich Winery → Villicana Winery and Vineyard → Adelaida Cellars → Tablas Creek Vineyard → Robert Hall Winery → Vino Robles

This area was once but another link in the travel chain of U.S. 101. Fuel, a soda perhaps, and it was time to move out on the highway again. An agriculture and ranching center, the town had little more to offer than the **Paso Robles Inn,** which in this case, is plenty. Visit www.pasoroblesinn.com or phone (805) 238-2660. The inn is a regular stop for discerning travelers who care about attentive service, gracious dining, and an imaginative garden setting. In its earliest incarnation, the inn was a popular hot-springs resort. That history is being revisited today, with new mineral-spa fireplace rooms—right in the heart of Paso Robles wine country. And for an on-the-road breakfast, the inn's landmark 1950s-style coffee shop is tops. Maps and guides for the area are available from Paso Robles Wine Country Alliance. Visit www.pasowine.com or Far Out Paso Robles Wineries at www.faroutwineries.com.

Villa Toscana at 4230 Buena Vista is without doubt one of the most romantic bed-and-breakfast inns to be found anywhere. Visit www.myvillatoscana.com or phone (805) 238-5600. Created by Martin & Weyrich in the style of a Tuscan village—with eight lovely guest rooms, plus cottage and private villa—it is an inspired design. At day's end, slip between luxurious 700-count Italian linen and fall asleep to the sounds of the courtyard fountain. Waken to the sun rising over acres of vineyards, all in perfect rows—sentinels of pleasure they seem to me—and drift into the bistro restaurant for a prepared-to-order breakfast. Villa Toscana is a place to be breathed in and admired. It will surely touch your sense of being in return. And to strengthen either your anticipation or fulfillment, be sure to stop at the **Martin & Weyrich Winery** tasting room at 2610 Buena Vista, on the northwest corner at the traffic signal just east of U.S. 101 on Highway 46. Visit www.martinweyrich.com or phone (805) 238-2520. Some of the most imaginative varietals and blends in the region are created in this winery and offered for winetasting. Some wineries produce an oak-free Chardonnay, others concentrate on the buttery tannins that barrel fermentation can achieve. But here you'll find Chardonnay fully aged in chestnut barrels, resulting in a full-mouth earthen experience with no hint of oak. For red-wine lovers, Estrusco is a unique blend of Sangiovese and the winery's Nebbiolo is a fine Italian-California treatment. And, as a grace note, these wines are attractively priced.

Across U.S. 101, where 24th Street becomes Adelaida Road, are several wineries worth exploring, and the drive through this countryside offers a wonderful look at the land, with pocket ranches and farms alongside big-time spreads. **Villicana Winery & Vineyard** is on the south side at 2725 Adelaida Road.

Visit www.villicanawinery.com or phone (805) 239-9456 for hours. Owners Alex and Monica Villicana are low-volume producers of a medal-winning Syrah and an Estate Winemakers Cuvée that is just lovely. Farther west is **Adelaida Cellars** at 5805 Adelaida Road. Visit www.adelaida.com or phone (805) 239-8980. This estate winery is committed to intense fruit flavors in their Pinot Noir and Chardonnay. And if you are a big-red fan, their Reserve Cabernet Sauvignon is excellent.

Just after the intersection with Vineyard Drive, to the south, keep watch for **Tablas Creek Vineyard** at 9339 Adelaida Road. This two-family estate winery is extraordinary in its vision and incorporation of French traditions in Paso Robles winemaking. Visit www.tablascreek.com or phone (805) 237-1231. In a unique partnership with Château de Beaucastel in Châteauneuf du Pape, Tablas Creek produces Rhône varietals.

The Rhône Connection

Châteauneuf du Pape (pronounced: shatto-nerf-doo-pop, as fast as possible) refers to the new house of the pope—but not in Rome. In the 1300s, France was unable to reach agreement on major issues with the Vatican, so they declared their own pope and set up shop in Avignon. Over the centuries, Châteauneuf du Pape became a top-tier wine region in the southern Rhône district and Château de Beaucastel developed into a major producer of premium Rhône varietals.

These Rhône vines are happiest in that range from rocky to crumbly, and a few favor limestone most of all—which is exactly what the winery's founders, the French Perrin family and importer Robert Hass, discovered in the soil at Tablas Creek.

Here, they found a perfect place to combine terroir with the romance and history of Rhône wines—following the eternal desire to bring something of great value from the earth and share it in an amiable way with others. This winery is also a marvelous place to tour. I spoke with Tablas Creek manager Jason Haas, an enthusiastic guide.

"The two families were set on making this an authentic Rhône project by bringing new cuttings from France and using only grapes grown on the estate. We also farm organically."

"Single varietals, or are you blending?"

"We blend. It's traditional in the Rhône Valley, and our winemaking is designed to let the signature of this special land come through. But we suggest that visitors sample the single-varietal wines on which our blends are based."

Jason led me toward a set of barrels—carefully finished and enormous.

"These hold 1,200 gallons each. High cost initially, but economical over the long run. We also use wild yeasts to make our wine."

And those wines are superb. Tablas Creek's Esprit de Beaucastel Blanc is a stand-alone wine. Less buttery and full than a Chardonnay, it approaches a Pinot Gris in its crisp fresh-fruit quality and light mineralization. With great potential in food pairings, this wine could become the California equivalent of a Rhône standard. Tablas Creek's Rosé is also a lesson in what can be accomplished in the Rhône style. Fresh, fruity, with no hint of that sugary quality that grandma's Rosé displayed at Thanksgiving—when wines sales faded and scotch soared. Tablas Creek's rendition is well-balanced, crisp, and inviting. Now, to the Mourvèdre, produced with flair and *joie de vivre* by Tablas Creek. If you enjoy both Cabernet Sauvignon and Syrah, yet sometimes imagine them together, this wine could be your grail. This varietal sagged in popularity with California vintners who follow trends, but Tablas Creek may hasten its return. Full-bodied like a Cab, yet at the same time elegant, with perfect mineralization displayed in a good Syrah, this Mourvèdre is well-balanced, fruity, and offers a splendid finish—all part of the Tablas Creek experience.

To the east of U.S. 101 on Highway 46E are several more exceptional wineries. **Robert Hall Winery** at 3443 Mill Road, is just off the highway to the south. Visit www.roberthallwinery.com or phone (805) 239-1616. This winery is of unexpected and stunning design. Cavern tours and tastings are offered, but take a little time to roam and get to know the place and the founder's philosophy that guided development of this winery.

"In the tradition of all the great châteaux, we know it takes time and vigilance to make great wine," Robert Hall says. "But after decades of planning and hard work, we also know nothing worth having comes easily."

The signature of that philosophy is all about the place and Robert Hall wines are well recognized with medals and points. Their Chardonnay's aroma and flavors are citrus-filled and the wine is crisp, with a firm body, and a lingering light oak finish. The Syrah and Reserve Syrah make for a good side-by-side tasting, with both subtle and significant differences in body and shadings in flavor. A relatively new release, Robert Hall Rhône de Robles is a lovely blend of Grenache and Syrah, with light touches of Cinsaut and Counoise, supported by a base of smooth tannins, and enough spice to suggest pairing it with a wide range of dishes.

Across the road, **Vina Robles** at 3700 Mill Road is a fine young winery founded by entrepreneur Hans Nef that will bring a Swiss signature to wines from the Paso Robles region. Visit www.vinarobles.com or phone (805) 227-4812. As you might gather, growing practices are both Old World and meticulous, with sensitivity to the land and the fruit it offers. Their Edna Ranch Chardonnay is big and fruit-filled, with a toasty base. But taste this side by side with a Vina Robles Jardine Sauvignon Blanc to discover qualities of terroir common to both—words just won't do. For red-wine lovers, the award-winning Estate Cabernet Sauvignon is big, with bold aromas and flavors, plus a long, rich finish. If you're not far from home, take some with you for dinner.

SOLEDAD AREA

Inn at the Pinnacles Bed & Breakfast → Paraiso Vineyards
→ Hahn Estates and the Smith & Hook Winery → San Saba
Vineyard → Pessagno Winery → Marilyn Remark Wines

Some stretches of U.S. 101 are as bleak as others are beautiful. So, the sight of stately vineyards marching up the Santa Lucia Highlands to the west can be welcome indeed. A good way to reach them is to exit the freeway at Soledad / Arroyo Seco Road (north of Greenfield) and continue west past the Stop sign. Paraiso Vineyards will be your first visit on this wine trail to the north that loops south again to the Inn at the Pinnacles east of Soledad. For a fine map and guide to this area, plus Carmel Valley and the Monterey Peninsula, visit Monterey County Vintners Associates at www.montereywines.org or phone (831) 375-9400.

For a memorable stay with owners Jon and Jan Brosseau

above the valley to the east, the **Inn at the Pinnacles Bed & Breakfast** offers both respite and companion destinations—the inn is close to Pinnacles National Monument and the award-winning Chalon Winery. It is an engaging drive up into the Gabilan Mountains and you may recall that the red pony in Steinbeck's classic tale was named Gabilan. All that and more blend at this unique inn at 32025 Stonewall Canyon Road. Visit www.innatthepinnacles.com or phone (831) 678-2400. Do obtain driving directions from the inn, however. You are unlikely to be lost on the way up, but it can feel that way. The Inn at the Pinnacles offers serenity found only in the rarest places, yet provides the possibility of action if you're a rock climber or hiker. Extraordinary guests turn up here, and conversations touch on everything from the human condition to flying—a pal of Jon's might even buzz the valley—or you may choose solitude in a luxurious suite, with its private entrance and patio. All this, and vineyards, too.

Paraiso Vineyards at 38060 Paraiso Springs Road makes a great first stop along the Santa Lucia wine trail. Visit www.paraisovineyards.com, where a lot can be learned about the nature of viticulture and the vision of founding vintners, or phone (831) 678-0300. Imagine being filled with ideas—but only fresh out of school—and coming into this area, with your kids in tow, to do something others have only hinted at before. That's what owners Richard and Claudia Smith did, and Paraiso (Spanish for heaven or paradise) continues to evolve as a result of their courage to work a dream to its fullest.

"Claudia and I take great pride in our accomplishments at Paraiso," Rich says. "We feel very blessed, very fortunate to live here among the vines. We raised our children and our grandchildren here in the vineyard and so feel a very close connection to the land. Everything we do here, from our careful, sustainable farming techniques to our limited release vintages reflects our love of this 'heavenly' place."

Paraiso wines reflect the fullness of the Smith family viewpoint. And here again is an opportunity for tasters to make side-by-side comparisons, in addition to tasting a variety of whites and reds—all splendid. Paraiso produces two wines in its flagship Pinot Noir line. Their Santa Lucia Highlands Pinot Noir is complex and well-balanced, with aromatic flavors of dark fruit supported by firm tannins and light smoke, for a long finish. Yet, oh my, the West Terrace Pinot Noir will tug at your heart. Little is produced, but taste—and buy—it if you can. Earthy and dark in a way that would have made Steinbeck smile and nod, this wine is a rush of aromas and fruit flavors, with just the right support from firm tannins. Finish is delightful and long-lasting, with light smoke, as if from distant workers' fires.

Continue north to **Hahn Estates** and the **Smith & Hook Winery** at 37700 Foothill Road. Visit www.hahnestates.com or phone (831) 678-4555. Nicky Hahn is a Swiss entrepreneur and a lover of California wines. That's how he and wife Gaby discovered and acquired the Smith & Hook property. Developing the Hahn Estates label is a major undertaking, but detracts in no way from Nicky as a conversationalist in the classic style. One can practically see him in Africa on the wildlife preserve he maintains. Yet what stands out most is his humanity. The Hahn family supports schools and children from tribes that saw no value in reading because it appeared to offer no hope for improvement in their lives. But as students earn success and return home, that condition stands to change. Hahn Estates wines are simply another facet of the family's focus and sense of commitment. From a wide range of current releases, all combining premium quality with value, the Pinot Gris is a lovely, fruit-filled wine, right on the cusp of mineralization between vineyards farther to the south and Willamette Valley wines to the north, with continuity between aromas and a long finish. Still, Hahn Estates reds display more of the terroir found on these unique hillsides of the Monterey region. Their Meritage is a broad canvas of intense but mannerly fruit, with layered complexity of unexpected dimension, plus bass notes of chocolate. Hahn Estates Cabernet Sauvignon is simply excellent: complex, with firm tannins, and an exceptional balance. But if there is any chance at all of tasting—and buying—the Smith & Hook Cabernet Sauvignon, do not hesitate. This is a marvelous yet unassuming wine, with broad shoulders and smoky tannins firmly under control. Sip and enjoy.

San Saba Vineyard is next at 35801 Foothill Road. Visit www.sansaba.com or phone (831) 678-2212. Cresting a hill on the highway just south of the vineyard, it's clear that this place is close to the heart and soul of Steinbeck Country. A fine old residence on the right, barely carrying the weight of its own ruin, is a reminder of how this valley is able to bring the mighty low, even as it rouses others to success—something Steinbeck well knew. San Saba reflects all this in the character of its vineyards and tasting room. The hum of purpose is present at San Saba but muted, with time for you to shake off the dust of the road, feel the sweet melancholy of this valley, and sample some of the wonderful wines to which owners Mark and Barbara Lemmon are dedicated.

"We want to remain a small producer of fine wine in the Salinas Valley and play our part in confirming the predictions of greatness for our valley," Mark says. "I set out thirty years ago to make wine with the elegance and artistic character of my favorite painting, *The Lions* by Rosa Bonheur. The exceptional climate and soil conditions of our vineyard are the canvas for San Saba wines."

Chardonnays from the Monterey area exhibit the mineralization found in this varietal in more northern climates, yet benefit from a lengthy growing season. San Saba Chardonnay is crisp, with lush fruit and spice, and a light oaken touch that is clearly present, yet does not distract from the complex aromas and flavors. San Saba also produces a no-oak Chardonnay, which, with its greater mineralization, is outstanding. A side-by-side comparison is enlightening, but both renditions are so good, that any preference is elusive. Blended with just a touch of Malbec, San Saba Merlot is superb. It conveys dense, dark fruit flavors that flood the palate, over currents of toasty oak and light smoke, to a lingering, light spice finish. A step up in body and powerful fruit flavor, with an earthy accompaniment and minerality, is San Saba Cabernet Sauvignon. The whites here are remarkable, but don't let them distract you from this winery's reds.

To reach **Pessagno Winery** at 1645 River Road, continue north on Foothill Road. At Chualar River Road, jog left on what becomes River Road. Visit www.pessagnowines.com or phone (831) 675-9463. For winemaker-partner Steve Pessagno, it is not only the pursuit of exceptional wines, but the setting and life rhythms of viticulture that drew him away from work as a mechanical engineer. I saw that firsthand when a neighbor stepped into the doorway. He'd come to borrow a few bins.

"How many are you taking?" Steve asked.

"I don't know. Eight, I guess."

"Take ten," Steve said with a smile. "You always underestimate."

It was an exchange between friends in an enterprise that includes all estate winemaking, and it was my privilege to witness its worth. Those same values are apparent in Steve's pursuit of handcrafted premium wines. Although he has been a winemaker and part of management at larger wineries, this is it for him.

"I'm able again to make those small batches of wine my grandfather introduced to me . . . wines with distinction and character. I must admit, I'm having the time of my life."

And you may, too, by tasting some of Steve's wines side by side. Two lovely Pessagno white wines are the Sleepy Hollow Vineyard Chardonnay and the Intrinity Chardonnay. The first is bright, with sightly mineralized fruit, and enough viscosity to cover the palate for a seamless finish. Ah, but the Intrinity can take you by surprise, with its whisper-light straw color and aroma, plus a remarkable depth that carries a different sense of place. One of Steve's sons coined the name *Intrinity*, with his notion that some pursuits simply carry on forever. Both wines will work well with seafood and light sauces, but consider the first wine for lunch, and save the second for dinner. Pessagno Pinot Noirs, both estate-grown, with similar intensity, invite another cross-tasting. Four Boys is an excellent, bright, fruit-forward wine, with northern aromas and flavors that a skilled winemaker can extract from this delicate fruit. But for subtlety, and a special come-hither quality that increases to a languishing finish, the Lucia Highlands rendition can bring both a sigh and a wink. Pessagno Zinfandel from Idyll Time Vineyard is a bold, full-bodied wine that takes aroma and flavor near the top without going over. And if you push a Zin too hard that can happen, but not here. This wine is complex and structured enough to stand up to anything from the grill, yet not overpower a dessert.

And might we not have a special tasters lane for dedicated chocolate lovers? Try this wine with a Lindt dark chocolate at 85 percent cocoa—and smile.

A delightful last stop on this trail is **Marilyn Remark Wines** at 645 River Road. Visit www.remarkwines.com or phone (831) 455-9310. Here is winemaking at its most straightforward and the only all-Rhône winery in Monterey. Owner-winemaker Joel Burnstein is a former stock trader, and partner Marilyn Remark remains a dedicated social worker when not at the winery. They produce Syrah, Petite Sirah, Marsanne, Rousanne, and Viognier. Yet it was Joel's Grenache that took top honors on its debut at the largest competition in the country. Other Marilyn Remark wines have won awards as well. Joel invited me into his office, which turned out to be an open space on the crush pad, and waved me to a barrelhead seat. I asked how he managed such a fast start. He'd probably heard the question a hundred times.

"We use the best fruit the land can give us and work hard not to screw it up."

"The prerogative of a boutique winery?"

"Exactly. We produce fewer than 2,000 cases each year and don't manipulate the wine."

That focus comes through in the Rhône-style wines at Marilyn Remark. If you've not sampled a Marsanne or Rousanne from this region, the Loma Pacific Marsanne and Lockwood Valley Rousanne can surprise and tempt you. Each is done in the classic Rhône tradition, with bright citrus aromas and flavors bound together in two varietals of near equal intensity. And if you are a fan of Châteauneuf du Pape wines, you'll find Joel's Grenache superb. This is a full-bodied wine of deep, intense fruit and sufficient complexity to cellar well. It is also quite approachable. Just give it some time to open up and offer the overtones present in this fine wine.

CARMEL AREA

Heller Estate → Bernardus Lodge and Winery →
Château Julien Wine Estate → La Playa Hotel

Despite the missteps of Silicon Valley and their effects on the Monterey Peninsula, Carmel-by-the-Sea continues to be one of the most charming spots anywhere along the West Coast. Once a trysting place for the rich and famous from San Francisco, it is now visitor- (and dog-) friendly. During winter, it's hard to imagine a moodier, more romantic place. In summer, the town simply floats along in the wake of its own charm, with candlelit restaurants and dimly lit streets, all within a short drive of Carmel Valley's wineries.

If you are heading back to the Inn at the Pinnacles, or farther south, return via River Road. Or, if you are moving on to the Carmel area, continue north to Highway 68 and turn west. Continue on to Carmel and your overnight stay in this area. Or, take a scenic shortcut to Carmel Valley. Watch for a right (south) turn on Laureles Grade / Highway G20, which will carry you through scenic hills to Carmel Valley Road / Highway G16. A left turn will take you to the tasting rooms for **Heller Estate** located at 69 W. Carmel Valley Road. (Visit www.hellerestate.com or phone [831]-659-6220), and **Bernardus Lodge and Winery** at 5 W. Carmel Valley Road (visit www.bernardus.com or phone [831] 659-1900). These tasting rooms are easily found and worthwhile to visit. Grounds and décor are lush and the wines are outstanding. South of the Laureles Grade intersection, just a few miles up from Highway 1, is **Château Julien Wine Estate** at 8940 Carmel Valley Road. Visit www.chateaujulien.com or phone (831) 624-2600. The winery and tasting room are accessible and architecturally intriguing. In the tasting room, wines are poured at a linen-covered table, amid interior design qualities that seem effortless. Owners Patty and Bob Brower have seen to it, as well as to so many fine details here. A garden courtyard is also available for picnics. Even parking is easy and pleasant. But aside from the wines, which are jewels, a tour here is fascinating. Vice president and winemaker Bill Anderson met with me early one Sunday morning for a tour of the winery. The processing layout seemed familiar enough until we reached what appeared to be a huge radiator, with its tubes covered by insulation.

"You won't see many of these around," Bill said.

"It looks like a giant heat exchanger."

"That's what it is. After our juice is extracted, it goes to a 13,000-gallon settling tank. Cooling a mass that great would be too costly in time and energy, yet we need to get the temperature down quickly."

"What's the rush?"

"We don't like to harvest at night. It's a safety risk for workers to be in the vineyards at night, so we bring the fruit in during the day and this chilling apparatus will reduce juice temperatures 45–50° as quickly as it can be done, and help protect the juice from wild fermentation."

"How fast is this system?"

"It's a tube within an insulated cooling tube. Instead of taking twenty-four to thirty-six hours to chill an entire tank, we can manage this in only three minutes. And it's also gentle on the juice."

It certainly is. Château Julien Private Reserve Merlot is absolutely splendid. Full-flavored, with traces of smoky oak and cedar, its tannins are firmly controlled to allow intense fruit flavors to emerge. Even dyed-in-the-wool Cabernet Sauvignon lovers can be seduced by this wine, with its full palate and languorous finish. The winery's Zinfandel Private Reserve is also delightful. In a wine world where some winemakers are jamming Zin alcohol levels toward 17 percent, this wine shows its true heritage. Still, it is a big wine. Robust in its expression of flavors, with layered textures, it offers a full-mouth experience, enough acidity to allow a wide range of food pairings—from artisan cheeses to Asian grills—and a great finish. For this wine, it's more a matter of taking time to appreciate its quality. A final note: Keep watch for Château Julien's new Sangiovese, under Bill Anderson's talented hand. It's going to be a winner.

Once into Carmel-by-the Sea, about twenty minutes from Carmel Valley, lodging possibilities are many. Yet few classic inns along the West Coast are able to coax a gentle past into the present like **La Playa Hotel** on Camino Real at Eighth Avenue. Fewer still are family owned. Stepping into the lobby or dining room, you may notice that guests speak in low tones. It harks back to an earlier, more refined time when having class was not confused with being showy. That distinction is evident at La Playa. Stroll the grounds as well; each planting is as it should be, and gardeners are as attentive to guests as skilled in their craft. Built as a Mediterranean villa in 1905, La Playa still stands guard over old-style hospitality. I asked manager Tom Glidden what brings guests back so often.

"People return to La Playa to be cared for and catered to, in the classic tradition. They tell us, after visiting, that they come away looking at life a bit differently."

"Any idea how you and your staff do that?"

"We keep the atmosphere serene, yet fun. That's part of it. La Playa does the rest."

Many rooms have ocean views, and guests drift off to sleep to the sound of surf on Carmel's famed walking beach just steps down the hill. For all the time I've spent in this dog-friendly village—many shops keep filled water dishes on the sidewalk out front—no inn reflects the character of Carmel better than La Playa. Visit www.laplayahotel.com or phone (831)-624-6476.

MONTEREY AREA

A Taste of Monterey → The Sardine Factory
→ Central Avenue Bakery & Deli

Whether tourists favor destinations in Carmel, Monterey, Pacific Grove, or Pebble Beach, the Monterey Peninsula goes all-out. Many of the attractions, plus a large number of restaurants and ocean-view bed-and-breakfasts vie for attention. For a wealth of tourism information, visit www.montereycvb.com. If you're already in the area, **A Taste of Monterey** at 700 Cannery Row, Suite KK, is a great first stop. Visit www.tastemonterey.com or phone (831) 646-5446. Close to the aquarium and several top restaurants, it's a good place to ferret out information from locals while tasting handcrafted wines from small producers that are otherwise hard to find. One note: if you're in Monterey on a weekend, park well up the hill and leg it on down to the center of things. Even if it costs a few bucks, it will save both fuel and frustration.

The Sardine Factory at 701 Wave Street has been a standard for fine dining here since it was established in 1968, with a shoestring budget and space in one of the shuttered canning sheds. Visit www.sardinefactory.com or phone (831)-373-3775. If you love seafood and care about sustainability—as well as service—this is a grand Monterey tradition.

Or, if you and your flip-flops are worn-out from strolling through Monterey's attractions, and you just want a simple breakfast or lunch in a place where you can put your feet up, head toward **Central Avenue Bakery & Deli** at 173 Central Avenue in Pacific Grove at Dewey Avenue. Visit www.centralavenue bakery.com or phone (831)-373-2000. Take a comfy chair and look through the library, or play Anti-Monopoly. This is gourmet organic dining in a homey atmosphere. Nonvegetarians—who love the cookies and just about everything else—are welcome. Everyone can choose from ten coffees or Chai tea, free-range eggs, and road goodies galore, including chocolate naughties.

SANTA CRUZ AREA

Historic Sand Rock Farm B&B → Nicholson Vineyards →
Windy Oaks Estate Vineyard & Winery → Bargetto Winery →
Vinocruz → Soif Wine Bar Restaurant & Merchants
→ Bonny Doon Vineyard → La Nebbia Winery

From Aptos to Davenport, Santa Cruz lazes in year-round comfort. A south-facing beach brings this fair benefit, and like Santa Barbara, university students hang on after graduation, lending the town an ever-young look and feel. But they are also role models for squadrons of pedestrians heedless of traffic, so take special care. Crosswalks mean little here.

Historic Sand Rock Farm B&B at 6901 Freedom Boulevard in Aptos is just shy of a mile from Highway 1. Visit www.sandrockfarm.com or phone (831) 688-8005. Established in 1885, this restored Arts and Crafts mansion was one of the original family wineries in the Santa Cruz area. The inn is glorious, with handprinted wallpaper, period furnishings, and views from every window. Sand Rock Farm's grounds are fascinating as well: acres of meadow, oaks, and redwoods give a sun-dappled quality to this suburban forest. Owner Kris Sheehan walked me down to the old winery's location.

"Our guests love to stroll through these gardens and paths." She pointed out a wine-barrel fountain. "Hummingbirds seem to have fallen in love with this place, too."

Gourmet breakfasts here, featuring local organic produce, are not to be missed. But you could fail to see the driveway on a first pass, since county regulations prevent Sand Rock's sign from being conspicuous. Watch for the yellow country mailbox (6901) and the sign hanging in a tree. Turn into the well-paved driveway between two wine-barrel planters and you're there.

Dozens of wineries dot the Santa Cruz Mountains, though most are much farther inland. But Sand Rock Farm makes an ideal entry point for the Corralitos Wine Trail and an experience of the Santa Cruz foothills that remains close to our main route. Corralitos area wineries are also small family vineyards that offer an intimacy with the land and vines. These wineries welcome guests, though tastings and tours are by appointment only. Family vineyards are a quiet treat, with time to savor and reflect.

Nicholson Vineyards at 2800 Pleasant Valley Road is a lovely introduction to winemaking—and olive growing—in this area. Just follow Freedom Boulevard from Aptos into the hills, turn left (north) on Pleasant Valley Road and continue on to the winery. Visit www.nicholsonvineyards.com or phone (831) 724-7071. Brian and Marguerite Nicholson planted this vineyard a decade ago. Both were, and continue to be, in the business of real estate appraisal. Growing and winemaking are their labors of love. I asked about their tipping point.

"Brian's family history goes back to the days of Padre Serra, and my family is Italian, so it probably was in our blood as much as anything. Brian sees a lot of properties and one day brought me up here. After that, we were committed. We sold the fruit at first. Now, we're into making the wine as well. Our children have grown to young adulthood here, and we find it a happy thing to do. The winery has become a way of life for our entire family and is our love."

Nicholson wines reveal that sense of a commitment fulfilled. The family produces about five hundred cases a year and will soon be up to a few thousand. Yet the wines will always be handcrafted, the land always nurtured, and many vintages will sell out early, so getting on the Nicholson mailing list is a good idea. Their Pinot Noir Limited Reserve is unmistakable (where some Pinots seem to wander far afield), yet unique. Given a moment to open, this wine is full, rich, and velvety. It is both elegant and able to stand up to most sauces and dishes, whether white or red. Structure and complexity allow the fruit to glide along for a full-palate experience and a long, fine finish. Nicholson Zinfandel can benefit from some time in bottle, but the body and bass line of this wine are fully intertwined. Intriguing aromas lead to complex flavors and a boldness that is well-rounded with fruit and the earthiness found in wines from this region.

Farther into the foothills and valleys, a sense of place, a feeling of a life fully grounded takes hold. So, take time to visit

Windy Oaks Estate Vineyard & Winery at 550 Hazel Dell Road. Visit www.windyoaksestate.com or phone (831) 786-9463. As with many small wineries committed to premium handcrafted wines, owners-winemakers Judy and Jim Schultze are pleased to have guests, but by appointment only. And it's worth it. The winery is surrounded by redwoods and the adjacent vineyard tops a one-thousand-foot ridge overlooking Monterey Bay. Judy and Jim honor this land with their commitment to sustainable Biodynamic practices. They are also minimalists in producing their estate Pinot Noir and Chardonnay—no filtering or fining, no added enzymes. The resulting wines are not only grand to drink; they are winning double-golds in major competitions. Windy Oaks Chardonnay is in a word: *dear*. Bright, eager to please when uncorked, with a fine body, color, and balance, it also presents that degree of mineralization that speaks of California and points to Oregon. But her Pinot Noir brother from Henry's Block is the athlete in the family—not football, though, more like the grace of archery or tennis. This is a big wine, but very light on its feet, with complex aromas and flavors moving over a smooth tannin base—bold enough to pair with most anything, delicate enough to enjoy on its own.

Few wineries in the Santa Cruz area can claim the heritage of the **Bargetto Winery** at 3535 N. Main Street in Soquel. Although the family first planted in 1918, their current vineyards were established in the early 1930s. Now under third-generation management, this family estate winery is as fresh today as it must have been back then. Visit www.bargetto.com or phone (831) 475-2258. The tasting room is minutes from U.S. 101. And the wines are marvelous. Italian varietals are finding renewed interest among wine lovers, and the Bargetto Winery produces superb wines and vintages. Yet something else is at work here. When visiting wineries like Bargetto that are decades or generations old, there is a calm—an easy orderliness—that pervades the atmosphere. Winemakers and workers in very large operations may be no less dedicated, but the sheer bustle of a large producer can obscure the care and commitment. At Bargetto, this becomes clear when you reach the door—and certainly when you taste their wines. Three favorites are from Bargetto's Regan Estate Vineyards in the Santa Cruz Mountains. The Pinot Grigio is a bright wine with a delightful aroma announcing citrus flavors with blossomy overtones, plus a spicy come-hither quality that invites unusual food pairings—an exotic chicken dish or Asian-spiced vegetable platter. Despite sideways slaps at Merlot, this genteel varietal is developing stronger nuances among wineries with long histories. Bargetto's Santa Cruz Mountains Merlot presents dark color and a fruit-oak aroma that are superbly balanced. Flavors are well developed, quite complex, giving the wine a robustness that remains approachable and quietly persuasive. In Bargetto's LA VITA Red Wine blend, however, can be found a dual sense of place: Santa Cruz and the Piedmont Province of northwest Italy. This stunning blend of Dolcetto, Nebbiolo, and Refosco reveals attention to detail, from its bottle design and the label of classic art, right on into the wine. LA VITA is not only a wine of color and depth, it carries complex, velvety flavors across the entire palate to an extraordinary finish. Muscular enough to complement grilled meats, yet elegant and expansive enough to serve as a centerpiece for lighter imaginative dishes—and with each sip, a connection to Etruscan beginnings.

At first glance, **Vinocruz** at 725 Front Street, No. 101, appears to be an upscale fashion shop. Except its high-tech contemporary surfaces are stocked with wine—all from the Santa Cruz region. Visit www.vinocruz.com or phone (831) 426-8466.

Chardonnay and Pinots are featured, though you'll find dozens of others. And an increasing degree of mineralization is present in these wines, as the big, buttery, oak-driven flavors of the south begin to fade into northern terroir. At a tasting here, you're almost sure to find wines that suit your palate. The Macchia California Red Wine from Muccigrosso Vineyards and the Cabernet Sauvignon from Martin Ranch are both excellent. Indeed, Santa Cruz wines as a whole are terrific, but most wineries are small hands-on operations that have little time or support for marketing.

"That's where we come in," says owner J-P Correa. "Our mission is to provide exposure for a number of hidden vineyards. Their wines deserve it."

Partner Jeffrey Kongslie agrees. "Some of the wineries we represent turn out as few as two hundred cases a year. No one at the neighborhood market or big-box store takes time to guide someone new to these wines through tasting flights that will help them find the perfect wines for them."

There's a saying around Santa Cruz: Come for the beaches, stay for the crazy. So, we'll scoot down a few blocks to **Soif Wine Bar Restaurant & Merchants** at 105 Walnut Avenue. Visit www.soifwine.com or phone (831) 423-2020. Soif (rhymes with *quaff*, and in French, means *thirst*) is where the idea of crazy like a fox has real meaning. In a minimalist building, which survived the earthquake here, the idea is to create a wine bar with worldwide offerings, personally selected by owner-chef Chris Avila. Indeed, she has given nearly half the space to ceiling-high racks of excellent wines from around the world, with more than fifty wines offered by the glass. Soif is also a top-tier restaurant. A few couples were enjoying wines, but everyone else—and the house was full on a weeknight—was enjoying food-and-wine pairings. Many of these are suggested on the menu, but the waitstaff is both patient and knowledgeable when you'd like to explore options. I joined chef Chris, sous-chef Patrick Boyle, and his wife, Patricia, for wine and small plates. We sampled Pinot Noirs from Oregon and France for a start, and moved on to pairings with crostini and white beans, roasted peppers and olives, and sautéed arugula with Parmesan. An artisan cheese selection carried us to an old-vines Pinot Auxerrois. House-made Yukon gold gnocchi with radish greens and morels was accompanied by a Canayli Vermentino di Gallura. And I called it quits with warm chocolate cake, coffee ice cream, and a Brande Maison Monbazillac. With stories told, mutual acquaintances discovered, fine wines, and superb cuisine, it was an evening to be remembered. Find your memorable evening here, too.

The coast above Santa Cruz is wild in an open way, and inviting, too. It also leads to the Bonny Doon turnoff for **Bonny Doon Vineyard** well up in the hills above the fog line at 10 Pine Flat Road. Visit www.bonnydoonvineyard.com or phone (831) 425-4518. Iconoclastic owner Randall Grahm was one of the first to favor the Châteauneuf du Pape blends now produced by Tablas Creek and Curtis—both on our wine trail—plus a few others. And Bonny Doon's Rhône-style wines are winners. As if to offset such a serious outcome, Randall fashioned himself a Rhône Ranger—he's probably heard any Tonto joke you can think of—and added such names to his wine labels as Old Telegram and Le Cigare Volant. Good fun and excellent wines. You may especially enjoy the Syrah Le Pousseur, which is not pushy at all, but produced through whole-cluster fermentation, yielding intense fruit flavors layered with firm tannins and a light smokiness. To paraphrase: Come for the wine, stay for the laughter.

At Half Moon Bay, you may continue up the coast to San Francisco and the Golden Gate Bridge. It's a pretty but rambling route, sometimes with ill-marked turns approaching the city. Or you can turn east on Highway 92 to link up with northbound I-280 and take your medicine all at once. I favor the inland route, but I also tend to pull Band-Aids off fast. One pleasant advantage to the inland route is the chance to stop at **La Nebbia Winery** on the right (south) side at 12341 San Mateo Road / Highway 92 just a few minutes east of Half Moon Bay. Visit www.nebbiawinery.com or phone (650) 726-9463. Formerly under the Obester name, this is a charming vest-pocket winery where neighbors stop in with the latest on the locals. La Nebbia focuses on big reds. Their Cabernet Sauvignon is an award-winner—bold, jammy, and well-balanced against firm tannins. A less burly wine is their Cabernet Blend, with Merlot to round off the edges, add fruit, and provide a long finish. Of special note is La Nebbia's tradition of Bottle & Cork days. On certain dates, guests bring in their empty wine bottles and the staff refills them with barrel select wine—free. So, do you feel lucky?

See you in San Francisco.

Northern California

Winegrowing moved north through California's coastal valleys with Padre Serra's chain of missions. But plantings and mission building stopped at Carmel.

Across Monterey Bay, it was Yankee territory, where whiskey was favored over wine. The first serious winegrowing in the north didn't begin until George Calvert Yount recognized the potential of Napa Valley's soil and climate. By the nineteenth century's end, at least 150 wineries were in operation. All seemed well until an outbreak of phylloxera wiped out many of the northern vintners and what was left fell under the ax of Prohibition.

SAN FRANCISCO AREA

Huntington Hotel & Nob Hill Spa → London Wine Bar
→ The Hidden Vine

Being sloganized is the price of fame, perhaps. Yet places like New York, Paris, and San Francisco are hard to capture in plain words. Despite a lurid and tumbledown past, San Francisco has come to define charm, from cable cars—moving national historic landmarks—to hilltop views second to none, and hotels of world reputation.

Among these is the multiple award-winning **Huntington Hotel & Nob Hill Spa,** which is equal to its prestigious address, yet in a manner that is as relaxed as it is elegant. Located at 1075 California Street, the Huntington is easy to reach, with cable-car access to both city and waterfront close at hand. Visit www.huntingtonhotel.com or phone (415) 474-5400. From doormen who are helpful rather than imperious, to an efficient staff at an inconspicuous front desk, the sense of family ownership is everywhere. Guests even pass the time of day with one another in the elevators, instead of staring up at the floor numbers. Everyone seems to feel at home.

The Huntington's Big Four Restaurant exudes the charm of an English club: a quiet bar to one side, with a dining area that feels sheltering and exclusive—deep green furnishings, walls of

Huntington and Company

Who were the Big Four? They're rarely mentioned today as the boundless tycoons they were. Californians reap the benefits of the group's enterprises, yet their accomplishments came at great cost in life and limb. Collis P. Huntington, Charles Crocker, Mark Hopkins, and Leland Stanford combined their energies and resources to link America's east and west, with the completion of the Union Pacific Railroad in 1869. Several got up to some mischief, but on the whole, no one could have accomplished what the Big Four did, nor performed it with such panache.

framed prints and historic photographs, plus servers who are attentive while remaining unobtrusive.

For a change of pace in a seafood city, try the venison and black bean chili, with onion crisps and a big California red. The entire experience of the Huntington Hotel is world-class. Not to mention an opulent new spa—complimentary for hotel guests—that is as dazzling as its view. Lounge inside or on the terrace; the city will be at your feet.

Ready for a winetasting expedition in San Francisco? The **London Wine Bar** located at 415 Sansome Street is a classic. Visit www.londonwinesf.com or phone (415) 788-4811. Located in a former Yokohama bank building, the bar exemplifies adaptive reuse. It also suits the cultural mix of a city in which the Chinese fortune cookie was invented by a Japanese gardener. The London has an English wood-paneled look to match its history—it was the first wine bar in the United States—yet the wine list is truly international. If you'd like to know how California wines differ from those produced in Latin America, Australia, Spain, or say, Hungary, this is a good place to start.

In **The Hidden Vine** at ½ Cosmo Place, it's a dream in the making. Visit www.thehiddenvine.com or phone (415) 674-3567. This is a sweet place, with easier conversation than many, and a lovely spot to conclude a San Francisco evening. An eclectic list of some thirty wines available by the glass complements a bottle list of more than a hundred.

As a rule, cities call to me less than open spaces and the next bend in a two-lane road. Yet I feel a certain Tony Bennett melancholy in leaving San Francisco, and especially the Huntington. Checking out early to beat the traffic I stepped up to the front desk, where the morning man was in a mood as bright as the sunrise. He had my paperwork ready and was humming a show tune softly to himself. I sang a little harmony over the last few notes. A woman standing nearby joined in.

"Do you know the second verse?" I asked the man at the desk.

"No, but I will know it by the next time you stay with us."

"Suppose I drive back over from Napa tomorrow?"

"I'll be ready."

Smiles and soft laughter all around—a personal moment early in the day of a waking city. I headed for Lombard Street and the Golden Gate Bridge. Driving across to the Marin County side is not only easy in the morning, there's no toll. The bridge was paid off years ago. Still, it's a nice bit of largesse from a city that doesn't need to nail you in both directions.

NAPA VALLEY AREA

Saintsbury → Cedar Gables Inn → Poetry Inn → Cliff Lede Vineyards → Plumpjack Winery → Frog's Leap → Louis M. Martini Winery

Serious winegrowing for the Napa Valley began in 1943, but stalled again after World War II. Two forces were at work against the development of premium varietal wines. One was a holdover from Prohibition, in which a bootlegging mentality and general suspicion of winegrowers persisted. The other was more a matter of internecine warfare among growers. While premium winegrowers like Martin Ray argued for high ideals in labeling premium estate wines, others lobbied for lax standards. The market drifted somewhere between.

Up from the Jug

Most wine buyers of the 1940s and '50s figured that a dollar was about the limit for jug wine. Bottled wine might fetch $1.50. Some semipremium wines reached $2, in a preview of Two Buck Chuck. In 1889, Cresta Blanca Winery had won a grand prize at the Paris Exposition, but by the 1940s it was reduced to radio jingles. Italian Swiss Colony, with the voice of Jim Backus as the Little Old Italian Winemaker, blitzed television screens in the '50s. Orson Welles promised to sell no wine before its time. Mass marketing was moving in. Apple wines and all the rest would obscure the few remaining premium winemakers.

It wasn't until the 1970s that Napa Valley premium winegrowers turned the corner. Their wines took top honors in several international competitions and thanks to that, the United States moved into new markets, with Napa and Sonoma Counties at the forefront. The Napa region produces relatively little of California's wine, but its name is recognized worldwide. And that's part of what brings both wine lovers and tourists here.

On your way toward Napa from San Francisco—here's where your maps will come in handy—plan a first stop at **Saintsbury** at 1500 Los Carneros Avenue, which is easiest to reach on the way into the Napa region. Visit www.saintsbury .com or phone (707) 252-0592 to make an appointment. Saintsbury wines are listed at many top restaurants along the California coast. And a visit can explain why: This place is the creation of Dick Ward and David Graves, two intensely curious—if laid-back—winemakers who regularly choose the road less traveled. They think a lot about wine here and what separates great from merely very good. Although Riesling was their first leap of oenological faith, other wines are what brought recognition to Saintsbury. Two lovely Chardonnays offer a chance at side-by-side tasting on the geographic scale where Southern California and Northern California traditions and terroir meet. Carneros Chardonnay is rich, yet not overly buttery, with density and character, plus texture and full-mouth flavors leading to a long, fulfilling finish. It is sun and beaches and holding hands. Brown Ranch Chardonnay from Saintsbury is dry and elegant in its structure and earthy minerality. Subtle as pale mountain light, this wine reaches places on the palate rarely touched by a Chardonnay. It is mist and gentle slopes—and holding hands. Tasting these two is a lesson in the winemaker's craft. Yet no more so than a three-way tasting with the stunning Saintsbury Pinot Noirs. The Garnet may surprise you, it is a subtle and quite approachable wine, with fruit flavors that develop nicely right in the glass, and the kiss of a light finish. Now sip the Carneros. Ah, a touch of the same earthy minerality exhibited in the Carneros Chardonnay, but in a red! Terroir will tell and this Pinot Noir speaks volumes of slope, soil, and climate. Bright, with strength of character, this wine will need a moment or two to deliver the full-fruit aroma and flavors, plus a delicate balance and fine finish. Now, to the Brown Ranch Pinot Noir that—it may as well be said—turns heads, brightens eyes, and finds its own place in wine lovers' hearts. This is a gorgeous wine from Dijon clones (including 777, which we'll meet later at Phelps Creek near Hood River, Oregon). Dark and full in its structure, this Pinot Noir is deep and velvety, with powerful fruit flavors, and a delightful see-you-again-soon finish. Make time for a visit and space for these handcrafted Saintsbury wines. You'll be well rewarded.

For the Napa area, **Cedar Gables Inn** at 486 Coombs Street is a bed-and-breakfast of special qualities, and a perfect base for browsing the town. Visit www.cedargablesinn.com or phone (707) 224-7969. Part of the task of a great inn is to get us out of our heads and into our experience. Cedar Gables manages that and more. From the welcoming columns of its portico, every part of this inn tugs at your consciousness: Tudor furniture, carved handrails, rich oriental rugs, soft lighting, rich velvets and brocades, and floral arrangements greet the senses at every turn. It is, in short, a mansion, done up in its finest—and yours to enjoy as a guest for as long as you stay. It's Victorian England, days in America before income tax, and wonderful tales of the maid and someone chasing each other about the house in search of a mystery—all very exciting.

Yet owners Susie and Ken Pope imbue the place with such calm and warmth that excitement drifts into sheer enjoyment, like pouring a glass of fine wine and slipping into a warm tub.

"Susie and I both come from large families," Ken says. "It's natural for us to have friends and family around. And that's how we treat our guests, like family. That's part of what is so special about our Old English Tavern. Curl up with a book. Sample some Napa Valley wine and see who turns up."

The tavern has hosted impromptu performances by opera singers, flamenco guitarists, a screen composer, and choirs. And all manner of tales are told around the huge dining table during the inn's gourmet breakfasts. Perhaps it's another wine-trail paradox: a beautifully furnished mansion that feels just like home.

Heading north from Napa, hook up with the Silverado Trail. You'll find several familiar names like Stag's Leap Cellars that have helped make this region famous. Approaching Yountville Crossroad on the left (west) side of the highway, keep watch for

Poetry Inn on the right at 6380 Silverado Trail. Unless you're driving a top-down convertible, the inn will be out of sight, so look for the sign. Visit www.poetryinn.com or phone (707) 944-0646. Poetry Inn juts from the hillside, high above the valley floor like the fabled monasteries of Greece. Head on up, past the helicopter pad on the right, and continue along the concrete drive to the main entrance at the back side of the inn. This inn is exceptional in every regard: an indoor-outdoor dining area, with a panoramic view of Napa Valley, luxurious accommodations, free-form pool, and a tempting glassed-in wall of wines on the way to the spa. The truth is, it's difficult to make too much of this place. Each detail works alone and in the company of the inn's overall interior. Just below Poetry Inn are the vines from which an excellent claret is produced by **Cliff Lede Vineyards** at 1473 Yountville Cross Road. Visit www.cliffledevineyards.com or phone (707) 944-8642. On entering the gate, visitors recognize this winery as special. Flanking vineyards are meticulously kept and the winery's tasting room enjoys the twin charms of openness and intimacy through its Craftsman-style architecture. Also, take time for the resident collection of sculptures and a gallery featuring front-rank artists. Cliff Lede still wines appear under his name and the flagship Poetry line. Sparkling wines are bottled under the S. Anderson label. Many of these are high-point winners and sampling these handcrafted wines from a family estate is both exciting and rewarding.

If you're looking for lively winetasting, be sure to visit **Plumpjack Winery** at 620 Oakville Cross Road in Oakville. Visit www.plumpjack.com or phone (707) 945-1220. A few of the winery's sister properties are Plumpjack Squaw Valley Inn, and Plumpjack's Balboa Cafes in San Francisco and Squaw Valley—each illuminating the notion of efficient exuberance among staff. The Falstaff-style logo helps reinvent the traditional tasting room and the wines are first-class. Plumpjack Reserve Chardonnay is well-rounded, yet bright, with nicely layered citrus and a crisp finish. Their Merlot is full, well-balanced, and eager to open. Give it a moment or two more and its aromatic flavors carry the high notes, with light tannins beneath. If you're able, sample one of the earlier Reserve Cabernet Sauvignons. These are outstanding wines, in barrel for almost three years, offering a powerful, but not at all burly, complex of flavors, with smooth tannins and a lingering toasty finish. Drink now or cellar for a decade or more.

Visiting **Frog's Leap** at 8815 Conn Creek Road in Rutherford is a treat for anyone of the green persuasion. Solar-powered, committed to dry farming, with energy-efficient structures, this winery is a tasting-room joy and a learning center for all. They are very serious about their dedication to the environment, yet like many on the leading edge, they don't take themselves too seriously. It's a pleasure just to enter the Big Red Barn. Now renovated, it was originally built in the 1880s. The winery is minimalist when it comes to winemaking. To the extent possible, what you see in the ground is what you get. Not that they don't have a little fun with labels. Leapfrögmilch—a takeoff on Liebfraumilch, once wildly popular—is a lovely Riesling and Chardonnay blend that brings some of the preeminent qualities of both to the glass. This wine is bright but not high-strung, with well-layered aromas and flavors, plus a long is-there-more finish. Frog's Leap Syrah is a single-varietal wine. Rich and dark, with fullness in the fruit and underlying structure, this is a terrific rendition. Their Cabernet Sauvignon is superb, but sample the Rutherford, if it has not sold out. This wine is from the Rutherford benchland and has a deep, velvety mouth feel, with complex flavors and tannins intertwined to produce an extraordinary wine. Visit www.frogsleap.com (it's one of the most entertaining winery Web sites), or phone (707) 963-4704.

Of the icons in winemaking, none carry more luster, foresight, and compassion than **Louis M. Martini Winery** at 254 South St. Helena Highway, at the southern entrance to St. Helena. Visit www.louismartini.com or phone (707) 968-3361. Emigrating from Italy in 1899, patriarch Louis Martini envisioned a market for premium wines in America. Third-generation vintners Mike and sister Carolyn now carry on the work and philosophy of a family estate vineyard dedicated to a long-term partnership with land. Mike has a talent for being outgoing even when focused on a task—and he is someone who would take in a stranded writer, see that he was properly wined and dined, then speed him on his way. In the family tradition, he also makes extraordinary wines.

"When Prohibition ended," Mike says, "construction on the winery was already complete and my grandfather, then my father, went on to establish a Napa Valley legacy. It is my great honor to carry on this family legacy. I strive to make Cabernets that speak of their vineyard sources and show power as well as elegance and finesse."

It is said that to make a generous wine, you must first have a generous winemaker. That would certainly be true at Louis M. Martini. Their Napa Valley Cabernet Sauvignon is an outstanding wine of deep color and full-bodied aroma and flavors. It opens quickly to reveal excellent structure, with a wide stance on firmly controlled tannins, and a long silky finish. Another superb Martini wine is the Alexander Valley Cabernet Sauvignon. Together, they offer another opportunity to sense the difference in terroir under the hand of the same winemaker. Martini's Alexander Valley Cabernet presents much of the same structure and balance, yet it also exhibits differences in subtlety and richness. The fact is that words fail here. Let's just say that these wines are, and will continue to be, outstanding.

SONOMA AREA

Les Petites Maisons → Ledson Hotel & Harmony Lounge → Sebastiani Vineyards & Winery → Buena Vista Carneros → the girl & the fig restaurant

After driving across the open floor of Napa Valley, Sonoma County can be a surprise. Hills rise up all around, often dense with oak, while roads follow winding creek beds. The beauty is striking, but it's not always easy to know where you are. And, take note, mailbox numbers alongside the road often make no sense whatsoever in their numbering. That said, load up with maps and enjoy the countryside! For a guide to Sonoma wineries throughout the area, visit www.visitsantarosa.com or phone (707) 577-8674. And for Healdsburg and the Russian River wine road, visit www.wineroad.com or phone (707) 433-4335. Without these two, I would have been a world contender for number of times lost in this area. Visit www.sonoma.com or phone (707) 522-5800 for a book-sized guide to attractions. The city of Sonoma offers a good map of its area through www.sonomachamber.com or phone (707) 996-1033. One other driving tip: fill up in Sonoma, Santa Rosa, or Healdsburg. Few service stations can be found out in vineyard country.

Because Sonoma wine trails are so diverse, they are easier to follow with an inn-and-vineyard pairing that can avoid traffic clumps along Highway 12. After a day or so, shortcuts will become clear to you. We'll concentrate on three areas: Sonoma, Healdsburg, and the Russian River–Dry Creek areas. For each, we'll suggest a top inn, special wineries, plus a fine restaurant.

Only a short drive from Napa, the town of Sonoma is a good starting place. And if you're here in season or on a weekend, consider working your way toward the east end of town and getting around by bicycle from there. Sonoma is a great browsing place. It is also the site of the Bear Flag Rebellion, in which a handful of ragtag American settlers rode into town, took General Vallejo captive, and declared themselves independent. Mexico's government considered the odds, took notice of how far north Sonoma was, and let the California Republic stand.

If a little pedaling and exploring seems right, head for **Les Petites Maisons** at 1190 E. Napa Street just a mile east of the plaza. Visit www.thegirlandthefig.com (same owner and, at press time, same Web address as the girl and the fig) or phone (707) 933-0340. These are charming little cottages, with kitchens and bicycles available, secure parking, a friendly staff, and a country-style deli for picnic supplies. If Clark Gable had wanted to hide out in Sonoma, this would have made a fine spot. Or, if luxury is your preference, **Ledson Hotel & Harmony Lounge** at 480 First Street East is elegant, historic, a short walk from Sonoma Plaza, and truly one of a kind. Accommodations and the restoration are exceptional, as is the dining. Visit www.ledson.com or phone (707) 996-9779.

Sebastiani Vineyards & Winery, at 389 Fourth Street East, is an icon of California viticulture and makes a grand first stop in the Sonoma area. Sebastiani has also made an art form of their tours and visitors center. You may even make reservations to stay at the historic Sebastiani family home, Casa de Sonoma. For information from a devoted staff on all these possibilities, visit www.sebastiani.com or phone (707) 933-3230. From the entry, bordered by trees and a charming old-country fountain, make your way into the tasting room and spend a moment taking it all in. The staff is welcoming and eager to answer questions about the winery, its history, and the Sonoma area. Sebastiani is one of the few large producers to combine quality with continuity and the entire range of wines reflects that philosophy. Their Barbera is a quintessential California interpretation of an old-vines wine from the Piedmont region of northwest Italy. Its deep purple color and smoky-oak aroma announce a dark body rich with fruit, softened by blending elements of Petite Sirah and Zinfandel. The result is a pasta-lover's dream. Sebastiani's Pinot Noir, Merlot, and Cabernet Sauvignon are just what you would expect from an innovative but cautious producer: ascending levels of intensity in the fruit and firm tannins unique to Sebastiani's terroir. Their Zinfandel is a fine expression—and a good preview—of the grapes produced in the Dry Creek Valley: fruity with intense flavors and notable acidity. These are all fine wines, but Sebastiani's Cherryblock Cabernet Sauvignon is what can blow your wine-colored socks off. This wine, from an old-vines block, is simply gorgeous from the moment its cork comes out. Complex aromas are immediately apparent, and with a bit of swirling, become compelling. The depth and breadth of this full-palate wine are remarkable. Tannins that can be distracting in a big red like this are firmly controlled, leading to utter satisfaction. Cross-taste Cherryblock with another excellent Sebastiani Cabernet to appreciate more fully what the vineyard and winemaker have created.

Buena Vista Carneros at 18000 Old Winery Road is

just a few minutes from the Sonoma plaza area. Visit www .buenavistacarneros.com or phone (707) 938-1266. To enter Buena Vista's tasting room in a historic stone press house is to step into a composite world of history: Old Europe, Mexico, and early California days are all present in the art, antiques, and noble tasting bar. Dating from 1857, Buena Vista Carneros is celebrating more than 150 years as California's first premium winery. It remains the largest landholder in the Carneros region, with a thousand-acre estate, planted in more than 167 blocks overlooking San Pablo Bay. Buena Vista's Chardonnay is balanced and luxurious, with aroma right on the mark, and light mineralization. Perfect for apéritifs or midday conversation. Their Syrah is luscious, yet leggy and lively where many Syrahs pale and fade. Winemakers might dislike me for this—but a grand Syrah can present as a light Cabernet Sauvignon: athletic while still displaying table-linen manners—a dancer, yes indeed. Buena Vista's Pinot Noir is complex and fruit-forward, but not in the least edgy. It opens quickly, with confidence, suggesting a larger red, yet this Pinot Noir carries a notable sense of place, with a nice, toasty finish. The terroir of Buena Vista is even more prominent in the Merlot. This is a rich wine, with superb balance and distinguishable layers of fruit and cocoa. Merlots this full-bodied are sometimes tannin-heavy, but this wine is smooth as well as robust and will pair with a variety of light meats, red sauces, and almost anything from the grill—altogether a lovely wine.

In the plaza area of Sonoma, **the girl & the fig restaurant** at 110 W. Spain Street is a gem. This small bistro didn't invent the word *eclectic,* but it could have. Visit www.thegirlandthefig.com or phone (707) 938-3634 and plan on making early reservations for dinner. Cuisine is Provençal as inspired by the marvelous produce, meats, and seafood available just minutes away. Starters and small plates include sweetbreads with foraged mushrooms, and a cannelloni ragout. A crab dumpling dish with pistachios and an apple-sage combo is amazing. I learned this from two charming young women at the next table—seating is close here, but it leads to easy cross-talk—while I whaled away at a polenta of portobella mushroom, onions, and spinach drenched in a roasted pepper-and-tomato sauce. The duck confit, two tables over, got rave reviews as well. And I'd go for the risotto again in a minute. Service is friendly and impeccable, the wine list is very good, and the atmosphere is perfect for a place on the plaza in Sonoma.

GLEN ELLEN AREA

Arrowood Vineyards & Winery → Mantazas Creek Winery

This area is known for some major labels, yet there are smaller producers of extraordinary quality. One special place is **Arrowood Vineyards & Winery** on the east side of the road at 14347 Sonoma Highway near Glen Ellen. By county ordinance, their sign is small, so watch for three flying banners, and turn up the drive. Visit www.arrowoodwinery.com or phone (707) 935-2600. Wine writers often cite Arrowood as a winery where each wine is at the top of its form. Toss in a visit to a New England–style farmhouse we might have always wished for grandma, and you've got it: flowers, a wraparound veranda, and always a warm welcome. Arrowood is on an invisible border throughout this area, between farms and wineries. So the architecture and landscaping, though new, are a fit. Arrowood's wines are as well and almost every one—perhaps all by now—are top-rated and award-winners. Among these, Saralee's Vineyard Côte de Lune Blanc is an absolute charmer, blending Rousanne, Marsanne, and Viognier in the Rhône fashion. The wine leaves the bottle pale and subtle as smoke. In the glass, layered fruit aromas and flavors convey light overtones of herbs and spice. If you care for Rieslings and crisp Chardonnays, this wine could easily capture your fancy. Arrowood's Merlot is almost the red side of the Côte de Lune Blanc. With perfect viscosity, it rises above Merlots that are too soft and rounded, delivering a delicate balance among textured aromas and dark fruit flavors, with a bass line of smoky toast—a Merlot that reminds us how much wine lovers once prized them, and will again. The Arrowood Syrah, also from Saralee's Vineyard, is a sensual wine of amazing complexity and dimension. It reclines in the glass, making lovely arched windows and waiting on your pleasure with a kind of royal serenity. Aromas and flavors are intertwined, yet distinguishable, and the enduring finish is but another invitation. Of course, you know by now that I may be genetically inclined toward big reds. So, Arrowood is a mother lode in this gold country of wine. Their Cabernet Sauvignon is an amalgam of earthy, dark full-bodied fruit, smoky oak, and layers that continue straight through a long finish. But for the true Cab lover, searching less for a wine than an experience, the winery offers yet another level: Cabernet Sauvignon Reserve Speciale. Owner-winemaker Richard Arrowood thought he might have something remarkable in this wine, and the proof is in the first pour. Bold, without being edgy, this wine is as intense and complex as you're likely to find. It simply sweeps you up in a choir of dark fruit, with deeper chords of smoky earth and tannins that make of this wine a hymn. You could drink this special Cabernet right away, but what a treasure it would be to open years from now—on a day when the wine itself would be the center of all attention for the pleasure it can offer.

Matanzas Creek Winery, at 6097 Bennett Valley Road, between Glen Ellen and Santa Rosa, is well worth the half-hour drive to reach it. Visit www.matanzascreek.com or phone (707) 528-6464. The curvy two-lane roads are sweet, roadside villages are charming, and the Bennett Valley terroir produces a complex of flavors and undercurrents not found elsewhere. Just take care to use their online or phone driving directions when visiting; other advice can be deceiving. Matanzas is a farm-turned-winery, which has an altogether different feel than grazing land or raw hillsides on which vines have been planted. The tasting room and its surrounds are equally fascinating. If Arrowood recalls the image of a family farm, Matanzas Creek is an architect's vision of an estate-sized tree house. To ascend the tasting-room steps is to enter another realm. It is a place, which if absorbed in every detail, can move visitors to tears. Matanzas Creek wines project all that, plus the earthy, unspoiled quality of Bennett Valley. The Sauvignon Blanc is excellent. Aromas and fruit flavors are rangy, yet closely bound, all delivered in a lovely pale shade. The wine also presents some mineralization rare in a California Blanc. True fanciers of Cabernet Sauvignon will enjoy—and perhaps be surprised by—the subtlety of the interpretation by Matanzas Creek. Aromatic and full-bodied, it is a complex blend with touches of Merlot, Cabernet Franc, and Syrah to round out the textures and acidity. Tannins are firm but restrained and the wine should age quite well. Yet it is the Matanzas Creek Bennett Valley Merlot that holds the greatest surprise. This award-winner is taller and more athletic than most Merlots and the wine shows its debt to this valley's soil and unique climate. Fruit-driven, with a toasty stance, the wine also brings a warm-earth quality to the midpalate, along with a lingering finish—altogether a wonderful rendition. A leader in creating premium wines, Matanzas Creek Winery is guided by a simple but profound commitment to a fulfilling experience of taste as an extension of the land and life.

RUSSIAN RIVER AREA

Farmhouse Inn & Restaurant → Iron Horse Ranch & Vineyards → De Loach Vineyards → Hook & Ladder Winery → Davis Bynum Winery → Arista Winery

In every regard, **Farmhouse Inn & Restaurant** at 7871 River Road near Forestville is a grand place to stay—and to enjoy a superb dinner. A perennial winner of awards, the restaurant is staffed by those who are masters of their crafts. Meals are not served so much as hosted by the waitstaff. It is a remarkable feeling. And in those moments when you are not fully involved with a meal, keep an eye on the sommelier's associate. She treats each bottle as an infant, with care, economy of movement, and full attention on her task. Vintners refer to their grapes as babies; she seems aware of that love. Food-and-wine selections live up to the Farmhouse reputation for top wine-country cuisine framed by chef Steve Litke. Focus is on organic dishes with harmonious yet distinguishable flavors, with sophisticated staff suggestions for pairing menu selections with wines from an extensive list. I found myself dawdling over a succulent dessert and a delicious Port, just to stay a bit longer. And do consider the Farmhouse Inn for an overnight as well—a wonderful

base for adventures in Russian River wine country. Visit
www.farmhouseinn.com or phone (707) 887-3300. Early reservations are advised.

Off Highway 116 south of Forestville, **Iron Horse Ranch
& Vineyards** is the first stop, at 9786 Ross Station Road. Visit
www.ironhorsevineyards.com or phone (707) 431-3646. Once
on that road, keep going. After a bit, you'll crest a hill to find a
view of 350 acres of vines. Up at the winery, the view opens
across Sonoma County to Mt. St. Helena. Park along a row of
trees and head over to the open-air tasting room. The first vintage of Estate Chardonnay was produced in 1978, and Estate
Pinot Noir made its debut the next year. Tasting takes place
right on the edge of a vineyard, and instead of using a dump
bucket, visitors are encouraged to pour their excess—if any—
right back into the soil. But if Iron Horse still wines are making
a name for themselves, their sparkling wines make headlines. If
you're a fan of suspense fiction, you'll find Iron Horse mentioned by more than one top author. Iron Horse Wines are also
regular fare at the White House and were served to diplomats at
the 1985 Reagan-Gorbachev summit meetings that ended the
Cold War. In short, if Iron Horse is being poured, you're likely
to be in interesting company. And these sparkling wines reap
awards and high points. Iron Horse Classic is what we imagine
bubbly to be: bright, saucy, and eager to please. This sparkling
wine is a blend of Pinot Noir and Chardonnay, aged four years,
and easily paired with apéritifs, fruit, or a light chocolate dessert.
Russian Cuvée is virtually the same blend, with a more fruit-
forward quality and a touch of sweetness. Wedding Cuvée is a
lovely wine: inviting in color, light in its fruit, and velvety across
the palate. It is celebration personified and pairs well with firelight . . . or a ring. Iron Horse Blanc de Blanc may be queen of

the realm for white-wine lovers. Pressed only from Chardonnay, this sparkling wine is aged six years, and when uncorked, brings a bouquet and lightness of flavor that one hopes for, yet rarely finds—a stunning wine, graceful in its exuberance.

Farther south on Highway 116, turn east on Guerneville Road and north again on Olivet Road to reach **De Loach Vineyards** at 1791 Olivet Road. Visit www.deloachvineyards.com or phone (707) 526-9111. This vineyard and winery was established in the 1970s by retired San Francisco firefighter Cecil De Loach, and attracted early recognition with a hit Zinfandel. Some thirty years later, the property was sold to Boisset America, and an ambitious program of expansion began, with emphasis on Biodynamic farming led by Ginny Limbrix. Award-winning, high-point Chardonnays and Pinot Noirs are a treat in the newly designed tasting room. But with culinary director Cyndicy Coudray on hand, food pairings interested me.

"What pairings would you recommend, Cyndicy?"

"For vegetarians, our OFS Sauvignon Blanc would enrich a tofu seviche with chili, lime, and cilantro, served in a chilled wine or martini glass with cubed cucumber and ripe avocado, garnished with tortilla chips. Plus basil crêpes filled with red onion, shiitake mushrooms, asparagus, and wilted spinach, with lemon-wine-butter sauce."

"And for meat lovers?"

"We have two fine Zinfandels. For either, I'd suggest you use the varietal to be served to braise chicken thighs with fennel, shallots, capers, and Kalamata olives on creamy polenta or orzo pasta with Parmesan."

And the Zinfandels are fine, indeed. De Loach Russian River Valley Zinfandel offers vivid aromas and red-fruit flavors, with soft hints of barrel spice and walnut. But Forgotten Vines Zinfandel is a trip back through time, with a classic old-vine jammy wine as your guide. This wine has firm, yet unobtrusive tannins and aging potential. For all that, the Forgotten Old Vines is a big, round, entertaining wine with a baritone personality and—with every sip— a story to tell about the early days in Sonoma County.

Driving away, I resolved to add another recipe to my collection. But I also wondered about Cecil De Loach. Where had he and his wife Christine gone? The answer turned up just about a blink north. On the opposite side of the highway stands a fire-engine red truck, with a tall ladder atop it. Cecil and Christine had just moved across the way with their family, to establish the **Hook & Ladder Winery** at 2134 Olivet Road. Visit www.hookandladderwinery.com or phone (707) 546-5712.

"Our previous incarnation, De Loach Vineyards, grew far beyond anything we imagined," son Michael says. "We were dealing day in and out with bankers, lawyers, and distributors, instead of growing grapes and making wine together as a family. My father is a hands-on guy. He puts the dog in his truck, goes all around the vineyards, checks in at the winery, and makes dinner for all of us here on the ranch. Now that we've sold the De Loach brand, we can make and keep it that way again on the four hundred acres we retained. Our wines are completely estate and we want to keep it profitable, healthy, sustainable, relaxed, and enjoyable."

And they have. Hook & Ladder is one of those extraordinary places where a traveler feels instantly at home with close family members, sampling handcrafted wines at attractive prices, and making new friends. Cecil was what so many of us aspired to be: driver at the rear set of wheels—the tillerman—on a huge hook and ladder engine. In fact, Hook & Ladder has both red and white Table Wines under the Tillerman label. The white is crisp and dry, while the red is a fine blend of Cabernet Sauvignon, Cabernet Franc, and Sangiovese, with berry and spice flavors delivered on an earthy base that leaves a satisfying finish. But Hook & Ladder Cabernet Sauvignon, Third Alarm Reserve, is a blaze of deep aromas in a big, bold wine, with tannins nonetheless held in check to produce a velvety full-mouth wine leading to a long finish of distinctive character. What a ride!

Not much farther north is **Davis Bynum Winery** at 8075 Westside Road. Visit www.davisbynum.com or phone (707) 433-2611. A visit here is another opportunity to step back in time. The grounds near the tasting room are so parklike, they bring out the child in visitors. And the winery is located in a renovated hop barn. This winery has been, and continues to be, a leader in creating an organic relationship with the land that is nearly spiritual—do visit the Bynum permaculture garden, if you can. It expresses, in the complex beauty of its existence, what it would take, and has taken, books to describe. Many wines here are high-point award-winners. Davis Bynum Limited Edition Chardonnay is on the cusp between full and crisp, with lovely fruit aromas and flavors, and a languishing finish. Their reds are exceptional, with two Pinot Noirs that invite side-by-side comparison, and a Meritage: Westside Road. Blended on a Merlot, this is an exciting, yet very approachable wine that maintains an air of delicacy while standing up to everything from roasts to Cajun. The Laureles Estate Vineyard Cabernet Sauvignon is at the top of its form. An expansive wine with nothing held back, it is what a big red should be. Paired with grilled beef, it can really present well.

Arista Winery at 7015 Westside Road is next. Visit

www.aristawinery.com or phone (707) 473-0606. Pulling up the drive, the tasting room seems almost a cultural island: a Japanese retreat rendered in California surroundings, trees, pathways for exploring and reflection, and giant, mossy rocks.

"Visitors often ask how we managed to get these boulders up here," Mark McWilliams says. "And we always say that we didn't. It was all here, just like this. Some find that hard to believe." And part of the grounds is landscaped, but more to consciousness than the eye. Winetasters, more than most, understand the distinction. They also recognize the quality in Artista's wines.

I asked Mark McWilliams what draws visitors here, other than the wine.

"They want a memory, a connection. The warm, almost homey intimacy of our tasting room creates that opportunity . . . they can completely escape the world, relax, and visit with our family as we share our passion."

That passion is in Arista's wines. Their Sauvignon Blanc is light, with elegant fruit aromas and flavors, on that fine line between bright and fullish. But it is their range in Pinot Noir that invites side-by-side tastings. The Russian River Valley Pinot Noir is a complex of fruit and tannin aromas that opens to display a rich, dark wine with a velvety texture and long finish. Arista's Longbow opens more slowly. Give it time—perhaps even recork overnight—to encourage greater expression. A complex, layered wine with deep earthy tones, the Longbow shows its close relation in fruit and style, but is more assertive. And where its sister displays an herbal finish, Longbow offers a longer, spicy finish. See what you make of the two. And be aware that the vintages of each sell out quickly.

HEALDSBURG AREA—WEST

Madrona Manor → Forth Vineyards → Lambert Bridge
Winery → Quivira Estate Vineyards and Winery

On the boundary of the Russian River and Dry Creek areas, **Madrona Manor** stands in Victorian splendor at 1001 Westside Road at the junction of W. Dry Creek Road. Visit www.madronamanor.com or phone (707) 433-4231. On acres of gardens and forest, this is one of the most delightful of the area's many mansion inns: fireplaces, romantic settings, a summertime pool, and all the amenities a discerning traveler would expect—with ceilings high enough to show up on radar. The Madrona is more than an inn; it offers a moment in time to be savored.

Three special wineries are ranged along W. Dry Creek Road, north of Madrona Manor. The first is **Forth Vineyards** at 2335 W. Dry Creek Road. Visit www.forthvineyards.com or phone (707) 473-0553. At present, Forth is open for tasting by appointment only, but they will be hosting a series of intimate hands-on wine education events. Not to be confused with crush camps, where guests do fieldwork, these are coaching seminars with a delicious meal included. All this stems from the elegant wines Jann and Gerry Forth are developing, plus their gift for sharing the romance and nuances of winemaking. The three of us walked out to the modest processing plant.

"Have you ever had a breakfast wine?" Jann asked.

I hadn't and wasn't sure I wanted to. With a grin, Gerry tapped the first fermentation tank for a sample. One sip was convincing:

I could indeed drink this partially fermented Sauvignon Blanc first thing in the morning, with its grapefruit-dominant chorus of berry flavors . . . and I would really like it.

"See what I mean?" Jann said.

We moved on to their Estate Syrah and All Boys Cabernet—both exceptional. These artisan wines are drinkable now or may be stored. They also share the Dry Creek Valley sense of place: earth tones coupled with a certain liveliness. The Forth Estate Syrah—yes, I'm sure they noticed the wordplay—reminds us that metaphors for wine can be art and perfume, as well as taste. This wine has great legs and composure to match. Subtle fruit flavors ask politely for your attention, and once in the mouth, they deliver. Just delightful. But for big-red lovers, hold your glass out for All Boys, which nearly reinvents Cabernet Sauvignon. Full-flavored, but not burly or edgy, this wine is deep in color and aroma, opens at a scholarly pace, and then simply floats onto your palate. Almost as soon as you discover the smoky tannins, these seem to disappear into the richness of this wine—a moment to be savored in good company on a Sonoma hillside.

Lambert Bridge Winery at 4085 W. Dry Creek Road is a marvelous place to visit, picnic, wed—whatever comes to mind—with a grand tasting room and excellent wines. Visit www.lambertbridge.com or phone (707) 431-9600. The Lambert Bridge tasting room is a study in contrasting elements that work well together. On one side, a wall of glass brings the barrel room into full view. Opposite, is a grand fireplace—the kind that calls to true wine lovers on a chilly February day. And hospitality is the hallmark of Lambert Bridge, with beautifully landscaped grounds and well-regarded wines to match. Their Chardonnay and Sauvignon Blanc are both award-winners. The Chardonnay is a lovely Sonoma-style sipping wine and will pair well with traditional seafood, while the Sauvignon Blanc is complex and dry enough to work with Asian spices. Lambert Bridge Merlot is medium-bodied and concentrated, flooding the palate with a closing flourish.

A few minutes farther north is **Quivira Estate Vineyards and Winery** at 4900 W. Dry Creek Road, and a lovely stop before crossing the Russian River to a loop east of Healdsburg. Visit www.quivirawine.com or phone (707) 431-8333. The Quivira property, at the confluence of Dry Creek and Wine Creek, was acquired by entrepreneur Pete Kight in 2006. An avid fly fisherman, he valued an opportunity to contribute to the Wine Creek restoration project—and yes, the steelheads are back. He also committed Quivira to organic farming and Biodynamic principles that treat the entire farm as an evolving ecosystem. It was all a major change from Pete's background in technology.

"In that role," Pete says, "at the end of the day I didn't have anything to hold in my hands. . . . With an estate winery you literally have the chance to sink your hands into the soil from the wine's conception."

So, Quivira's wines are organically true as well as handcrafted by winemaker Steven Canter in small lots. The Zinfandel, exceptionally well developed and complex, is a wine for all seasons, with a robust crispness that carries well over the palate, and a long, leggy finish that brings satisfaction with each sip. Quivira Fig Tree Vineyard Sauvignon Blanc is a delightful blend that brings the character of Sémillon and Sauvignon Musqué to the wine for a strong sense of place, with bright overtones of fruit and spice on a base of muted oak. Also sample new single-varietal releases of Grenache and Mourvèdre, sure to be excellent additions to Quivira's superb line.

HEALDSBURG AREA—EAST

Honor Mansion → Seghesio Family Vineyards →
Jordan Vineyard & Winery → Hanna Winery
→ Stryker Sonoma Winery and Vineyards

The extraordinary **Honor Mansion** at 14891 Grove Street has long been a favorite among bed-and-breakfasts along the West Coast. Visit www.honormansion.com (the Web site is a treat in itself) or phone (707) 433-4277. Service is gracious, as are the furnishings and grounds, including a waterfall and pond. Honor Mansion cuisine has also attracted a national following. Imagine a three-course breakfast by dappled morning light, with fine china, crystal, and silver, and you have the idea.

Seghesio Family Vineyards at 14730 Grove Street in Healdsburg is practically across the street from Honor Mansion. Visit www.seghesio.com or phone (707) 433-3579. The Seghesio tasting room carries a deep, traditional look, though being right in town, it can spill over with young locals meeting one another for wine, conversation, and bocce ball. A cork tree on the grounds is there to remind us of the origins of our partnership with the vine. Seghesio Family Vineyards began in 1895 and Zinfandel is their hallmark. They also feature Barbera, a fine Pinot Grigio, and a lovely Sangiovese. But the Zinfandel line is gorgeous. Seghesio Sonoma Zinfandel is excellent. It will benefit from a little time to open. After that, the nature of growing and winemaking will make itself evident: aroma and flavor are singular, yet rich, with light spice and a long, smooth finish. With Old Vine Zinfandel, though, it's time to pause. We are sometimes amazed at the degree to which animals and plant life are able to communicate with us, if we understand or allow it. Here is an opportunity to notice that old-vine wines are indeed different. Open your senses and you can taste the age. These vines and the Seghesio family have been speaking to each other for nearly one hundred years, and the result is right there in your glass. Still doubtful? Move on to Home Ranch Zinfandel. The language is clearer, deeper, more complex, and beautifully structured, with an amazing wealth and no edginess whatsoever. It is a Zinfandel of uncommon quality, yet with an attractive price. Is it magic? To put it in perspective, taste the Seghesio Sangiovese. A different wine? Certainly, but this wine also comes from vines put down as early as 1910. Take a moment, not only to enjoy the wine, but to imagine how long, and on what intimate terms, we have been speaking with these vines.

Jordan Vineyard & Winery at 1474 Alexander Valley Road is just a bit east of Healdsburg and one of the most handsome wineries to be found anywhere. Visit www.jordanwinery.com and phone (707) 431-5250 to reserve space in Jordan's popular tours and tastings, offered by appointment only. Designed in a manor house style, each detail of the winery is sweet to the eye—it appears as a fine engraving come to life—from meticulous land-scaping to ivy-covered walls that soften the structure's proportions. Founded by geologist Tom Jordan in the early '70s, this winery and its vineyards represented an enormous invest-ment in the untested notion that this region could produce pre-mium wines that would find worldwide recognition. The gamble paid off and Jordan wines now top many wine lovers' lists. At a time when California reds required years to become approach-able with their muscular tannins, Jordan moved in a different direction, a philosophy reflected in the winery's pursuit of pre-mium white wine as well. Their Russian River Chardonnay sweeps from the bottle, opening in a swirl of aromas that lead to a creamy, yet not buttery, complex of flavors that are both crisp and well mineralized. Jordan's Cabernet Sauvignon is a celebration of what a red wine from Alexander Valley can be. With light touches of Merlot, Cabernet Franc, and Petit Verdot, this wine has both breadth and a sense of the highly refined. Color and aromas are dark and deep, with firmly controlled tannins on an unobtrusive base of cedar and smoke. Jordan's Chardonnay and Cabernet Sauvignon can both be savored alone and are robust enough to pair well with a whole spectrum of dishes. Exquisite wines created in a superb setting. What more could one ask?

Continue east toward Highway 128 and turn right (south) to **Hanna Winery** at 9280 Highway 128. Visit www.hanna winery.com or phone (707) 431-4310. A beautifully landscaped tasting room in a Mediterranean style, plus the open feeling that Northern California so encourages. Sample wines in the well-appointed room, or, as is my favorite, out on the formal deck—vineyards in close and reaching across the Alexander Valley and just below, a helicopter pad for special arrivals. Sound like a stretch? Not at all. Direct flights are offered to Sonoma County Airport from SFO, SEA-TAC, and others. You could be here within minutes to sample Hanna wines and take in the good life.

Return north on Highway 128. Just beyond the jog is **Stryker Sonoma Winery and Vineyards** at 5110 Highway 128. Visit www.strykersonoma.com or phone (707) 433-1944. The winery is an architectural award-winner and a grand exercise in transparency, with an indoor-outdoor fireplace, and commanding views.

"We wanted to offer our visitors a 'room with a view,' of both the vineyards and the inner workings of a small winery," partner

Craig MacDonald says. "We feel that wine tasting should be fun and educational, not stuffy or intimidating. The tasting room is a glass pavilion offering visitors the feeling that they are in the vineyards as they taste our wines. From the crush pad to the barrel room, all without going on a tour."

The design is an unqualified success, and you may want to get an early start here. Response from visitors to the tasting room and Stryker Sonoma wines has been immediate and strong.

Continue north on Highway 128 and rejoin U.S. 101 for an unhurried drive north into quite different wine country—and a breathtaking loop through California redwoods.

MENDOCINO COUNTY AREA

Milano Family Winery → Brutocao Vineyards & Cellars →
Jeriko Estate → Parducci Winery-Mendocino Wine Company
→ Redwood Valley Cellars

Traveling the old routes of pioneers and stagecoaches, it's clear that state boundaries have little to do with the land or its people. Except for taxation and the like, California doesn't extend nearly so far north as its border suggests.

Instead, what we recognize as Oregon begins farther south, below Eureka and most of Humboldt County. For a map and guide, visit www.redwoods.info or phone (707) 444-6634. Up here, the energy level softens. Mountains and forests encircle the valley with increasing intimacy. Smiles begin slower and last longer. Winters are less easy, sunshine more valued. Driving along in our steel cocoons, it can be difficult to discern these changes.

But if there is a place where the overlap between Oregon and California begins, it's close to the **Milano Family Winery,** located in an ancient hop kiln at 14594 S. Highway 101 south of Hopland. Visit www.milanowinery.com or phone (707) 774-1396—and watch for the highway signs directing you to a hard left turn (west) down from the highway. Once parked, and before ascending the steps to the second-floor tasting room, take a look around. You may know by now that most vintners escaped from another profession to make wine and that most are committed to the land and exceptionally curious. Here, you'll find that same blend. The picnic area is surrounded by an entire menagerie, yet their keeper, Ted Starr, is not only the winery's manager, but a software developer for the wine industry. Former nurse Deanna Starr is the winemaker. Most everyone visiting here feels at home, and Milano's wines are frosting on the cake. Milano's Merlot has won Best of Class and other awards, their Cabernet Sauvignon is an award-winner as well, while sales of Milano's Disaster Relief Red dedicate 10 percent to disaster funds. And it gets better. Milano's Sunshine is as pale as the light that appears just before dawn: present, but almost invisible. This is a fine blend, both sleek and satisfying, with a full-mouth quality, and a lingering finish. The Carignane may be the most widely planted varietal in France, yet it's not well known here in the United States. It should be, with its depth in color, ample spices, and vanilla overtones. But if you're looking for a daily Table Wine with top varietal qualities, be sure to sample their Big Ass Red. Give it a few minutes to relax from the bottle and it will be surprisingly full-flavored, with no rough edges. You can almost hear an old upright piano playing as you pour. And as a conversation starter, it's hard to beat.

Near the southern edge of Hopland, be sure to visit **Brutocao**

Vineyards & Cellars in an adapted schoolhouse on the west side at 13500 S. Highway 101. Visit www.brutocaocellars.com or phone (707) 774-1664. Brutocao's tasting room is spacious and welcoming, with an extensive gift shop. Step through the side door and you'll be on a bocce court. To the rear of the tasting room is the Crushed Grape Restaurant, family-friendly, with a varied menu. On weekends, the Lion's Den Bistro features five-course wine-and-food pairings.

"Out of our line of twenty-five wines, we always have a dozen or so open for tasting," Steve Brutocao says. "Visitors come in for a whole day experience, tasting and learning about wine from our staff, playing bocce ball, enjoying the grounds and our food. It's a lot of fun and we're usually not very crowded here in Mendocino County, so winetasting is never hurried." Brutocao follows both Tuscan and French traditions of gentle winemaking, which produces superb wines. The emphasis is on estate-grown fruit, not masked with too much oak. Their Zinfandel is both delicate and moderately priced, with its fruit flavors balanced by a light flavor of smoky chocolate. But if you're looking for a wine to stand up to game or spicy foods, be sure to sample the Primitivo. Brave, but with excellent manners. Do take some time to taste Brutacao's line of Estate-Bottled Merlot. Stepping through these to sample the subtle but discrete differences is an education in itself. And if you are of the view that blends are too often lacking in character, be sure to sample Brutocao's Quadriga—a blend of Sangiovese, Primitivo, Barbera, and Dolcetto—it is said to be an inspiration of the gods, which may not be far off.

Jeriko Estate, its vineyard, grounds, and winery are the vision of designers-vintners Daniel and Linda Fetzer. North of Hopland, this expansive estate is stunning, especially as it calls more attention to the land than to itself. Visit www.jeriko estate.com or phone (707) 744-1140. Wines produced here are handcrafted, following stringent organic and Biodynamic practices. From Jerikos's Chardonnay, Pinot Noir, and a lovely Sangiovese, to their Merlot and Syrah, you'll find a pleasant tasting-room experience here.

From Hopland north, U.S. 101 follows the course of the Russian River toward its source north of Redwood Valley and the population thins. Yet here, near the tip of California's winegrowing regions, classic California labels have conveyed the virtues of quality and value since the 1850s.

In Ukiah, be sure to sample the wines and make a tour of **Parducci Winery-Mendocino Wine Company** located at 501 Parducci Road. Visit www.mendocinowinecompany.com or phone (707) 463-5350. The winery's history is remarkable. So is the view, held by the winery's partners, that we cannot lag behind the planet's needs, but must foresee and meet those needs. Partner Tim Thornhill walked us over to the winery's cellar. This underground room is filled with such tanks—vertical barrels, all handmade and huge—as you may never have seen. And they have capacities of up to 20,000 gallons each. It's winemaking in a striking tradition.

"We have twenty-seven tanks from the 1930s or earlier, all of old-growth redwood," Tim said, "plus nineteen redwood tanks dating from the 1960s."

"Why redwood?"

"It's a neutral wood that imparts no flavor. Yet it allows the wine to breathe a little as it develops. You could say that it's 'alive' in there."

"These tanks seem to have a majesty about them."

"They do. When we were acquiring the winery, I was down

here to complete due diligence by estimating the board-feet of redwood as an asset. A winemaker mistook what I was doing and later chained himself to one of the tanks to let us know they wouldn't be going anywhere."

History and commitment like that can still be found under the Parducci label. The Cabernet Sauvignon is big, yet well-rounded by blending with trace amounts of Merlot and Syrah, enhancing both the deep fruit flavors and the wine's long finish. A delightful surprise is the Parducci Petite Sirah. This Sirah is full, well-rounded, able to stand up to almost anything grilled, and a bargain among big, expansive reds: jammy fruit flavors, a bit spicy, with toasted oak, and a lingering finish. If you like Cabernet Sauvignon and sometimes prefer something a bit lighter, be sure to sample this wine. Mendocino Wine Company also has some fun with its labels. Big Yellow Cab is a traditional Cabernet Sauvignon that will remind some wine lovers of the ubiquitous Marathon Checker Taxis that prowled the streets of every major U.S. city in the 1940s and '50s. Not a blend, this wine is dark and broad-shouldered, with deep fruit and firm tannins leading to a flourishing light-oak finish. Mendocino's Tusk 'N Red is a fanciful, roly-poly blend of Syrah, Zinfandel, Sangiovese, and Petite Syrah, with a touch of Grenache—perfect for red sauces, wood-fired pizza, and light game. Done up in a northwest Italian style, with character and a whisper of smoke, this is a wine to make you smile. Zig Zag Zin is a blend that retains the essential character of Zinfandel, with fruit-forward aromas and complex flavors. Bold, but with good manners, this wine has the structure to pair with a wide range of foods, from grilled meats to bold sauces. Mendocino's Sketchbook is a Cabernet Sauvignon blend, with just enough Merlot and Syrah to ease the palate, yet maintain a strong sense of place. Structure and firm tannins underlie deep and complex flavors, with a whisper of smoke and earthiness for balance. Pair with fine meats or hearty dishes, just bring conversation.

Redwood Valley Cellars is just about ten minutes north at 7051 N. State Street in Redwood Valley, and it's easiest to follow State Street north from Ukiah. Visit www.barraof mendocino.com or phone (707) 485-0322. Even if you're still on U.S. 101, you'll recognize this unusual tasting room by its domed shape. Inside, the curved wood beams are even more striking, with a tabernacle quality. Meditrina and Dom Perignon would both feel at home here. The Barra family knows this land and the estate has been organically certified for more than twenty years. Charlie Barra, as charming a storyteller as you'd want to know, is in his eighties and we are talking about the upcoming harvest—his sixty-first—while Martha is making sure that my plate is never empty.

"It looks good for so far," Charlie says.

"I heard that wineries in Eastern Washington and Santa Ynez started about the same time."

Charlie smiles. "I've learned not to ask too many questions when it comes to weather," he says.

It's a good policy. And the wines here are outstanding. The Barra of Mendocino Pinot Blanc is both rare and well turned out. Bright and light on its feet, this white is crisp, with complex citrus flavors that will stand up to spices from Cajun to Asian, and remain a light summer treat. Barra's Zinfandel is what wine lovers always hope to find in that varietal. This wine is from a gnarly old-vines block that Charlie planted in 1955, expressing his dedication to leave a vineyard better than he found it. Zinfandel is not typically a shy wine, but many take time to open. Not this one, Barra's Zin is bold and eager for the glass, yet sophisticated. Dark and rich in flavor, with a light toasty base, this wine is seamless from aroma through its lingering. I'd drive a long way for more of this wine . . . and most likely will.

HUMBOLDT AREA

The Benbow Inn → Carter House & 301 Restaurant

South of Liggett, the mountains begin to close in as you approach some of the finest stands of redwood still in existence. Watch for Smith Redwood State Reserve and directional signs for Avenue of the Giants—the drive of a lifetime, or many lifetimes, in redwood years. Dark and shadowy, even on sunny days, these trees are both comforting and mesmerizing. Take time to pull over for a stroll among these forgiving giants. If you spot a circle of these trees, you've discovered a family mystery extending back thousands of years.

The Benbow Inn at 445 Lake Benbow Drive in Garberville is a heartwarming sentinel to times gone by and times to come. Visit www.benbowinn.com or phone (707) 923-2124. This very special inn is on the National Register and now welcomes reservations all year-round. First opened in the 1920s, the Benbow Inn once hosted biplanes on the lawn and the likes of Clark Gable—yes, we're still on his trail—in its earlier days. Yet the inn is more comfortable now than it ever was. Choose a room in the inn proper for the feeling of glamour past, or stay in one of the terrace rooms with decks extending into the wooded area adjoining this remarkable property. The dining room alone draws regulars from everywhere, and in summer, patio dining is sweet beyond compare. The Benbow's wine list is extensive and well chosen. Waitstaff is friendly as well as accommodating and finds true delight in suggesting food-and-wine pairings. The Benbow is a prized stop along the north coast and I am always pleased to be among their guests. I'm sure you will be, too. Bring an appetite for food, wine, the '20s, and perhaps a parasol. . . .

In Eureka, a stay at the **Carter House & Restaurant 301** is unique in the truest sense. Visit www.carterhouse.com or phone (707) 444-8062. Here, at 301 L Street in Old Town, Mark Carter has created an award-winning boutique hotel and restaurant, complemented by three renovated Victorian homes across the way. Done up in shades of sun-yellow, with varying trim, these Painted Ladies are rich in history and guest amenities. The main inn, right on the corner and housing Restaurant 301, is surprising in its wealth of detail. It also carries an air of seclusion that recalls—in an elegant way—Edward Hopper's painting, *Nighthawks*. To sit before the fire or take a meal at Carter House is to be insulated from the traffic or weather outside. Nothing is left to chance. To be certain that the freshest produce is available to executive chef Joseph Beaubien's exquisite menu, the Carters have created extraordinary herb gardens (tours on request), plus Carter Cellars from which superb Napa Valley Cabernet Sauvignons add to what is already an amazing wine list. Visit www.cartercellars.com. Carter wines are faithful to their heritage and a joy to sample at winetastings offered to guests in the afternoon or with dinner. Carter reds are deep in color and aroma, eager to be out of the bottle, and velvety, with an exceptional finish. These wines remind us why we sip wine with care and appreciation. The Carter House staff is warm, knowledgeable, and, as you might imagine, very good at offering guests an unforgettable experience. Early reservations are advised.

From Eureka, we'll continue along our tour in a brief dash through Crescent City toward the Applegate-Ashland area in Southern Oregon. From Eureka, continue along a breathtaking stretch of U.S. 101, with the highway alternating between shady forests and sandy tidelands. North of Crescent City, take the eastbound exit for U.S. 199, which follows a spectacular, tree-lined river gorge through to Cave Junction.

Oregon

If California is a state of mind, Oregon is a state of being. And that being seems always in transition. From Lewis and Clark forward, Oregonians have been on the cusp of change.

Early Oregon vintners gave up on wine grapes, as these were first introduced in the 1850s, yet the state now embraces a wine renaissance that began in the 1970s.

"Well, Oregon didn't exactly embrace us," recalls Dick Ponzi, one of the architects of the wine revival. "At the beginning, farmers would ask us what we were planting, and when we told them that we were putting in wine grapes, they'd shake their heads. About half of them told us to go much farther south. The other half told us we should be way up north, maybe in Washington. Which didn't seem to leave us much room," Dick says.

"Maybe that was their point.

"It certainly could have been. But we figured that by averaging out what all those farmers were saying, we had to be in exactly the right place."

The early vineslingers who rode into Oregon were correct. They became the godfathers and defenders of that delicate, thin-skinned little Pinot grape for which the Willamette Valley is well suited. So, to the twin strands that underlie viticulture in California—mutual support among winegrowers, plus a sense of stewardship for the land—must be added the idealism found in Oregon's wine industry, from the early days right on up to the present.

"It extends from the character of our founders, those who persevered over the Oregon Trail and settled in the Willamette Valley," says David Adelsheim, cofounder of Adelsheim Vineyard. "It leads to endurance."

That's part of what it took for David Lett, Dick Erath, David Adelsheim, Dick Ponzi, Susan Sokol Blosser, and others to experiment and learn—to express through their wines what could be done with grapes in Oregon. These visionaries were among the first to regard hilly, rocky soil as something other than marginal orchards or poor grazing land. In following their dreams, they established an industry that already contributes about $1.5 billion annually to the state's economy and could soon double that.

Of equal importance, Oregon now enjoys a reputation for world-class wines. Paul Pintarich provides a rousing personal history of some of those pioneers in his book, *The Boys Up North*. (See Connections.)

Yet the question arises: how can such energy be expressed through cooperation while competing toe-to-toe in a reluctant marketplace? I asked Allan Carter of Domaine Serene Vineyards and Winery about it. A twinkle comes into his eye.

"I've thought about that," he says. "The best example I know comes from the Warner Brothers cartoons with Sam Sheepdog and Ralph Wolf."

"How so?"

"Well, in the first scene of each episode, they're walking along, chatting, with their arms draped around each other's shoulders. They're the best of buddies. Then, they come up to a time-clock station in the meadow. Each one punches in and . . . off they go! Running around like mad as Ralph tries to corner the sheep market and Sam has to catch him. Both are doing everything they can to gain an advantage. And one of them almost prevails . . . when the whistle blows. Each one punches out again, and off down the path they go, still the best of friends."

You'll find more of the underlying culture of the Pacific Northwest during your own travels through wine country here. To be sure, you'll discover special inns and wineries and restaurants, but the emphasis is on relaxation and enjoyment, often in unfussy surroundings. Even the term *laid-back* doesn't work as a description up this way, for it conveys attitude—something you'll rarely find in either Oregon or Washington.

On being invited to a fine restaurant owned by a chef of stellar reputation, I asked my innkeeper about attire for the occasion.

"Whatever makes you feel most comfortable," she said. "You'll see everything there from formal wear to Carhartts."

And there's this: in very few areas of agriculture will you find so little emphasis on yield. That's much of what other farming is about: yield. Even among California wineries, volume is often a major goal. Yet among Pacific Northwest vintners, the issue is more often how to *limit* production in order to encourage the fruit to provide the most complex and intense flavors with which a winemaker can work. Often a vineyard that could easily produce six tons per acre is held to less than two.

Which leads to another question: When was the last time you heard of someone sending back some bread because the dough was no good or the wrapping had tainted the loaf? Yet that's what vintners contend with. Of course, they will tell you that it's all worthwhile. They will tell you that most days.

APPLEGATE-JACKSONVILLE AREA

Schmidt Family Vineyards → Troon Vineyard → Wooldridge Creek Winery → Valley View Winery → McCully House Inn

Continue east on U.S. 199. Approaching Grants Pass, prepare for a right turn and follow signs for Highway 238. You'll be making an extended U-turn and heading back west, but to reach Applegate Valley wineries on the east side of Applegate River, this is a less complicated way to go.

If you are near the end of your day, you may wish to spend the night in the Grants Pass area, at Weasku Inn Historic Lodge or the Lodge at Riverside, for a fresh morning start on a tour of Applegate Valley, Jacksonville, and Ashland.

Ashland has become a wine-and-cuisine destination to complement its cultural investment in the long-running Oregon Shakespeare Festival—not that they're against a little Molière from time to time. Meantime, Applegate Valley wineries are on the rise. It can help to imagine this area as a triangle, with Grants Pass at the apex, the Applegate Valley along the western side, extending through Jacksonville and Ashland, and I-5 / Highway 99 forming the other side. This entire area is in transition. The Applegate Valley is likely to become a prime viticulture area, Ashland is expanding, and renovation is going on throughout Grants Pass. This southern region is a lovely place to find part of the spirit of Oregon.

On hillsides flanking the Applegate River are wineries well worth visiting. For a rack card-sized map of the area—with road names displayed—visit www.applegatewinetrail.com or phone (541) 846-9900. En route, if you find yourself back across the Applegate River and on Highway 238 only, swing around and pick up the turn on the east side of the river. Applegate Road is a charming route through trees and hills, with small farms, ranches, and distractions of all kinds. So, keep watch for the Kubli Road sign on the left (east) side. It is a loop that leads to Schmidt Family Vineyards, Troon Vineyard, and Wooldridge Creek Winery. If you overshoot the northernmost Kubli Road turn, you'll have another chance to turn left at the loop's southern end. The wineries will simply appear in reverse order, and you'll be looking for Slagle Creek Road, leading to Wooldrige Creek Winery first.

Schmidt Family Vineyards is at 330 Kubli Road. Visit www.sfvineyards.com or phone (541) 846-1125. If, at first, the tasting room appears to be a roundhouse, that's what it was. The former owner was a backyard railroad fan, with live steam locomotives to tend. Look closer and you'll see what owners Cal and Judy Schmidt have accomplished here. He is a master cabinetmaker and his touch is everywhere, from joinery work to wood inlays in the tile floor. Judy's plantings have created wonderful surroundings in which to stroll or picnic. From their joy of growing—Cal grew up on a farm and Judy is a master gardener—plus their love of wine, you might say this vineyard was inevitable. The Schmidts' first vintage year was 2004, but the lineage of their wines seems much longer than that. Schmidt Family Chardonnay is bright and light on its feet, with a subtle blend of fruit and spice. Oak is present but in character with the mineralization that marks Pacific Northwest wines and adds crispness. The Merlot is an abundant wine and expansive as a medium-bodied red should be. Fruit flavors are concentrated but not overly intense, playing well across the palate with excellent balance and structure. This wine will pair with almost any grilled or broiled meats, yet not intimidate light sauces. Schmidt Cabernet Sauvignon is a big red in the grand manner, which means it is paradoxical: well structured, yet not too aggressive. The result is a wine with firm but not overbearing tannins, with a fullness that can serve equally well with red-sauced dinners or elegant fireside conversation. Which brings us to the Schmidt Syrah. This is an exhilarating wine right from the start, able to open quickly and still not disappoint. Fruit flavors are rich and forward, with a fullness and balance that lead to a decadent, lingering finish. All these wines signal marvelous vintages to come from this very special family estate.

Troon Vineyard is only a bit farther south at 1475 Kubli Road. Visit www.troonvineyard.com or phone (541) 846-9900. One of the first vineyards established in the Applegate Valley, Troon Vineyard produces more than twenty-five wines and does so with sustainable practices that are Salmon-Safe and include Blue Sky renewable energy sources. It's a unique winery to visit, with contemporary touches mixed in with the old—and a grin or two. A blend of Merlot, Syrah, Zinfandel, and Cabernet Sauvignon is called Druid's Fluid and, for a red-wine fancier, can be like a bottled cafeteria. Troon Vineyard Limited Reserve is a fine blend of Cabernet Franc and Cabernet Sauvignon, with the latter playing a supporting role. The award-winning Reserve Cabernet Sauvignon is a traditional, though minimalist, wine, with enough brawn to satisfy big-red lovers, and the balance needed to fill the palate and finish well. Troon Vineyard Zinfandel Reserve is also an award-winner. Full-bodied, it takes a moment for aroma and flavor to open fully, but the reward is ample. This superb wine, with a subtlety rare in Zinfandels, delivers full-mouth flavor right through to its extraordinary finish—an excellent choice for firelight and conversation.

Wooldridge Creek Winery is a few minutes east at 818 Slagle Creek Road. Visit www.wcwinery.com or phone (541) 846-6364. Wooldridge Creek wines are very popular and typically sell out before release. Still, the winery offers a friendly tasting room and requests that guests phone ahead for an appointment.

"We thought about closing our tasting room," says Kara Olmo. "But we really do like to talk with other wine lovers, and share the handcrafted small-lot wines we make here, so we remain open for tasting."

Which is a good thing for wine lovers; Wooldridge Creek wines are superb.

Continue south along Applegate Road, beyond the junction with Highway 238, to **Valley View Winery** at 1000 Upper Applegate Road on the right, in the town of Ruch. Visit www .valleyviewwinery.com or phone (541) 899-8468. Valley View was a pioneer in this area back in the 1850s and the present owners are proud of their contributions to surrounding communities. The tasting room is easygoing, and the range of wines offered by this family-owned winery is exceptional—all at attractive prices. Several are outstanding and worth special mention. Pacific Northwest growing conditions favor Viognier and Valley View offers a lovely introduction to this singular white wine; their Anna Maria Viognier is excellent. Light in color and subtle in aroma, this wine covers the full palate with well-structured fruit and a marvelous finish. Valley View Cabernet Sauvignon is a hearty, rich wine that opens quickly for a big red. Yet the Anna Maria Cabernet Sauvignon is all that and more, with greater depth and complexity of aroma and flavors, plus concentration and well-controlled tannins that speak to its capacity to age well. For lovers of a deep, spicy Syrah, the Anna Maria Syrah is excellent. Color and aromas are deep and rich, leading to full-mouth textures and a languorous finish. A fine Tempranillo is also offered under the Anna Maria label. This dark, sultry Spanish wine is catching on in California and one sip of Valley View's rendition can result in instant affection. Aromas are as rich and complex as the wine, which has the bright quality of a big red and will need a bit of time to open properly, but the reward is ample. Look for this wine to cellar well and bring pleasure for years to come.

From Ruch, continue on Highway 238 into Jacksonville. The village itself is a wonder, one of many small boomtowns from the 1850s when mining, timber, and commercial fishing led the economy. When natural resources were played out, or in a state of desperate preservation, these little towns did not decay so much as slow to a crawl. Ashland has a similar history, as does Aurora and Hood River. We'll visit them all—and the nearby vineyards that now bring wine-and-cuisine tourism to each area.

In Jacksonville, the top-rated **McCully House Inn** at 240 E. California Street is a wonderful place to dine and spend the night. Visit www.mccullyhouse.com or phone (541) 899-1942. Accommodations are luxurious, with splendid antiques, and a relaxed air that makes it at once a bed-and-breakfast, plus a full-service inn. And if you've ever admired a sitting room with walls of books and a library ladder to reach the top shelves, there's a room here just for you. Dining is superb, with a catch of the day straight from the Rogue River, Cajun chicken fettucini, and plenty for vegetarians, including wild mushroom and tomato pesto lasagna or layered grilled eggplant and mozzarella. All this and timeless streets to walk make McCully House Inn a special treat.

ASHLAND AREA

Iris Inn → The Winchester Inn, Restaurant & Wine Bar
→ Peerless Restaurant → Weisinger's of Ashland

The **Iris Inn** at 59 Manzanita Street is celebrating twenty-five years or more in Ashland, and continues to be a destination for new travelers and former guests. Visit www.irisinnbb.com or phone (541) 488-2286. Vicki and Greg Capp have made this 1905 Victorian into such a special place that guests return simply to celebrate their first stay here. Of course, there's the Oregon Shakespeare Festival and grand places to browse or visit in town. Vicki knows them all. Yet it's being here on this quiet, shaded street, joining other guests for a superb breakfast, witty conversation, and shared memories that make the Iris Inn such a standout.

Downtown Ashland reminds travelers of both Napa and Port Townsend, with trendy shops, no one in much of a hurry, and terrific restaurants. One of the most honored is **The Winchester Inn, Restaurant & Wine Bar** at 35 S. Second Street. Spend the night, make reservations for dinner, or drop in for a winetasting in the bistro-style wine bar. Appetizers and small plates in the wine bar carry a master's touch, from mini beef Wellingtons and wonton chicken swimming in apricot vanilla sauce, to lovely soups and cheeses, all tuned to flights of excellent wine. The service is impeccable. Visit www.winchesterinn.com or phone (541) 488-1113.

Among a line of volcanic cones, Baileyana-tangent Vineyards welcomes cooling sea mists.
COURTESY OF BAILEYANA WINERY

Built by farmers in 1909, this schoolhouse is now the Baileyana-tangent Tasting Room.
COURTESY OF BAILEYANA WINERY. PHOTOGRAPH BY MARYA FIGUEROA

Bargetto Winery's lovely Regan Vineyard in the Corallitos region of the Santa Cruz Mountains.

The good life: luscious wines, delectable foods, friendly conversation.

In California's Glen Ellen area, Matanzas Creek Winery's tree-house quality speaks volumes about life in the Bennett Valley. Courtesy of Matanzas Creek Winery. PHOTOGRAPH BY JARED MEININGER

Historic Sand Rock Farm B&B south of Santa Cruz, where twilight is cause for celebration. COURTESY OF SAND ROCK FARM

What better than a balcony room at Villa Toscana in Paso Robles, with vineyards greeting the morning? COURTESY OF VILLA TOSCANA. PHOTOGRAPH BY INSIGHT ARCHITECTURAL PHOTOGRAPHY

Buena Vista Cellar's Ramal Vineyard reminds us that winegrowing remains farming of a special nature. COURTESY OF BUENA VISTA CARNEROS

LEFT: *California's first commercial winery, Buena Vista Cellars' hand-cut stone structure was built in 1857.* COURTESY OF BUENA VISTA CARNEROS

ABOVE: *Oregon's Dundee Bistro features wine, local fish, fresh foraged foods, and a smile from chef Jason Smith. Courtesy of Ponzi Vineyards.* PHOTOGRAPH BY STEVE PACKER

La Playa Hotel in Carmel, where murmurs of the Golden Age float in on breezes from the Pacific. COURTESY OF LA PLAYA HOTEL

Jordan Vineyard and Winery: sheer elegance on the eastern side of Healdsburg, California. Courtesy of Jordan Vineyard & Winery. Photograph by Caitlyn McCaffrey

The Ponzi family's Aurora Vineyard on Oregon's Chehalem Mountain slopes just after harvest. Courtesy of Ponzi Vineyards. Photograph by John McAnulty

Year-round skiing, fine wines, and superb dining at Oregon's Timberline Lodge.

Stone, wood, and furnishings all joined by hand during the Depression to create Timberline Lodge.

Barrel cave of Terra Blanca Winery and Estate Vineyard near Benton City, Washington. COURTESY OF
TERRA BLANCA CAVES. PHOTOGRAPH BY REBECCA WOEHLER-MOSS

The stunning Cave B Inn and Estate Winery at Sagecliffe, near Quincy, Washington.
COURTESY OF CAVE B AT SAGECLIFFE. PHOTOGRAPH BY BASIL CHILDERS

Peerless Restaurant at 265 Fourth Street is another top-tier restaurant and a definite don't-miss-it in Ashland. In addition to choreographed service, owner Crissy Barnett has created an extraordinary restaurant-wine bar. A fine, yet unobtrusive music system is part of the ambiance, perfectly complementing dining and conversation. And the four-course menu items are a marvel, with plenty of choices for meat lovers and vegetarians alike: bison tostadito with avocado cream, Manchego, and jalapeño; Hawaiian blue marlin; chanterelle mushroom and sweet corn risotto; and Yukon gold potato lasagna—plus lavender ice cream. Visit www.peerlessrestaurant.com or phone (541) 488-6067. Did I mention that the Peerless is also one of the foremost people-watching places in Southern Oregon?

Whether you're headed north or south from Ashland, plan to drive over to **Weisinger's of Ashland,** a charming family-owned winery and winery at 3150 Siskiyou Boulevard, two minutes off Highway 99 and I-5, just 4 miles south of town. Visit www.weisingers.com or phone (541) 488-5989. The tasting room is homey and Robert Trottmann is an amiable host who cares deeply for Weisinger artisan wines and the guests he and the staff greet. The tasting room enjoys beautiful views and the winery has accommodations for wine-trail travelers at a vineyard cottage. The first vines were planted in the Weisinger Vineyards more than twenty-eight years ago and the winery remains committed to producing award-winning wines. Offering their guests a quality winery experience is the goal of everyone at Weisinger's.

Eric Weisinger, a second-generation winemaker, is off to New Zealand and Europe to further his winemaking knowledge, and winemaker Chanda Beeghley has stepped in to bring her knowledge to the Weisinger line of premium wines. Fruit flavors in their dry Gewürztraminer are crisp and supported by spices, allowing balance and structure to take the wine to an excellent, recurring finish. Try this wine with a salad of romaine lettuce, sun-dried tomatoes, and gourmet albacore grilled in a spritz of extra-virgin olive oil. Red blends are increasing in response to a need for approachability. Most wine consumers do not cellar wines, but allow them to age on their way from the car to the dinner table. Weisinger's award-winning Petite Pompadour shows the value in that—plus the structure for moderate aging—with a lovely blend of Cabernet Franc, Merlot, Cabernet Sauvignon, and a touch of Malbec that produce a balanced, well-structured wine. Full fruit flavors are present, and increase as the wine opens, yet there is an unflustered quality in this wine that will stimulate conversation while standing up to sauces from Italian red to fishing-boat Asian.

GRANTS PASS AREA

Weasku Inn Historic Lodge → The Lodge at Riverside
→ Riverside Inn → AJA Restaurant

If a wilderness river setting tugs at you, **Weasku Inn Historic Lodge** at 5560 Rogue River Highway is a one-of-a-kind place to stay. Visit www.weasku.com or phone (541) 471-8000. First, it may help to know that the name was once printed as *We-ask-u Inn*. Nothing Native American about it, just down-home marketing. And there's been plenty here to draw travelers since the 1920s. The entire place has been renovated with care, to preserve the feeling—and the fishing—that brought Clark Gable here.

When Gable Was King

During Hollywood's golden era, through the early 1930s and '40s, no star captured more attention than Clark Gable. He was a ladies' man, no doubt, yet had that masculine gruffness that men admired as well. And the entire West Coast was his playground. He stormed all through Oregon and parts of Washington as a bit player in local theater companies, and sometimes as a deckhand. He was an avid fisherman and hunter and became a regular at Weasku Inn, often with one or another companion, until he met and married Carole Lombard. After her death in a tragic Arizona plane crash, he came here to grieve.

Gable was practically part of the family, and his memory still is. The main lodge will carry you back to those times, while the newer cabins and suites preserve the riverfront mystique.

On the river's opposite side, closer to restaurants and attractions, **The Lodge at Riverside** at 955 SE Seventh Street in Grants Pass is a good choice. Visit www.thelodgeatriverside.com or phone (541) 955-0600. Just across the way, the **Riverside Inn** at 971 SE Sixth Street is a landmark and a step up in luxury. Visit www.riversideinn.com or phone (541) 476-6873. Both properties are on the Rogue River and feature pools, full amenities, and recent upgrades.

Like many towns along old U.S. 99 and now I-5, Grants Pass was once known largely as a fuel stop. No longer, if only because **AJA Restaurant** at 118 Northwest E Street has taken up residence here. The restaurant business is risky, but locals and travelers alike are delighted that owners Tim Mock and Sandy Shizury have opened here. The place is a gem, and even if you've dined there before, it feels like a new, personal discovery. Pronounced as *Asia*, the name comes from the Steely Dan album of the same name. The restaurant is a small place, yet has no crowded feeling, in part because the host moves from table to table so swiftly, and always with a pleasant word or story, the surroundings simply recede. And the food is grand—far better than what often passes for Pacific Rim cuisine. Chicken with Asian barbecue sauce, wrapped in rice paper, will have you dreaming of Hong Kong, the marvelous Indonesian corn fritters will carry you to far-off temples, while smoked salmon blintzes in herbed goat cheese will bring you right back to the Northwest. It's not just wonderful food; it's a travelogue. Seating is limited, so phone (541) 471-1228 for reservations.

EUGENE AREA

Excelsior Inn and Restaurant → Campbell House Inn → King Estate Winery → Silvan Ridge-Hinman Vineyards → Sweet Cheeks Winery → Benton-Lane Winery → Van Duzer Vineyards

Home to the University of Oregon, Eugene is a small yet cosmopolitan city that leads to the Lorane and Willamette Valleys. It also hosts **Excelsior Inn and Restaurant** at 754 E. Thirteenth Avenue. Visit www.excelsiorinn.com or phone (541) 342-6963. Because space is tight around the university, double-parking is permitted in front of the inn to allow for check-in. Step through the lovely patio and look for the inkeeper's office on the left side of the path a bit farther along. Parking for overnight guests is provided in back.

It is not difficult to imagine the original 1912 property as it

was built for Kappa Kappa Gamma and occupied by the soror-
ity until sold to a fraternity in the mid-1930s. Each room must
have entertained secrets—whispered or wished—by the young
women who attended the university at a time when most were
expected to stay home. With the onset of World War II, college men left for the service and fraternities were closed
down.

After the war, the structure became a rooming house and of-
fices, including a radio station. But its architecture was still eye-
catching and after a brief life as a café, chef Maurizio Paparo
bought the place and undertook a full redevelopment into guest
suites, a full dining room, and the bar. Excelsior Inn and Restaurant now offers fourteen rooms, each themed for a classical composer. The Chopin Room overlooks the front courtyard and offers
a fine view of the passing parade. Nearly all who walk by look up
involuntarily at Excelsior's single arched eyebrow. Some guess at
the building's history.

"Dad, what's that place?" a young boy asks, pointing above
the courtyard.

The boy's father, wearing U of O colors, pauses for a
moment.

"It was a movie studio, son, back in the silent days."

Of course, it wasn't, but such is its mystique that the place
inspires curious suppositions. And the fascination doesn't end
out in front. In addition to the full breakfast included with each
room, the restaurant offers surroundings and dishes that are
pure delight.

Menus change frequently, depending on what is in season, and
organic hormone-free products are paramount. Fresh fish specials
are offered daily. And when available, range-fed Kobe beef from
the Snake River Valley is featured, along with house-made pastas.

Try the three-cheese Tortellini Valentino in a vodka-rose cream sauce, served with grilled breast of chicken. And if you are a vegetarian, you'll find several entrées on both luncheon and dinner menus that are small wonders in themselves. Keep a close eye on the dessert display, too. Diners often browse the selection before deciding on their entrée.

The Excelsior offers an excellent wine list with fine Oregon and Italian wines. But if space is not available at the Excelsior, consider the **Campbell House Inn** at 252 Pearl Street in Eugene. Visit www.campbellhouse.com or phone (541) 343-1119. The inn is well furnished, its staff most hospitable, and the grounds are lovely. Campbell House Inn provides a full breakfast for guests. Other dining is on a prix fixe basis.

Now let's head for the hills. **King Estate Winery** at 80854 Territorial Road is a southern introduction to the Willamette Valley. Visit www.kingestate.com or phone (541) 942-9874. Regardless of your route west from I-5 or Eugene, your first glimpse of King Estate, set atop a hill with vineyard rows cascading in every direction, can be startling. And as you continue through the gates and up the entry road, the image becomes more remarkable. Hilltop views in every direction are themselves worth the visit, and everywhere is evidence of the estate's continued development and dedication to its mission of producing excellent wines.

The 1,033-acre estate is fully certified as an organic operation dedicated to sustainable practices. In a market where U.S. sales of organic food products topped $13.8 billion in 2005, King Estate is a leader in its commitment to organic enterprise—surprising in a vineyard of this size—with a goal of producing more than 170,000 cases of premium wine annually.

Founded in 1992 by Ed King, Jr., and son Ed King III, the

winery benefits from the imaginative foresight of both men. Ed King, Jr., brought King Radio from a small company to a world leader in avionics. The King name even graces the side of Dick Rutan's global *Voyager,* now on display at the Smithsonian Air and Space Museum. Ed King III has a law degree and an M.B.A., plus a wide range of business experience. Yet wine-making was drawing them closer to this time and this place. Young Ed recalls that he had two small vineyards and an expanding interest in the wine industry. On a day when he was out looking for hay for his horses, he saw the glorious hills that now make up King Estate from the top. He called his father soon after.

"Dad, do you remember when we talked about building a winery of our own?"

"Yes, I do."

"Well," young Ed said, with no further preamble, "I've found the place."

By 2005, King Estate Pinot Noir was garnering both medals and awards. The Domaine Collection, a new line at King Estate from the finest estate blocks, features outstanding Pinot Noir, Pinot Gris, and Vin Glacé. These wines are grand now and hold great promise for aging. King Estate's Pinot Noir is bright, and well-balanced, with full fruit and a long finish. Their Pinot Gris is excellent, with a light spiciness and complex aroma. Both these wines are food-friendly. The Pinot Noir will stand up to game, and the Pinot Gris will work well with a variety of shell-fish. King Estate's Vin Glacé is especially interesting. Ice wines are difficult to produce and this one holds rich, intense flavors that work well with fresh fruit and tarts. Try this ice wine with a lemon-peach sorbet to savor the wine's body and excellent finish.

King Estate's tasting room offers wine in several flights. The opening flight is complimentary. Others are accompanied by fees that vary up to about the ten-dollar mark.

Food pairings are also available, from roasted garlic gnocchi with white truffle oil to asparagus crêpes, along with artisan cheese plates and estate-baked bread. These menu items change with the season, but you may often find Northwest Chinook Salmon Served Three Ways. It is a King Estate signature dish.

King Estate is celebrating its fifteenth anniversary this year and you'll no doubt find, as I did, that with its magnificent architecture, grounds, and presence, it is a place difficult to leave.

Oregon Giant

North of the Applegate, Umpqua, and Lorane Valleys lies Oregon's giant. The Willamette Valley is perhaps 120 miles long and comprises some 12,000 square miles, of which more than 5,000 square miles are now planted in wine grapes. And even with that much viticulture already in place, it is said that another 23,000 acres are suitable for winegrowing. By any standard, that's a lot of future.

Farther north on Territorial Road, follow blue directional signs onto Briggs Hill Road for **Silvan Ridge-Hinman Vineyards** at 27012 Briggs Hill Road, just south of the village of Crow. Visit www.silvanridge.com or phone (541) 345-1945. Established in 1979, Hinman Vineyards in the Rogue River area near Ashland was soon producing Oregon's top-selling wine.

With such public acceptance, the winery introduced a line of reserve wines under the Silvan Ridge label and has expanded its attraction to couples and families in the exurbs of

Eugene. The tasting and event rooms have recently been re-modeled, yet none of the European style has been lost. Bringing your own picnic is still encouraged, and the banquet room remains an inspiring blend of medieval and down-home styles. General manager Liz Chambers recognizes the balance necessary between offering premium wines and maintaining approachability and she is eager to be true to the vision of Silvan Ridge.

"I'm not interested in seeing who can make the wine with the biggest muscles," she says. "I want to drink wines that have table manners."

Parent winery Hinman has a strong history in producing wines that are not merely approachable but downright friendly. Try their Rogue Valley Red Wine with almost anything. No kidding. I poured the wine at a Memorial Day barbecue where it was paired with whatever anyone happened to be grilling: salmon, steak, chicken, or veggie burgers. And it worked with every one. This red presents as something between a Merlot and a subtle Cabernet Sauvignon. It opens quickly on being uncorked and is both good-natured and rewarding. It's an accommodating wine, though recent vintages may benefit from additional time in the bottle.

In addition to Cabernet, Merlot, Riesling, Chardonnay, and Syrah, Silvan Ridge produces outstanding Pinot Gris and Merlot varietals and an Early Muscat. The Pinot Gris is bright and lively, with good midpalate presence, and a crisp finish. Silvan Ridge's Merlot ages well and brings a full, rich body, with a satisfying finish. All have been awarded their share of medals. The Early Muscat is a surprise, with its somewhat sweet Asti-like flavors and a semisparkling nature. Try it at brunch with crêpes and a variety of light fruit.

If you agree with the *New York Times* columnist Frank Prial, that more humor is needed in today's wine business, head right across the way to **Sweet Cheeks Winery** at 26961 Briggs Hill Road in Eugene. Visit www.sweetcheekswinery.com or phone (541) 349-9463.

But before we get to the name—which makes most folks chuckle and a few wine stewards blush—spend some time in the tasting room. Actually, it's more of a tasting area, for the room leads out onto a patio with a sparkling view.

The winery's Chardonnay is bright with a touch of oak, and the Pinot Gris offers an interesting contrast with a balanced fullness. A very nice Pinot Noir is also represented, but the Riesling is both fine and surprising in its aromas and approachability. Serve it alone or with light salads and pastas.

Which brings us to the winery's name. When the vines were first going in, owner Dan Smith still had no clear idea of what to name this winery in which he had such faith. Standing out by the road one day, he noticed the curved shapes of the twin hillsides. It seemed obvious what they looked like, so Sweet Cheeks it would be. Check out the label for yourself . . .

Return to Territorial Highway and turn north for Benton-Lane. After crossing Highway 36, continue on north. Just 1.5 miles short of the town of Monroe, keep watch along the west side of the highway for **Benton-Lane Winery** located at 23924 Territorial Highway, just south of Monroe. Visit www.benton-lane.com or phone (541) 847-5792. The owners, Steve and Carol Girard, are California expatriates who became convinced that the grail of a great Pinot Noir was not to be found in the south. And they wanted to push ahead on production frontiers as well. The result is an extraordinary vineyard, certified sustainable by L.I.V.E., and a facility that calls little attention to itself, yet is sophisticated in its processing methods—from pulse air to screwcap closures. That's a lot for a family-owned winery to undertake. I asked Steve what first drew him to viticulture and prompted the move to Oregon.

"My dad traveled the world for Jeep and he'd bring home French wines. Even at age seven, I was fascinated with every aspect of wine. Some years later, that led me to Bad Idea Number One. My father was retiring, so we talked about buying a winery. I found a run-down place in Napa Valley and we set up shop. Of course, I was still holding down a corporate job in San Diego, so I was only home on weekends, and a lot of that time went into the winery. After a while, we were producing some good wines. But not the Pinot Noir my wife and I enjoyed. Not the killer Pinot Noir I wanted."

Steve laughs. I can practically hear him keeping score in his head.

"All that led to Bad Idea Number Two. We decided to buy Oregon fruit and haul it down to the winery in Napa. At first, I was doing it with a pickup truck. That didn't work. We were beating up the fruit and the wine was terrible. So we went all out one year and contracted for ten tons of Oregon Pinot Noir grapes. Which was manageable. We rented a huge truck, loaded it with empty poly tanks, and drove north. The plan was to do the crush and drive the juice home that night, so it wouldn't heat up. Except the facility trotted out a crusher about the size of a Fisher-Price toy. What should have taken an hour or so, kept us at it until three in the morning . . . and we had four extra tons to process, so the tanks were full with no expansion room. We started driving. By midday, the valleys were at the hundred-degree mark. The tanks were overflowing. We had this red guck streaming down out of the truck. Cars behind us were all red and drivers had turned on their windshield wipers."

By now, I'm thinking that this story can't get any better, but it does.

"So that was our condition when we pulled into the California Agricultural Inspection Station. We could hear the juice dripping on the ground all around the truck. We were sure we'd be busted, when a lovely young agent looked up at the cab and asked if we had any fruit with us. I just said, 'Umm, no, we don't,' and she waved us on through. That memory is part of what sustained me while we spent five years looking for exactly the right place, which turned out to be an old sheep ranch where we are now. The bank had foreclosed on the place. They didn't want it and I did. We're almost fully planted in a vineyard focused on Pinot Noir. We're sustainable, we're certified Salmon-Safe, and we're making interesting wines."

Steve's story ends as it should, with Benton-Lane's wines as the test. Of special note in the vineyard's pleasant tasting room is a red duo. Benton-Lane's Estate Pinot Noir presents a nuanced blend, with a well-knit texture, and a long, long finish. If a wine can be subtle and robust at the same time, this is it. Yet their First Class Pinot Noir is deeper and more intense, with a light oaky overtone to complement the spices, and a luscious, jammy finish. Pinot Noir can often be fruity but still thin. Benton-Lane's First Class Pinot Noir is creamy with great depth. Two whites are also exceptional. The Pinot Gris is well-balanced, with a long, clean finish that is light and vibrant with fruit. The Pinot Blanc is surprising in its excellence: bright yet quite warm, with complex citrus flavors and a decadent finish. Moderate pricing, especially for award-winners gaining ever more recognition. At home, as you're about to open one of the wines, notice the fine design work in the label—the etched look of a bottle-sized postage stamp, with a wavy postmark pointing your way right up to the screwcap. Good. Very, very good.

All these wines will pair well with a wide range of food, yet they are also front-porch wines, meant to accompany conversation and the sound of a breeze across the vine-covered slopes.

From Benton-Lane, continue north toward Monroe. It will be much easier to navigate wine-country roads with the guide from Willamette Valley Wineries Association. Visit www .willamettewines.com or phone (503) 646-2985. Most wineries and inns north of Corvallis will have copies on hand. If requesting the guide through the association, be sure to allow time for delivery through the mails before your departure. A phone call can be speedier than the online form.

As Territorial Highway merges with Highway 99W, traffic can become an issue—and this is where having the Willamette Valley map will pay off. An alternative to 99W is to turn west on Greenberry Road, 10 miles north of Monroe. Continue west and turn north on Bellfountain Road, west again onto Chapel Drive, then north on Thirteenth Street into Philomath and the intersection with U.S. 20. These are peaceful roads and well worth a bit of extra time. And if you are drawn to covered bridges and the early railroading era, you'll find a special treat along U.S. 20 west of Philomath at the now-lapsed town of Chitwood (near mile marker 17). Before this area was timbered out, Chitwood was a water-and-fuel stop for steam locomotives in the 1900s. The rails are still in use, as is the wonderful Chitwood Bridge. Renovated and rededicated in 1986, it is a local treasure.

Continue west on U.S. 20 and turn northeast on Highway 223 through the small town of Dallas to Highway 22. Turn west once again and be prepared for **Van Duzer Vineyards** on the north side at 11975 Smithfield Road in Dallas. Visit www .vanduzer.com or phone (503) 623-6420. The winery is remarkable for its location in a coastal corridor favored by winds that produce temperature variations favoring a long hang time and the resulting intensity in flavor for which their Pinot Noir is known. Van Duzer's Pinot Gris is also receiving excellent reviews. Reserves, when available, are outstanding. And if you enjoy the romantic intricacy of Art Nouveau and know Mucha's intricate nineteenth-century artwork on French champagne labels, you'll be taken with this winery's style. Moderate pricing and several new offerings.

McMINNVILLE AREA

Youngberg Hill Vineyards and Inn → Maysara Winery-Momtazi Vineyards → Evergreen Aviation Museum and Vineyards → The Eyrie Vineyards → R. Stuart & Co. → Panther Creek Winery → Nick's Italian Café → La Rambla Restaurant & Bar → Bistro Maison

Continue west on Highway 22 to the interchange and head north on Highway 18 for Youngberg Hill Vineyards & Inn, a wonderful base for the entire McMinnville area, with Maysara Winery close by. After passing the two entrances to Old Sheridan Road, prepare for a left turn on Masonville Road and continue for 2 miles, following the blue winery signs. Turn north again onto Youngberg Hill Road and continue uphill to the inn. I found this winding, intimate drive drawing me into the surrounding landscape. But the sight of the inn, just over the last rise, tops everything.

Youngberg Hill Vineyards and Inn is on a hilltop more than 700 feet above the valley floor at 10660 SW Youngberg Hill Road, just minutes southwest of McMinnville. Visit www .youngberghill.com or phone (503) 472-2727. In the foyer, you'll be taken by the inn's attention to detail and the warm welcome of Wayne and Nicolette Bailey. For Youngberg Hill Inn is more than a top bed-and-breakfast, it is a prime attraction of the Pacific Northwest. Four guest rooms and three suites are featured, all with private baths, plus central heating and air-conditioning. The first-floor library is cozy and inviting, along with a lounge and spacious dining room—all looking out onto the wraparound veranda and the valley view beyond. Indeed, it takes some time for the length and breadth of this place to unfold along with a panoramic view of the Willamette Valley, stretching out for miles to the south and west to the coastal mountains, with Mount Hood and Mount Jefferson to the east. And it gets better. For just below, viewed best from the inn's veranda or the path that winds around the hilltop, is a vineyard of twelve acres.

Closer in, the inn's gardens and waterfalls tug at the romantic in us all, with a lovely arbor for weddings—or whatever commemoration might be imagined. The blocks of vines, each planted with clear purpose as well as loving care, merely add to the sense of place here. Yet the wines are no afterthought. These are award-winners, with an expressive die-cut label design to highlight their qualities. A selection of wine is available in the salon on the honor system: a thoughtful touch to ease guests through a transition from everyday rush-minutes into a time of relaxation and enchantment. The Baileys, originally in

Chicago sales and marketing jobs, knew they wanted a change, but to what?

"Preparation meets opportunity is the best way to describe finding Youngberg Hill," Nicolette says. "I don't believe in luck. In 2003, I came out here to find investment property and ended up taking an unexpected turn in the road. And what a beautiful road it has been."

Nicolette is also very clear about the mantle of stewardship. "Youngberg Hill is too amazing for someone just to own it. It's our responsibility to take care of it and protect this beautiful location in Yamhill Valley. . . . We're fortunate to be able to share it with those who visit—to feel the wonderful energy of this place, which in a quiet moment can take your breath away."

Later, as we tasted two vintages of their Estate Pinot Noir, Wayne agrees. "Almost all of us came from somewhere else."

Youngberg Hill's vineyard is further blessed with Van Duzer weather patterns that produce more precipitation and sun, with cooler temperatures, giving more intensity to the fruit. And the wine itself?

Nicolette describes a vintage Estate Pinot Noir as being "like a whisper on the wind . . . well-balanced and as much a pleasure to drink now as it will be in ten years."

Youngberg Hill's Pinot Noirs are expansive, with rich flavors and a long, subtle finish. Yet their Pinot Blanc, from the fruit of a neighboring vineyard in the coastal foothills is remarkable as well—gentle handling lets the fullness and complexity of the wine show through, with more body, and a svelte finish uncommon in a white wine.

For all their qualities, both the inn and Youngberg Hill's wines are moderately priced—a sum of experiences not to be missed.

Maysara Winery-Momtazi Vineyards is at 15765 SW

Muddy Valley Road, also southwest of McMinnville. Visit
www.maysara.com or phone (503) 843-1234. From Youngberg
Hill, turn west on Masonville Road, and south on Muddy Valley Road and into the winery. Maysara is more than a quiet
place, with a long, winding drive alongside a pond and through
shady oaks, you'll also find a curious sense of peace here. Their
tasting bar is set up in the barrel room, which maintains a feeling of intimacy with the wine. And you might want to bring a
jacket.

The winery was established in the late '90s by Moe and Flora
Momtazi, who surveyed an old wheat farm and envisioned vines
on its barren slopes. From the first block planted with Pinot
Noir, Maysara revealed a family history of devotion to the
land—using low-impact Biodynamic practices.

Sour Grapes

The folklore of winemaking is one of its most endearing qualities. In
Persian legend, a princess who was given to fits of depression fell
out of favor with her king. In despair, she tried to poison herself
with the liquid from a long-forgotten jar in which grapes had
spoiled. Well, you can imagine how that turned out. Her mood
lifted, so she drank a bit more. Even better. Upon learning of this
sour-grapes miracle, the king not only restored the princess to his
favor, he shared her discovery with his court and by extension, with
all of us. Moe Momtazi is a messenger.

The Persian king was Jamsheed and one of the Pinot Noirs
in an extensive line from Maysara bears his name. Their Pinot
Gris is fruity but crisp, with a velvety finish, which would pair
well with Asian spices and lighter Indian foods. A quartet of

Pinot Noirs are outstanding. All are leggy and smooth, with re-fined tannins, and are gaining recognition in the wine press. I asked winemaker Todd Hamina about the lineup.

"Our Jamsheed is always ready to go, so I look for barrels with ripe fruit and an open texture. It's designed to be con-sumed in the first few year of its life. So, it's restaurant-friendly with firm, balanced tannins. Our Estate Cuvée needs time to come around, though. The next blends won't be on the market for a couple of years. More red fruit and firm tannins."

"I liked the Delara. It has an uncommon richness."

"Yes. Lots of power and presence with promise for aging. This is not a shy wine, but it has accessibility now. It will soften some with age."

Maysara's reds are dark but not moody. All are well-balanced and rounded in their finish. Each can pair well with a number of white or red meats and pastas. Moe Momtazi would be pleased with the idea that his wines are both robust and peaceful. Mid-priced to upper mid-priced, and for collectors, a bargain.

Departing Maysara, it's easier to continue south on Muddy Valley Road until a hard left bend leads directly to Highway 18. Turn north toward McMinnville. The town has several excellent restaurants and interesting urban wineries. But just before traf-fic bound for McMinnville continues on 99W, consider bend-ing east to follow the Highway 18 Bypass, which becomes NE Three Mile Lane. On the north side, opposite the airport, you'll find an extraordinary attraction: **Evergreen Aviation Mu-seum and Vineyards,** off Cumulus Avenue at 3685 NE Three Mile Lane in McMinnville. Visit www.sprucegoose.org or phone (503) 434-4180. Well, I suppose the Web address gives away the last of any surprise.

If not, the 121,000 square-foot museum building that houses Howard Hughes's flying boat makes the announcement. Hughes disliked the plane's nickname; it is largely constructed of laminated birch. Regardless, this museum is a major item on any tour of the Pacific Northwest—and in true Oregon fashion, you'll find that Evergreen has its own vineyards, planted right alongside the entry drive.

If the giant Hughes HK-1/H-4 is the main attraction by size—wingspan greater than a football field, with a tail eight stories high—the rest of the exhibit shows attention to history and detail equaled by few collections in the world, and surpassed by none. Even a mach 3.5 (at least) SR-71 Blackbird is on hand. Civilian entries include a rare executive version of the Curtiss A-22. Don't recognize that one? I didn't either. She's a beauty, though, turned out in polished aluminum and looking eager to go.

Yet for all the aircraft displayed, there is no sense of crowding or loss of perspective. Interactive stations, plus flight simulators are also available as part of the educational program for youngsters. Nicole Wahlberg of the Evergreen Aviation Museum sums it up.

"From Evergreen's acquisitions and restoration staffs, through our flight-experienced docents on the floor, we've all worked hard to create a space that will nurture both the dream and reality of flight."

An inconspicuous tasting bar is located just inside the museum's main entrance, where you'll find several wines to sample under the commemorative Spruce Goose label. The Pinot Noir is not too muscular or bright, yet carries a full cargo of fruit flavors. The Pinot Gris is quite good, with a light presence and a well-rendered finish. Of special note, for those about to fly or drive, is a semisparkling nonalcoholic Pinot Noir grape juice.

Most visitors wish they could have spent an hour longer at the museum, and a few might have wanted to spend an hour less. But every kid—which would include lapsed pilots—might wish to stay forever. It's that kind of place.

Three outstanding wineries have tasting rooms in McMinnville. The first of these is **The Eyrie Vineyards** at 935 NE Tenth Street. Visit www.eyrievineyards.com or phone (503) 472-6315. Over forty years ago, owner-winemaker David Lett and wife Diana were first to recognize the Willamette Valley as a perfect place for the delicate Pinot Noir grape, and the first producer of Pinot Gris in the United States. Now a second-generation operation as well, a visit to this tasting room is like finding history in your glass. **R. Stuart & Co.** is only a few blocks away at 845 NE Fifth Street. Visit www.rstuartandco .com or phone (503) 472-6990. Rob Stuart and wife Maria were once the winemaker-marketing duo at Erath Vineyards when Dick Erath decided to slow down a bit to sublight speeds. Now, Rob and Maria are in an adaptive-reuse place that still has a weight-scale out front. **Panther Creek Winery** is just across the street in a former electric power station at 455 NE Irvine Street. Visit www.panthercreekcellars.com or phone (503) 472-8080. Now under new ownership, Panther Creek continues the reputation built here by Ken Wright, who had been winemaker at Domaine Serene before creating Panther Creek. These three wineries enjoy wide recognition as well as loyalty among wine lovers throughout the region.

Return to Third Street and turn west through McMinnville's historic district to find a trio of excellent restaurants within walking distance of one another. We'll start with Nick's, because if you happen to be in town on a Tuesday, nearly everyone else will be closed. Nick takes Mondays off. **Nick's Italian Cafe** is

semivisible at 521 NE Third Street. Visit www.nicksitaliancafe
.com or phone (503) 434-4471. Chef Nick Pierano opened his
unpretentious restaurant in 1977, just after Pinot Noir from this
area began attracting notice. Oregon wine pioneers held congress
here over their latest vintages . . . and their chances in the world
market. Nick's and the wine industry grew up together and both
have been the richer for it. Nick came to the valley ready to put
his own dream on the line. He had cooked with his family and
had some experience with the Santa Fe Railway, plus a degree in
political science. Meals at Nick's are prepared with the style and
flavors found in the north of Italy on a prix fixe basis (ordering à la
carte is okay) and Nick's serves dinners only. The wine list is extensive and prices are attractive, as well. Of course, if you have a
few hundred dollars to spare, you may choose a bottle from David
Lett's 1975 South Block Oregon Pinot, one of the few remaining.
Menu items change daily, but look for the Genovese minestrone
or the lemon-tarragon artichoke among the appetizers. For the
main event, the lamb lasagna is a favorite among regulars. Either
a local Pinot Noir or Sangiovese will excite the rich flavors of this
dish. But whatever you choose, it'll be hard to go wrong.

Evidence that regional wines will draw interesting new food
offerings can be found at **La Rambla Restaurant & Bar** at
238 NE Third Street. Visit www.laramblaonthird.com or phone
(503) 435-2126. But take note: This is not a Mexican-style
restaurant. Instead, La Rambla features Spanish wines and cuisine fashioned to Pacific Northwest tastes. And if you're like
most travelers—we get too little exercise on the road—the
restaurant's tapas, either hot or cold, are a year-round treat and
an easy way for travelers to explore delightful dishes without
overdoing it.

Bistro Maison is at 729 NE Third Street and rates a place on every traveler's A list. Visit www.bistromaison.com or phone (503) 474-1888. Chef Jean-Jacques and wife Deborah have created a French restaurant we've all dreamed about. Just the right atmosphere, with weather-friendly seating inside or on the patio, plus a touch of Provence. Deborah's greeting at the door is welcoming, the waitstaff is courteous and helpful with wine-and-entrée pairings, and the food chef Jean-Jacques prepares . . . *mon dieu*, you must find out for yourself. Vegetarians will find locally grown items in profusion, plus a superb penne pasta with oven-roasted tomatoes and wild mushrooms. A bit of white truffle oil? But of course. And the line-caught salmon with green lentils and mustard sauce makes its own recommendation. Attractively priced, Bistro Maison is but another motive to extend your stay in this area.

Note: *McMinnville does not ignore scofflaws, and visitors are advised by locals to adhere to posted speed limits.*

YAMHILL-CARLTON AREA

Lobenhaus B&B and Vineyard → Trappist Abbey → Adelsheim Vineyard → Penner-Ash Wine Cellars and Dussin Vineyards → Cuneo Cellars → Carlton Winemakers Studio → The Depot → Cuvée Restaurant

For a loop through the Carlton and Yamhill areas, an excellent base for your touring is Lobenhaus. This stylish bed-and-breakfast is central to wineries and restaurants. Depart McMinnville to the north and bend east along Highway 99W. In just a few minutes, the highway becomes W. Third Street in the town of LaFayette. Watch for the Trappist Abbey sign on Bridge Street and turn north. Bridge Street becomes Abbey Road. Continue a little over a mile.

Lobenhaus B & B and Vineyard is on the west side at 6975 NE Abbey Road. Visit www.lobenhaus.com or phone (503) 864-9173. The inn is at a near midpoint for Carlton, Yamhill, and Dundee. You'll recognize it by the lush gardens and landscaping that line the approach to this well-appointed inn. From the road, it appears to be a one-story rambler, but it's really a trilevel lodge on a site that slopes away into a wooded area, a brook, and vineyards beyond.

Owners Joe and Shari Lobenstein have taken great care in designing and constructing this inn. Wide guest decks reach out at tree-level to a mixed-stand forest. A gentle stream flows from pond to pond as an invitation to relax and be present. In an exploring mood and ready to stretch a bit? Follow the path on down from the inn to the troll-bridge crossing the stream. A path leads into the woods, toward the upper vineyard.

It's not hard to imagine the Lobensteins leaving a life in blistering Phoenix for this.

"It was time for us to go. We knew that. We just weren't sure how or to where. But we have family here, and once we found this site, other decisions started making themselves. The Pacific Northwest is where we want to be."

Yet life is a great blend of experience. Throughout the inn, you'll find subtle touches of the Southwest in textures, decorative pieces, and even in the finely radiused corners of each room and doorway, done in the pueblo manner. Coming from the Arizona desert, noted for fickle extremes in weather, prompted other decisions: each room is individually heated and cooled, and the entire structure is sheltered by nature from wind and sun.

The inn also looks practically brand-new. I wanted to know how the owners manage that.

"One thing I learned," Joe says, "is that if there's a problem, it's got to be handled right away. Otherwise, anyone who comes along only adds to it."

My kitchen at home is the better for remembering Joe's advice. Still, what I recall in vivid detail is that my visit was on a Tuesday, when most of the restaurants on the itinerary were closed—and the rest, not surprisingly—were crowded. In short, I hadn't done all my homework. After miles of chasing a restaurant meal, I finally let go and bought a takeout bowl of tomato-basil soup. Restaurants were for another day. I drove back to Lobenhaus, and with some stand-by crackers from the car, I settled in on the deck under a canopy of trees for the quiet. A couple of birds joined me, not pestering for food, just hanging out. It was one of the grandest gourmet meals ever—having dinner with Oregon.

Now this next visit may be a long shot, so check with Shari and Joe to be sure it's something you'll enjoy. It's the **Trappist Abbey,** a bit farther on at 9200 NE Abbey Road. Visit www .trappistabbey.org or phone (503) 852-7174. The thing is, that along with the rest of us, the monastic population is aging and its traditional works are slackening. Some years ago, income from the monks' pew factory began to decline. But where others saw empty prospects, Father Pascal—once a corporate attorney— saw a wine warehouse that could offer storage to local wineries. As is often said: Monks don't think the way other people do. Today, the Trappist Abbey serves about 150 wineries in the area. You'll recognize several: Adelsheim, Domaine Serene, Erath, Penner-Ash, and Sokol Blosser, among others.

Continue north on Abbey Road past the intersection with Hendricks Road. Abbey will become Kuehne Road. At Highway 240 turn east and after the bend, turn north again on Ribbon Ridge Road. At the next intersection, turn east again on North Valley Road and travel 1 mile, to the intersection with Dopp Road. Continue east and, at the first opportunity, turn north on Calkins Lane to **Adelsheim Vineyard** on the right-hand side at 16800 NE Calkins Lane. Visit www.adelsheim.com or phone (503) 838-6013. This is a premier winery, as you'll realize on pulling into the courtyard. Exceptional details everywhere, and it all fits together in a fashion that is at once exotic and understated. Like many others, David Adelsheim's degree (in German literature) was of greater value to the man than the vine. But unlike so many others, David did not immigrate to Oregon. He and Ginny (whose degree is in art) moved to the Chehalem Mountains from Portland after touring Europe, where they fell in love with winegrowing. Still, despite the demands of a full-on winery, David is ever the gentle, patient scholar. When I ask for a little history on the winery, he smiles.

"All right. The story begins about two million years ago—"

"Do you suppose we could begin with something a little more recent?"

David laughs gently. He has me hooked and knows it.

"Much later, then," he says. "About ten thousand years ago . . ."

It's a great line, and instructive at the same time, for David is explaining how the Willamette Valley became what it is, with slopes and soil just waiting for the kinds of wine grapes now grown here. As with many lovely things in the universe, a cataclysm plays a big part in the story. A great ice dam periodically formed a lake of some 500 cubic miles in the Missoula Valley of

Montana all those years ago. Whenever that ice dam buckled under the load, a flood equal to half the volume of Lake Michigan was released. Roaring down the Columbia channel, these floods carried boulders embedded in ice rafts, along with a mass of sediment, which filled the Willamette Valley to depths of 400 feet or more. The boulders were scattered across the valley, while sediment from various releases created deposits that are often found at elevations of above 250 feet—hence the demand for higher slopes.

"We have a souvenir from Montana here on the property," David says. "A rock so big that it stopped our D-9 in its tracks."

Now, it bears mention that while a D-9 isn't the largest bulldozer made by Caterpillar, it does weigh forty-nine tons and packs about 500 horsepower. When a big boy like that gets rolling, its momentum is staggering. Yet the rock that stalled such a machine had been bounced into the Willamette Valley like a giant ping-pong ball, so great was the flood's force.

The resulting terroir and three decades of Adelsheim winemaking pair well. The Willamette Valley Pinot Noir is subtle, not so much fruit-forward as oblique. Complex aromas and body, good length, and a nice finish. Elizabeth's Reserve from Adelsheim begins there and takes Pinot Noir to a different level. This wine's aroma is like a rediscovered friend, recognized but now more sophisticated. Rich and elegant, with deep fruit and layered spices, all rendered with exceptional complexity. It opens quickly, yet should cellar for a decade or more. A side note is that the portrait on the label is of Diana Lett, who along with her husband David Lett, helped lead the effort that resulted in the Oregon wine industry of today.

On the white side, the Pinot Gris is marvelous. The fruit opens further, even as you taste it, and conveys its memory of the barrel, as it should. Very nice balance, with enough acidity to pair well with a wealth of dishes. Whether you are a Chardonnay fan or not, Caitlin's Reserve from Adelsheim is outstanding, with firmness in its structure, just the right note of oak, and a perfect blend of fruit and spice. This is a gorgeous wine for any time, any season.

From Adelsheim Vineyard, return to North Valley Road and turn west. Just beyond Dopp Road, turn south on Ribbon Ridge Road, following winery signs to **Penner-Ash Wine Cellars and Dussin Vineyards** at 15771 NE Ribbon Ridge Road. Visit www.pennerash.com or phone (503) 554-5545. As you reach the winery, it will appear to rise anatomically from its surroundings, joining structure with land. Ron and Lynn Penner-Ash—along with the winery's proprietors Tyanne and Chris Dussin—are committed to handcrafted Pinot Noir. Plus the new kid on their block, Syrah. The depth of their commitment emerges both in reviews of their product and the degree to which their lifestyle fits the land. I found Lynn with her dog, who was fully engaged in excavating a gopher hole.

"Nice day, if you're not a gopher," I said.

"That's what's so good about this life," Lynn says. "During planting and fieldwork and harvest, it's a deep plunge into all-out labor. Then, there are days like this, with the sun and a breeze over the ridge here. The rows of vines curving over the hillside below."

Not to mention the winery itself which, though state-of-the-art, is perfectly designed and sited, a blend of Northwest and Craftsman styles. Wines from Penner-Ash range from their Willamette Valley blend and a lovely Viognier, through a superb Goldschmidt Vineyard Pinot Noir, and their Dussin Vineyard Pinot Noir. Be aware that much of each vintage sells out early, so be clear about release dates and time your visit.

From Penner-Ash, return to Highway 240. Turn west toward Yamhill and then south onto Highway 47. Continue south a little more than 2 miles and turn west on Lincoln Street for **Cuneo Cellars,** at 750 W. Lincoln Street. Visit www.cuneocellars.com or phone (503) 852-0002. Nestled in a land dedicated to Pinots, owner and winemaker Gino Cuneo is renewing his Tuscan heritage by developing a fine Sangiovese.

Seghesio Gift

Oregon, with its terroir so suited to Pinot Noir, has not embraced this excellent varietal. Nor, truth be told, has the public. In California, Sangiovese became confused with Chianti and ended up in blends marketed as Zinfandel. Yet Sangiovese is more like an Italian Cabernet Sauvignon, and it was introduced from Tuscany in the 1890s by the Seghesio family at their Chianti Station in Sonoma County. Soften the tannins a bit and you have a rich, complex, approachable wine that will age well—robust enough to stand up to meats, heavy (but oh-so-good) red sauces, and foods laden with spices.

With winemakers like Gino Cuneo taking the lead, plus the availability of certified Brunello Sangiovese, the wine may find a strong new following. Cuneo Cellars also features an award-winning Pinot Noir that combines brightness with depth and a firm, complex structure that rushes along to a fine finish. And don't overlook Cuneo Cellars Del Rio Syrah. Also an award-winner, this is a big fruit-laden wine, with a powerful, complex structure, and superb balance, leading to a lengthy bring-me-some-more finish.

An extraordinary ecoenterprise, the **Carlton Winemakers Studio,** is a few yards west of Cuneo Cellars on the same side of the street. Visit www.winemakersstudio.com or phone (503) 852-6100. Imagine, if you will, a dormitory for barreled wine. That's part of what the studio is. It's also a processing facility and self-training ground for winemakers in transition who require private access to their stored wine. They share floor space, state-of-the-art equipment, a lab—and lucky for you and me—a tasting room. Lynn Penner-Ash handcrafted her wines here before planting the vineyard on Ribbon Ridge. It is the first facility of its kind in Oregon, and so bold was the idea that a whole stack of state laws had to be altered to allow the studio's cooperative nature to emerge. Even the structure reflects the earth-friendly views of both founders and winemakers in residence. The barrel room and a portion of the processing facility is bermed to support natural temperature control. Walls contain airflow passages, excess water is captured, and nearly everything you see is recycled. Oregon Pinot Noirs are well represented. But look for top-notch whites and dessert wines as well. Several flights are on hand from which to choose. To fully appreciate the Carlton Winemakers Studio and its potential role in the Oregon wine industry, call ahead to inquire about a tour.

Continue south into Carlton and turn east on Main Street. The tasting room for Ken Wright Cellars' Tyrus Evan label is in **The Depot** at the corner of Main and Pine Streets on the north side. Visit www.tyrusevan.com or phone (503) 852-7010. A delight to the eye, this depot was built in 1923, fell into disrepair after Southern Pacific's rail service faded away in the '50s, and has now been restored in detail by Ken Wright. Take a moment to walk around the structure. Notice the old

Railway Express Agency dock and, farther along, the ticket-master's window, all preserved for each of us to enjoy and for grandfathers to reminisce about with the young ones. Inside, you'll find the waiting room perfect for displays of Tyrus Evan and other Oregon varietals, gourmet food selections, and collectibles.

Across Main and a block west from The Depot is **Cuvée Restaurant** at 214 W. Main Street. Visit www.cuvee dining.com or phone (503) 852-6555. It is a testament to Carlton's future as an emerging wine village that it is attracting quality restaurants. Cuvée offers Country French cuisine fashioned by chef Gilbert Henry. The menu favors seafood specialties, though vegetarians will enjoy the mushroom fritatta with tomatoes, zucchini, and Abbey Road goat cheese. Desserts—with French press coffee—are varied, but death by chocolate is the recommended coup de grâce.

DUNDEE-DAYTON AREA

Wine Country Farm B&B → Domaine Serene Vineyards and Winery → Sokol Blosser Winery → Erath Vineyards Winery → Dundee Bistro → Joel Palmer House

Rolling farm country and vineyards embrace **Wine Country Farm B&B** at 6855 Breyman Orchards Road, between Dundee and Dayton. Visit www.winecountryfarm.com for a preview of this remodeled 1900s farmhouse done in French country style or phone (503) 864-3446 for information. With its magnificent views and an efficient staff, this bed-and-breakfast is a regular stop for travelers from Portland to the coast. Most of the nine rooms have views and balconies or decks, all have private baths. Guests may also explore trails and forests on horeseback or pic- nic nearby.

Just a breath or two down the hill from Wine Country Farm, turn southwest to **Domaine Serene Vineyards and Winery** at 6555 NE Hilltop Lane. Visit www.domainserene.com or phone (503) 864-4600 to check on tours and tasting-room hours. This winery has an extraordinary presence, produces outstanding wines, and is magnificent to tour. As you wind up the curving drive, continue beyond the first estate building to the winery at the top of the hill. Inside and out, the winery is stunning to visit, and its source is surprising as well.

Wineries—inns and restaurants, too—are capital-intensive. Many wineries depend on corporate support, partnerships, or venture capital. In the case of Domaine Serene, the story is a bit different. Some thirty-five years ago, Kenneth Evenstad in- vested everything he had in Upsher-Smith, a laboratory that had developed a form of digitalis, of great value for certain heart conditions. As it happens, the granddaughter of the lab's found- er is Ken Evenstad's wife, Grace. Over the years, Ken's vision led the Minnesota company to success in both prescription and nonprescription generics focused on cardiovascular support, dermatology, and women's health. Grace has pursued her own good works, raising substantial funds for children's charities across the country by opening the Evenstad home and winery. It's a fine way to put Domaine Serene's reputation for quality to its highest use.

And that quality shows everywhere in design and execution of the winery. One of the first to use gravity-feed processing from crush to bottling, the work proceeds according to Grace's instructions.

"These are tiny babies," she says of the fragile Pinot Noir grapes. "We must treat them with great care and intervene only as we must to produce the wine that lives in them."

And that philosophy pays off. Domaine Serene's releases typically span the moderate-and-up range, each with value beyond its price, reflected in high points and awards. The Côte Sud (south hillside) Chardonnay is produced from the estate's own Dijon clones. And unlike many Chardonnays, this wine is both fermented and aged in French oak in a fashion that will attract even dedicated red-wine lovers. Rich, with bright citrus, and buoyant oak overtones, this Chardonnay expresses itself over the whole palate, with a lingering finish to invite pause and reflection.

Among Domaine Serene's remarkable award-winning reds, Seven Hills Vineyard Rockblock Syrah is a good place to begin. It's also something of a preview, since Seven Hills is located in an apellation that straddles the state line from south of Lowden and Walla Walla, Washington, into Oregon. The aroma of this Syrah is subtle, like a delicate hint of perfume left by a wearer moving through a quiet room. Color is deep, nearly opaque, and controlled tannins add to its depth. Still hesitant about Syrahs? Rockblock will turn your head. A marvelous collaboration at Domaine Serene has created this exceptional wine. The winery's Evenstad Reserve Pinot Noir is a step up to a big, bold red. Although Reserve releases are not guaranteed on an annual basis, this is one to watch for. With just a brush of brightness, this Pinot Noir is smooth and lush, with layered undertones of spice combined with a fruit-forward presence. Next comes a Pinot Noir trio—and a chance to savor fine differences. Each of these wines comes from one of Domaine Serene's estate vineyards: Winery Hill, Mark Bradford, and Jerusalem Hill. Of course, we live in a world that urges us to see something as better or not so good as something else. So step around that and notice how each Pinot Noir—from the same estate and the same wine-maker, but a different slope—exhibits unique, almost Zenlike qualities. The Winery Hill is of a delicate ripeness, with fleeting aromas, yet a firm, earthy body. Its finish is generous and long, with a return to an initial impression of delicacy. If you are mov-ing toward reds and haven't quite made the leap, Winery Hill will encourage you. It is both relaxed and very special. The Mark Bradford is a bit more robust, announcing itself with an enviable aroma that delivers on a promise of fullness and struc-ture. Tannins are firm, yet controlled to produce a lush, out-standing finish. The Jerusalem Hill simply steps up the intensity. With a full-mouth taste and subtle overtones, this wine presents a fruity aroma that opens to an experience of dark fruit and complementary spices. Try pairing any of these with onion tarts of light pastry and mellow flavorings. A tasting with just these three would provide a focus for conversation and an evening's pleasure. It's rare to find wines able to provide their own music. These do.

Sokol Blosser Winery at 5000 Sokol Blosser Lane is the next road north from Breymann Orchards Road on Highway 99W. Visit www.sokolblosser.com or phone (503) 864-2282. Each Oregon winery is unique, yet many display similar qualities. This family-owned winery holds a list of accomplishments for the area: established in 1971; first to build a tasting room, and to do so with grace and panache; one of the first wineries with a woman at the helm. The vineyards are certified as organic and L.I.V.E., tractors operate on 20 percent biodiesel, and the winery's barrel cellar was first in the nation to qualify as a Green Building. Cov-ered with earth and planted over, it's quite unexpected, yet blends with its surroundings. Inside, two fans hang high overhead in the chilly air. Still, I wondered how effective this bermed design could be.

"How often do the fans cycle?" I asked Alison Sokol Blosser.

"See the cobweb way up on that fan?" Alison answered. "It wouldn't be there if the fans turned on. Temperature in here stays constant by itself."

There's more, but you get the point. I asked Alison about the legacy of Sokol Blosser—what her feelings were about being a second-generation winegrower.

"Growing up, family life was intertwined with the business. Our family time was often spent working together, and playtime always took place with the vineyards as a backdrop. It was a fabulous childhood, but at the time, I continually resisted the idea of growing up to work in the family business. Instead, I wanted to work in the 'real world.' After a short but adequate amount of time in that world, I realized just how lucky I am to have been born into this incredible winegrowing family. My mother and father were role models in the truest sense—hardworking, honorable, and unwavering in their drive to put Oregon wines on the international stage. Now it will be up to my brother and me, along with other second-generation winegrowers, to carry on the legacy. The future looks good. I'm going to make my parents proud."

This winery continues to be unique as well as a leader in the industry. Susan Sokol Blosser comments in her insightful book *At Home in the Vineyard* (see Connections). From the shaded parking area, your first glimpse of the tasting room amid trees, plantings, unique glasswork—and rocks—will both intrigue and inform. Inside, a glass wall frames a view of Mount Hood to perfection. All this is only a prelude to premium wines in a surprisingly moderate price range.

Among the reds, Dundee Hills Pinot Noir is a big wine, yet displays restrained tannins forming an earth subtext for the lush fruit. A sense of structure is present—the wine should age well—but after relaxing a bit, it is very approachable. This is an excellent Pinot Noir, but a surprise awaits with Sokol Blosser's Meditrina. It is a Pinot Noir with blendings of Syrah and Zinfandel, and it greets you with an aromatic intimacy. Meditrina also exhibits both subtle textures and strength of character. The wine is very feminine though, for the wine's namesake is a Roman goddess of wine and health, long overlooked and now celebrated in this blend. Meditrina is also—and I shrink from using this term, but it's apt—a *fun* wine. Sokol Blosser's good humor is both in the bottle and on the reverse label. Ever think of what a great letter an *M* is? The label will duly inform you.

Sokol Blosser's whites are excellent as well. The Dundee Hills Cuvée Pinot Gris is crisp, with a richness that will develop even more over time. Unlike Meditrina, which you could probably age on the way home, you'll be rewarded if you allow this lush Pinot Gris to recline in its bottle for a while. Perhaps the most interesting of Sokol Blosser's whites is a nine-way blend of white varietals called Evolution. Russ Rosner, the winemaker, has commented that the wine is his most difficult effort: like mixing nine colors on a palette that becomes a rainbow, rather than a dull brown. Yet in spite of its complexity, this extraordinary wine works with a wide range of foods from down-home Cajun to a light crème brûlée—standing up to spice while not overpowering a fragile dessert. Put it on your take-home list along with Meditrina. Check some of the cookbooks listed in Connections and be inventive. . . .

Continuing north to Dundee on Highway 99W, watch for Ninth Street, and turn west. The street becomes Worden Hill

Road and will lead you to **Erath Vineyards Winery** at 9409 Worden Hill Road. Visit www.erath.com or phone (503) 538-3318. Dick Erath is one of the patrons of the early winegrowing efforts in Oregon. So, a visit here will close the circle for readers who have followed the development of the wine industry in the Willamette Valley. Only days after my visit, it was announced that Erath Vineyards Winery had been sold to Chateau Ste. Michelle in Washington. So, while a bit of melancholy might accompany the change, most agree that the deal is a good one for Erath, for Chateau Ste. Michelle, and for Oregon winegrowing. Chateau Ste. Michelle will gain a top producer of Pinot Noir and a respected name in the industry. Oregon winemakers will gain a level of expertise in the U.S. and international markets that could have taken years longer to develop. And Dick Erath retains control of prime vineyards in the Dundee Hills. In short, the transition will relieve limitations while adding opportunity. For all, it seems a win-win outcome. Erath wines are more than iconic, they hark back to what vineyards and winemaking are about—and more than 20,000 wine lovers per year drive up the curving road to the Erath tasting room. The wines found here are the essence of Oregon, of high quality, and affordable. Erath is also adopting the twist cap. The Pinot Gris is a lovely exercise in growing and winemaking, with complex fruit that is as subtle as it is lively, and just the right degree of mineralization. Aroma and taste are so intertwined that the wine provides a continuous experience from nose to a languorous finish. And it can be paired with everything from Brussels sprouts to shellfish, and Asian spices. Erath's Pinot Noir is almost as adaptable and well constructed, with care and subtlety. Fruit-forward and spicy, but not the least bit pushy. And skipping over the Brussels sprouts, this Pinot Noir will pair well with everything from grilled meats through light Thai and red-sauce pastas. Throughout, the wine beckons; it does not insist. Erath's Prince Hill Pinot Noir is in the same form—Oregon through and through—yet invites comparison. This Dundee Hills wine has a splendid sense of place. Cross-tasting the two Pinots, one can almost feel a difference in altitude and slope. Sip both, enjoy, and consider.

Return to Dundee and whether you're ready for lunch, dinner, or more winetasting, head straight for the **Dundee Bistro** on the corner of Highway 99W and Seventh Street. Visit www .dundeebistro.com or phone (503) 554-1650. A neatly fenced parking area is behind the building, which has a distinctive Mediterranean-Northwest quality. Landscaping is lush and patio seating is screened from the long afternoon sun so treasured in this part of the country. This project by the entire Ponzi family is faultless in design and execution, from architecture and art to place settings and presentation. Every aspect is just as it should be, from the commissioned painting over the bar, to the Reidel crystal. Yet there is a sense of ease about the place. The eye flows naturally from one detail to another—elegance in a casual atmosphere. Local vintners gather here, often still in field boots, bringing in a few bottles of wine to share.

The Dundee Bistro is also a place where wine and cuisine meet each other on even terms. Chef Jason Smith crafts a new menu daily, depending on which of Oregon's bounty is brought to the door of his display kitchen.

"Of course, we can order delicacies from our regulars like the Duck Egg Lady and a woman who grows our arugula salad greens for us. We also get fresh line-caught salmon and age our select prosciutto in Dick Ponzi's wine cellar. Much of the rest comes from foragers."

I should have known there'd be a surprise for me. At an evening meal with Tamara Belgard of Ponzi Vineyards, my selections included tomato panzanella with basil vinaigrette and house-made mozzarella. Soon after, a braised fiddlehead fern arrived, standing coiled on a small plate. Now, at first glance, this green can look downright intergalactic: a vegetable from *Star Trek*. No matter, it is delicious—so maybe I really could live in the woods. Mushroom cannelloni followed, with creamed Oregon corn and arugula with blood orange oil. A five-cheese course was equally delightful. Across the table, Tamara's albacore poached in olive oil, with tomatoes, spinach, fingerling potatoes, olives, and hard-boiled duck egg looked wonderful. Each course paired well with tastings from the Ponzi Vineyards. The Pinot Gris was bright with a fruity, well-developed nose. Midpalate fullness leads to a crisp, lean finish. An excellent wine. Pinot Blanc is not a common wine in the Pacific Northwest. As a clone of Pinot Gris, which is itself a clone of Pinot Noir, we're talking second cousins here. Yet this Pinot Blanc from Ponzi is no shrinking violet. Full and zesty, both aromas and flavors are complex, with a lustrous structure and long, memorable finish.

Tamara was quick to notice that a certain light was coming into my eyes. "Aren't reds your favorites?" she asked.

"They usually are, but this is *really* nice."

From its origins in a certified vineyard to a screwcap to let you enjoy the wine on separate occasions without fridge drippings—this Pinot Blanc is special. And it tells you so.

In our red selection, the Ponzi Pinot Noir came through as fruit-forward, quite bright, with smooth tannins that fill the palate, but not in a pushy way. This is an accommodating wine that will pair with a wide range of foods. Poured gently but with some panache, a Ponzi Pinot Noir Reserve rounded out the meal and tasting—a fine conclusion.

The Ponzi family tradition pours with each wine. It is present in this Reserve, crafted by second-generation winemaker Luisa Ponzi. Relaxed, with neither hesitation nor abruptness, the wine holds mellowed spices, is generous with its fruit, and brings controlled tannins along for the ride—right down to an elegant finish. With care, it can enrich an entire multicourse meal, or stand on its own for an evening's conversation. This is a wine with winning ways. I asked Maria Ponzi Fogelstrom for a bit of history. When did the Ponzi vineyards go in?

"With a passion for Pinot Noir, my mother and father, Dick and Nancy Ponzi, moved our family up to Oregon's North Willamette Valley from Northern California in 1970. At that time, there were virtually no vineyards or winemakers in the region—my parents were real visionaries. Our first harvest came in 1974, with just four barrels of Pinot Noir. We've now grown to a 15,000 case production winery, and own and care for more than 140 acres of certified sustainable vineyards."

Are Dick and Nancy still involved?

"Oh, yes. But the family business is now under second-generation management with my sister, Luisa, as head winemaker, our brother, Michel in operations, and I direct sales and marketing. We take great pride in our wines."

In most restaurants, diners may sample wine before accepting it when a bottle is ordered. At the Dundee Bistro, even wine offered by the glass is presented and poured at the table for approval. Such a level of commitment to diner satisfaction marks this as a world-class restaurant. Awards for excellence from top wine and culinary organizations, plus regular mention in leading publications are standard. Prices are moderate. Reservations are a good idea. Ah, if my driveway were only closer . . .

If you are enticed by images of a historic Northwest colonial home and rare cuisine, head southwest on Highway 99W from Dundee and follow Highway 18 toward Dayton for the **Joel Palmer House** at 600 Ferry Street in Dayton. Visit www .joelpalmerhouse.com or phone (503) 864-2995. Which brings up the question: Who was Joel Palmer? The answer is that he was a Canadian immigrant who crisscrossed the United States in the mid-1800s, followed the gold rush, and worked to secure tribal lands in Oregon. In the end, he was sacked for being too caring toward Native Americans.

Palmer's home, now owned by chef Jack Czarnecki and his wife Heidi, has become the Northwest epicenter for mushroom-based cuisine of quality and inventiveness. Not that you'll faint away for lack of other choices: filet mignon, duckling, crab cakes, and scallops—all flavored and sauced in an imaginative style. Plus truffles and a specialty: Heidi's three-mushroom tarts. Not to slight the desserts: a strawberry-rosewater sorbet with angel food cake, carmel-walnut cheesecake, and a chocolate-hazelnut torte drenched in raspberry sauce. Oregon wines? Of course. And much more than can be listed here. Meals are moderately priced. The history is free.

TIMBERLINE AREA

Aurora → Timberline Lodge

Water and sky are like Oregon, always in transition. Mountains are a different matter. They're right there, right now. Yet what we see in them is eons of history, even as we view the present in snow or clouds streaming across their faces. Mountains offer an anchor for our wandering minds—a bookend against which our lives can lean.

Of all the mountains in the Pacific Northwest, Mount Hood is one of the most fascinating. Intimate, too. You can get right up close, without being a champion climber. Nearly everyone in the Willamette Valley relishes a view of this peak. So, off we go to Mount Hood, Timberline, and down the northern slope to a town that is reinventing itself: Hood River.

From the Willamette Valley, you'll have two main choices. One is northeast along Highway 99W through Newberg and Sherwood, and on into the Portland area. Prettier and more leisurely is a two-lane route east from the Dundee area. This southern path takes you to **Aurora,** Oregon's first National Historic District, and a magnet for antiquers with more than twenty shops to browse in the village. Visit www.auroracolony.com or phone (503) 939-0312 for a visitor's guide.

Aurora is more than 150 years old, a breakaway German commune from Pennsylvania. Unlike so many other communes from that wonderful utopian period in America, Aurora was a success. Built with reverence for the principle: "From each according to his ability, to each according to his need." Original colony buildings have been preserved—it's quite moving to see them—and dozens of shops line Main Street.

For the route to Timberline through Aurora, head northwest on 99W. Just beyond Newberg, turn right to go south on Highway 219 / NE St. Paul Highway, which becomes River Road NE. Another 1.5 miles will bring you to McKay Road NE. Turn left and continue for about 3.5 miles as McKay Road becomes Yergen Road NE, then Ehlen Road NE. A landmark will be the

I-5 underpass. Don't worry, you're getting close, and folks around here are helpful—if, as an Oregon farmer said, you can find any folks around here.

From Aurora, continue north on Highway 99E through Canby. Just beyond Oregon City, you'll need to enter I-205 northbound for about 5 miles. Take Exit 12, marked Highway 212 / Clackamus, and continue east about 15 miles, through the village of Boring, and turn right to go southeast on U.S. 26, which will lead you along a scenic stretch past Government Camp to the Timberline turnoff.

Winding up through the lower Cascades on U.S. 26, you'll find some small-town traffic at the lower elevations, but that eases. Even in winter, roads are usually well cleared above the snowline. Check the Timberline Lodge Web site for the latest, if weather seems iffy. Often it will clear as altitude increases.

Timberline Lodge is at the 6,000-foot level of Mount Hood, and is a world-class destination. Visit www.timberlinelodge.com or phone (503) 622-7979. If there is a testament to Oregon's claim of being a year-around destination, Timberline Lodge is a clear demonstration. It is a worldwide draw for year-round skiing, with a heated outdoor pool, spa, corridors of fancy that wind through the lower levels, and the award-winning Cascades Dining Room—with art and craftsmanship extending in every direction.

The lodge is also a gathering of history in a region where the fortunes of Oregon and Washington intertwine. The short version is that in 1929, with Americans' savings at an all-time low, the weight of speculation in the stock market exceeded our nation's capacity to sustain it. A terrible crash resulted, with no legislated protection for anyone, putting almost every worker on the street, jobless.

---------------- *Relieving Depression* ----------------

At the depth of the Depression in the mid-1930s, President Roosevelt created national programs to employ workers so they could feed their families. Construction of the great Bonneville Dam was underway, along with other projects across the land that are still marvels today. It wasn't an easy political sell and the government even hired folksinger Woody Guthrie to write songs that would both entertain and inform. His tunes helped, and, in so doing, made the Pacific Northwest familiar to generations. The power and irrigation projects here were once called a conspiracy. It's a good thing most people knew better.

Timberline Lodge was begun in 1933 and was dedicated by the president in 1937, during a tour of the Northwest in which he also heard proposals for Olympic National Park. The lodge was completed by project workers the next year. Artists and craftsmen were thrilled to receive 90¢ an hour. Many worked overtime without pay, just to be part of such a noble project. Main supporting columns that rise over three stories were all shaped from giant firs by one man—for $25 per column. No doubt, he was grateful to make such a contribution. It is the kind of thing we, as a people, feel when pressed by adversity into one another's grateful company. These builders, and their energies, offer a chance for us all to reflect on our common fortune.

Travelers who pass this way recognize the lodge from Stanley Kubrick's film *The Shining*, with Jack Nicholson. Some of the exterior shots were indeed made here. Good choice. For the lodge, by sun or moon, or swept by snow, is magnificent to see. As for those dull institutional interiors of the movie—not filmed here. No, sir. That will be clear as soon as you step through the main entrance. Before you will be a soaring hexagonal fireplace and hand-hewn timbers everywhere, all in the National Parks tradition. A special charm at each turning of the main stairway to the rooms above is a newel post hand-carved to remind you that everything here is a part of the Pacific Northwest, with all its birds and beasts and myths. Each one is a beauty.

Up from the lobby level is the Ram's Head Bar. Actually, it's a family-style restaurant, with a small bar, panoramic view windows, and even personal writing alcoves—all arranged around the open gallery. So, even if you only have a short time here, be sure to enjoy a lunch at least. For guests spending an evening or the night, there's the Cascade Dining Room, one of the finest in the Pacific Northwest. Executive chef Leif Erik Benson has directed food services at Timberline Lodge for more than twenty-eight years, is the author of the bestselling *Timberline Lodge Cookbook* (see Connections), and has won countless awards for his imaginative Northwest cuisine. It's gourmet dining in a beautiful setting of hewn wooden beams and hand-planked flooring, with a casual atmosphere.

Together with the award-winning wine list maintained by cellar master Nick Andrews, you'll find the perfect combination of dishes and wines to complement your stay at this enchanting lodge.

HOOD RIVER AREA

Mt. Hood Winery → Hood River BnB → Columbia Gorge Hotel → Cathedral Ridge Winery → Phelps Creek Vineyards Tasting Room → Pheasant Valley Vineyard & Winery → The Pines 1852 Vineyard and Winery → Celilo Restaurant and Bar

From Timberline, follow Highway 35 north toward Hood River. It's a beautiful, easy drive from mountain slopes and alpine meadows into rich farmland, with sweeping turns and straight-aways. Which is by way of mentioning that state troopers pay a lot more attention to the downhill lanes of traffic. That said, plan about an hour for the drive.

Two very nice—and very different—Hood River inns would normally be listed at the beginning of this section. But Highway 35 passes right by the **Mt. Hood Winery** at 3189 Highway 35. Visit www.mthoodwinery.com or phone (541) 386-8333. It's on the right-hand side, about 33 miles from the intersection near Government Camp, and well worth a stop.

Dick and Christie Reed have opted for adaptive reuse of a roadside stand, once part of the Hood River County Fruit Loop. So, you'll be looking for a large Mt. Hood Winery façade painted up in a fruit-stand style. Coming up on it, the place just makes you smile. Once inside, you'll find a cozy tasting room opening onto a tree-shaded patio and deck. A new waterfall is on the way. It's a welcoming place, but not run by a stopwatch. Hours are listed as "Noonish to five or so daily from mid-April to late October." That sums up the winery's philosophy.

"We're not out to sell a gazillion cases. We do about 1,500 a year now. After that, the business starts chasing the winemak-ing. That's not what we're here for," Dick says.

Except for Adelsheim and Sokol Blosser, who favor wonder-ful vineyard cats, most vintners up this way favor dogs. Some wineries even get busted by the health police for allowing a dog on the premises—as if having a dog around hasn't been com-mon since Etruscan times. Either way, Mt. Hood Winery offers an end-of-August deal: bring in a picture of your pet and they'll set you up with a glass of wine for a buck. If you miss that date, go for the deal anyhow. It might work out. Enjoy the wine inside or out on their patio and wave your picture around. Someone is bound to talk to your about your Wonder Pet.

Mt. Hood's Pinot Gris is inviting and relaxed enough to serve chilled and all on its own. Fruit-forward, but not pushy, with a long, satisfying finish. It is well layered for a white and carries a light aroma and taste of peach and pineapple, with slight spice on the palate. The Pinot Noir is full-flavored, yet quite stylish. The fruit is well-rounded, balancing the body of the wine. And the finish is both fine and long-lasting. This is an outstanding wine. It should stand up to all but heavily spiced foods or sauces and makes you want to hum "Mellow Yellow." For a young vineyard, these are great offerings.

Remain on Highway 35 toward Hood River, about 5 miles, and turn left into town at the Stop sign. The **Hood River BnB** at 918 Oak Street can be easily reached by their directions. Visit www.hoodriverbnb.com or phone (541) 387-2997. However, if your visit is on an event weekend, you can avoid downtown traffic by continuing west on State Street. Turn right on Ninth Street and left again on Oak Street. The inn will be on your right just down the block. A parking space for check-in is in front, with overnight parking available one level down.

This bed-and-breakfast is an elixir of homey adventure, just as Jane and Jim Nichols intend it to be. A living room with fireplace, plus a sitting-entertainment room, help ease away the day. And at breakfast, the dining room offers a panoramic view of the river. Most rooms have river views, and a larger upstairs room commands not only a changing river scene, but a whirlpool tub and walk-in closet. The room is also an absolute blessing for the taller traveler—high countertops and plenty of space for longer arms. But the big attraction is the view downhill to the Gorge.

At dusk, it's as though the river is busy changing sets for tomorrow's scene. And at false dawn, mists gather over the water, lifting to form clouds, and revealing homes and forest on the Washington shore. The changes are not hurried, but may repeat themselves several times before sunrise.

If you're headed to Hood River for water sports, this is a great base. Jane runs the inn. Jim is an electronics superdude, and a breakfast chef extraordinaire. Jane has been swimming at the master's level for some years and is swim coach at Hood River Valley High School. She knows the river and most water sports.

"Hood River has changed from a dwindling town to a destination, mostly due to windsurfing on the Columbia, and everything that goes with it," Jane says. "This weekend, Hood River is hosting bicycle races. It's always something, and we're glad to have sports people stay with us."

The inn is attractively priced and but a few blocks from downtown Hood River, which has artfully reinvented itself, with boutiques, shops, and restaurants. It's a great overnight destination on the way east toward wine country in the Tri-Cities area and Walla Walla.

A different experience awaits travelers at **Columbia Gorge Hotel** at 4000 Westcliff Drive, just west of Exit 62 on I-84 westbound. Visit www.columbiagorgehotel.com or phone (541) 386-5566. With its classic architecture, tile roofs, and lush gardens, the inn is one of Oregon's finest, and perhaps one of the few on the West Coast to offer high tea. Each room is well appointed, with a comfortable feeling. And guests are free to wander the grounds, its bridges, and watercourses—all within what seems to be touching distance of the Columbia below.

The hotel's five-course farm breakfast is offered to all guests— from baked apples and hash browns to pork chops and grilled mountain trout, it's up to you to control yourself. Haven't had enough? How about a stack of pancakes with maple syrup? I know, it's shameful, but so good. . . . Lunch and dinner are special as well, with attentive service and seasonal entrées.

The Columbia Gorge Hotel projects a timeless presence, right down to the operator-controlled elevator. It's marvelous and a favorite of children and adults alike. If you're a film buff, you may also be aware of a major Hollywood sin. In a film noir, presumably set in the 1930s or '40s, at least one scene opens with a private detective character stepping into an elevator. He pushes a button, or the elevator doors close by themselves, and . . . what's wrong here? An elevator in those days was run by a uniformed operator (with a little folding stool for the slow times) who stood in the front with a levered wheel.

"Floor, please?" the operator would inquire. It can make you feel special. Like someone with a story or on a mission. Even with a heavy load, an experienced operator could hit each floor right on the money, with no more than a half-inch either way. Of course, the neatest part would be when the operator didn't get it just right, and the car had to be jiggled up and down a bit. So, right here at the Columbia Gorge Hotel, you get a historic E-ride for the price of a room—you could be on your way to meet a lover, or a killer, with your gat hidden neatly in a jacket or purse. I tell you, a dozen films could begin right here, and dozens more in your mind. . . .

To tour several top wineries, head west as Oak Street becomes Oak Avenue and merges into Cascade Avenue in Hood River. Just after a bend, at an intersection with Country Club Road, a blue wineries sign will be on the left at the intersection. Turn southwest up the hill and continue 1.5 miles. Turn left on Post Canyon Drive and continue to **Cathedral Ridge Winery** at 4200 Post Canyon Road. Visit www.cathedralridgewinery.com or phone (541) 386-2882. This winery is special. Nestled against its vineyards, the tasting room is warm and inviting, with shade trees and flowers, between the Columbia River Gorge and the western slopes of Mount Hood. In short, this place is what many imagine a family-owned winery to be. And that's owner Robb Bell's focus. After enough traveling for the corporate world, he acquired these vineyards so he'd miss fewer of his daughter's soccer games. Michael Sebastiani has signed on as winemaker and Lonnie Wright (we'll meet him later), among others, handles field management for Cathedral Ridge. I asked Robb about the region.

"Rain forest to desert in thirty-five miles lets all the varietals grow close together and ripen to perfection. We make a full line of wines with a nice cluster of whites. Chardonnays, Pinot Gris, and Rieslings. But reds are most likely our destiny over the long term. The flavors and quality of red grapes here are unsurpassed and we're going to extreme lengths to create high-quality wines. Lonnie is helping us develop premier vineyards and Michael practices his black art with unusual yeast selections. He builds our reds to be approachable and food-friendly, with the capacity to age over extended periods of time."

The whites are very good as Robb suggested and the reds are excellent. Cathedral Ridge Pinot Gris is blended with a touch of Chardonnay. Color and body are clear and light, with muted citrus, low tannins, and a warm finish. The Zinfandel is a medium-bodied wine, with a deep garnet color. Give it some time to open and it will reward you with bold fruit on a light oak base, with well-controlled tannins. The wine is approachable now, but has the capacity for developing into a real winner with a little time. Cathedral Ridge Cabernet is a deep, inky color with bold fruit on earthy tannins, and a finish that lengthens as the wine opens. But it is the Syrah that can ring your bell. This is a hearty blend of Syrah and Cabernet, with the full aroma of a Northwest red, rich, deep flavors, and slightly smoky tannins. Drink it now or in three or four years; it's a grand wine.

Wine and golf? Why not? Returning to Country Club Road, continue for about a half mile to **Phelps Creek Vineyards Tasting Room** on the grounds of the Hood River Golf and Country Club at 1850 Country Club Road. Visit www.phelps creekvineyards.com or phone (541) 386-2607. Adjacent to the Oak Grove Restaurant, this fine tasting room is a gathering place for local vintners and wine lovers alike. Owner Bob Morus is a senior airline pilot also committed to viticulture—and a good story. Perhaps it's written somewhere that pilots must be storytellers in order to be licensed. I don't remember it from flight school, but then I may have missed that part.

In any case, Bob was planning on putting in some new vines on one his vineyard's hillsides. And since Phelps Creek fruit is used by wineries like King Estate and Ponzi, Bob wanted the new vines to be an excellent possible match for his terroir. Being trained in analytical matters, he studied the available Dijon clones for Pinot as carefully as preflight weather on an iffy day. Three clones emerged: numbers 667, 115, and 777. Bob checked with Oregon State University, he read, and considered. Still, despite his research, the proper choice seemed to elude him. A short time later, he was assigned to a new aircraft, the Boeing 777. That event pointed to the answer in clearest terms. Bob planted his hillside in 777 vines.

"It was as good a number as I was going to get," he says.

Bob is probably right, for Phelps Creek wines have a good deal of art in and around them. Judith Cunningham's work graces the label on Phelps Creek Pinot Noir Reserve, and Ellen Dittebrandt's work highlights Phelps Creek Chardonnay. Ellen's work also hangs in the Celilo Restaurant and Bar in Hood River. I admired the labels.

"It worked out all right," Bob says. "Judith and Ellen lived in a drafty farmhouse, so I traded firewood for art. They're warmer and we're prettier."

Not to mention that the wines are excellent. The Reserve Pinot Noir is dark and creamy, with a whole-mouth taste and feeling from the fruit and very light tannins. The wine's finish is extraordinary and sustained. Phelps Creek Chardonnay is tops as well. Neither too buttery nor too dry, the tropical fruit flavors are firm and not overbearing. This Chardonnay will pair well with a spectrum of foods extending well beyond white meats and seafood. And it will draw out complex flavors from mushrooms and stand up to Asian spices as well.

Continue south along Country Club Road and turn east on Barrett Drive. At Tucker Road turn south again and continue past Portland Drive, through a curvy section to Acree Drive. Turn right for **Pheasant Valley Vineyard & Winery** at 3890 Acree Drive on your right, uphill into the parking area. Visit www.pheasantvalleywinery.com or phone (541) 387-3040. Once in the tasting room, you'll be charmed by the great mahogany backbar straight ahead, with a massive stone fireplace to the right. And the backbar has a story. It was shipped around Cape Horn in the early 1900s and finally found its way into a drugstore in Hood River. After the sale of the drugstore, the backbar languished in long-term storage as an heirloom. A local attorney offered to buy it. The owner declined. But when owners Scott and Gail Hagee were building their tasting room, they both thought it would be perfect. Rather than trying to buy the backbar, Scott asked the owner if he'd like to "store" the bar in the new tasting room. A deal was struck, and there it stands for all to enjoy and admire.

Among the vintners we've visited thus far in Oregon, Scott and Gail are a bit unusual; they farmed for some years before converting part of their orchards to wine grapes. Yet Scott accomplished even more. He converted his farming to sustainable organic practices.

"That's a big change. What was the tipping point?" I asked.

"Oh, there's a little creek that runs down the hill here. I was up top, spraying chemicals, and on my way down, discovered my neighbor's horse down on the ground near the creek. His hooves were twitching. He looked terrible. So I called the neighbor and we got the vet. Well, it turned out that a vet had an antidote for the poison that was running down through the creek."

"But you kept thinking about the horse."

"Oh, yes," Scott says. "And about all of us. I knew a number of farmers, too many, that had cancer of one sort or another. I didn't want to be one of them, and I didn't want anyone else to go the same way. So I changed and never looked back."

"Is it difficult here?"

"No more or less than anywhere. But you just have to stay with it. You put out plants that attract pests away from the vines. We use efficient irrigation and keep the soil healthy naturally. Some days, it's a struggle."

"But worth it?"

"You bet. It's not just this place, you know, it's everything. Everywhere."

We were all silent for a moment. I haven't heard it said any better.

My guide through this Hood River loop has been Lonnie

Wright. Originally from Midwest farm country, in addition to being a vintner, he now runs a vineyard management business and has a farm of his own south of The Dalles. It's a lovely spot out in the hills, established in 1852. Its hillside vines probably date to the 1800s, when the first wine grapes appeared in the Pacific Northwest. Lonnie's daughter, Sierra, finished her college studies and chose to come back to the farm, to be part of the wine industry with her dad.

"I feel pretty good about that," Lonnie says. "And about the place our family has here. It's a lifelong dream."

So, Lonnie's tasting room is next on this loop of four top Hood River wineries and tasting rooms. Return to Hood River. **The Pines 1852 Vineyard and Winery** tasting room is located next to Westwind Art Gallery at 202 State Street, one block south of Second and Oak Streets—right across from the waterfalls. Visit www.thepinesvineyard.com or phone (541) 298-1981. A cherrywood bar, backed by antique Asian bookshelves, brings a contemplative air, just the right mood for winetasting. Bistro tables are arranged both in and outside, and hors d'oeuvres are available. From elegant bottles and labeling, this winery is one to watch. The Pines offers premium Pinot Gris, very much an Oregon wine, and a Merlot with a smoothness characteristic of Hood River wines. Old Vine Zinfandel is leggy, with fruit-forward aroma and low tannins. Give it plenty of time to open and light foods for good pairings. Big Red is a Merlot-Syrah-Cabernet Sauvignon blend, with a touch of Zinfandel. And it is big by Oregon standards. For those who find California and Washington reds a bit dominating, this wine offers a lighter touch on the palate with slim tannins. It will pair well with aromatic cheeses or pasta dishes, and it is a lovely sipping wine. Just the thing for a relaxed bit of Gorge-watching.

In the tide of Hood River's rebirth as a sports and wine-tour town, **Celilo Restaurant and Bar** has a deserving reputation and is downtown at 16 Oak Street. Visit www.celilorestaurant .com or phone (541) 386-5710. Celilo's focus is on local sustainable food sources and environmental responsibility. Everything possible is recycled and cooking oils are transformed into biodiesel fuel. Even the restaurant's beams are salvaged timber booms. The work of local artists grace the restaurant's walls with Impressionist paintings, structures, and glass that reflect qualities found here in the Columbia Gorge. Chef Ben Stenn trained in the Burgundy region and New York City. Menu items reflect that training and a near reverence for this grand seaway. Small plates range from greens to sweet potato fries and fish croquettes. Appetizers and entrées feature organic and free-range items, with an emphasis on seafood. The wine list reflects several local vineyards you'll recognize, including the Phelps Creek label, with a design by one of the artists whose work hangs in the restaurant.

Before crossing into Washington, it's a good idea to fill up in Hood River—a gas station is just short of the Oregon side of the bridge—because a sign out on Highway 14 advises that no fuel is available for 82 miles. It isn't kidding.

Washington

The western frontier came to Oregon with Lewis and Clark. Yet Washington carries a greater sense of the frontier period. Except for gold fever, which had just about everyone shooting at possible claim-jumpers, California had little real frontier. The Spanish had already established great land-grant ranchos in the south and transplanted a lifestyle of music, wine, cattle, and crafts. The United States simply annexed all that when California became a state.

Washington had no such advantage, nor a particularly benign climate. Yet Washingtonians carved much from a rough territory—even as promises by railroads, the federal government, and timber barons were broken as a matter of course. The result is that Washingtonians have learned to take the long view and to regard their environment with increasing concern.

So, where does that leave the wine industry? Actually, viticulture represents another aspect of Washington character: growth with sensitivity. After an early start—some vines were planted by the Hudson's Bay Company in 1825—Washington still had only a dozen or so wineries by 1980. Yet a scant twenty-five years later, that number has exceeded 450. And organic, sustainable farming is moving ahead despite the frustration and high cost of being in the vanguard of low-impact, earth-friendly practices.

Marketing helps. Although most winegrowers here put their sticks down a full decade after their Oregon contemporaries, Washington leaped ahead with marketing leadership from Chateau Ste. Michelle. The result is that the state's growers are now second only to California—which still produces some 90 percent of U.S. wine—and Washington is gaining, with the help of new marketing alliances with Italian and French vintners. The state's wine industry is even attracting attention from out-front vintners like Randall Grahm, who created the famous Bonny Doon Winery in the Santa Cruz Mountains of Northern California. Grahm is especially attracted to champion Rieslings and has announced plans to build a major winery nearer the source. And that would be Washington.

> **Note:** *Washington winegrowing is diverse and somewhat spread out. The Washington Wine Commission offers an excellent booklet-and-map combo,* Touring Washington Wine Country, *helpful in locating current appellations. To request a copy, visit www.washingtonwine.org or phone (206) 667-9463. Most winegrowing activity in the state is east of the Cascade Mountains, so we'll focus on a loop from the Hood River crossing, through the Tri-Cities area, Walla Walla, the Yakima Valley, with a jog north to Quincy, and westward to Woodinville. Keep in mind that many fine wineries, inns, and restaurants are to be found along the way—leave time to explore on your own!*

From Highway 35 or Exit 64 on I-84, head north to the Hood River Bridge, built in 1926, and a beauty. For traffic information, visit www.portofhoodriver.com. Pedestrians and bicycles are not allowed, however, and it's a good idea to inquire locally about the easiest times to cross. Depending on what you're driving, it costs only a buck or less to cross over into Washington and head east along the northern shore of the Columbia on Highway 14. This well-maintained two-lane is one of the most beautiful—some say inspiring—drives in the Northwest and avoids the whoosh and crush of the interstate for most of the distance to Walla Walla. From the Hood River Bridge east, the Gorge is a study in change of climate and landforms. Cloudy days can turn sunny, rain showers disappear, and the rocky cliffs of the Dalles give way to round-shouldered hills and undulating plains. The Columbia changes as well. Gone are the windblown stretches filled with windsurfers and kite-boarders. Instead, you'll find boiling rapids until, at last, the river becomes a wide, inviting plane of water that seems not to be moving at all. The Gorge also wears its geology on its sleeve and you'll be following a Lewis and Clark route. So, take time to enjoy this lovely bit of time travel on this historic two-lane highway.

Note: *You'll have a couple of choices on this Washington loop, depending on your starting time. The first is to head straight for Walla Walla, a little more than three hours distant, plus time for visits to Syncline Winery, Maryhill Winery, and the Maryhill Museum. If you prefer to stay over in the Tri-Cities area, the driving time will be a little more than two hours. Driving time from Tri-Cities to Walla Walla is about an hour and a half. A choice-point will come up at the junction of Highway 14 and I-82 in about 130 miles.*

At that junction, turn north for Tri-Cities. For Walla Walla, jog south on I-82, just over the bridge, and follow U.S. 730 northeast along the river. At the junction with U.S. 12, turn east. In Lowden, you'll find two fine roadside wineries: Walla Walla is only a few minutes farther along.

GOLDENDALE AREA

Syncline Wine Cellars → Maryhill Winery
→ Maryhill Museum of Art

Of the young, vibrant wineries in the Columbia Gorge region, **Syncline Wine Cellars** at 111 Balch Road, Lyle, is producing some splendid wines. Visit www.synclinewine.com or phone (509) 365-4361 for tasting-room hours. James and Poppie Mantone are producing—and gaining wide recognition for—limited quantities of fine Pinot Noir, but Rhône wines are their focus. Of the several Syrahs offered, the Mckinley Springs is deep in both aroma and color. This is an intense Syrah, with complex, well-balanced flavors. Exceptional fruit, yet not too forward. Instead, the berry and citrus are cradled in deeper toasty flavors. Silky and elegant overall. In whites, Syncline's Viognier and Rousanne are outstanding. Voignier can sometimes get out of hand, but James has created a full-mouth wine that retains its manners, with subtle layers of citrus and complementing mineral qualities leading to a long, exceptional finish. Syncline's Rousanne will take you by surprise as it opens to exotic aromas and rich flavors that are like the play of light on water. A fruit-and-nut blend that produces a wine to satisfy the palates of those typically dedicated to red wine. Exceptional in every way. Syncline's Rhône wines are food-friendly and encourage unusual pairings by bringing both grace and accommodation to the table.

Maryhill Winery, a few miles farther east, at 9774 Highway 14, is a showcase for Washington as well as the state's wines. Visit www.maryhillwinery.com or phone (509) 773-1976. Live music welcomes visitors on weekends to this popular wine-trail destination. Outside is a shaded patio and deck, with stunning views of vineyards and the Columbia Gorge. Inside is an impressive tasting bar, plus aisles of wines from which to choose. Cabernets, Merlots, Syrahs, and Sangioveses are popular here, along with rarer Malbecs. Gourmet snacks and gifts have always made this a special tasting room to visit as well. Now, there are bocce ball courts—the game is almost as old as wine—and a permanent stage, plus fine new box seats, for the amphitheater. A new 10,000-square-foot barrel room adds to the experience and tours are by appointment as staffing allows.

A joint venture of Craig and Vicki Leuthold, together with Donald Leuthold and Cherie Brooks, Maryhill follows a guiding principle. I asked Craig about it.

"Our philosophy is to provide top quality wines at affordable prices. We want Maryhill to be seen as a winery producing wines that people can afford to drink on a daily basis."

And Maryhill's wines are excellent. The Columbia Valley Zinfandel is a precocious red with plenty of body and excellent balance. If you are a Zin fan, this is a wine to sip and consider at length. A real standout is Maryhill's Proprietor's Reserve Cabernet Sauvignon. A lush and elegant wine, this Cabernet greets you with no hesitation, yet will grow warmer and more accommodating as it opens. A full-mouth wine, with a long finish, this offering from

Maryhill is both food- and conversation-friendly, with strong aging potential. Buy a bottle (or more), settle in on Maryhill's patio for a Columbia Gorge sunset, and enjoy.

Every wine-and-cuisine trail has its surprises, and just a few minutes east, the **Maryhill Museum of Art** at 35 Maryhill Museum Drive is one of these. Visit www.maryhillmuseum.org or phone (509) 773-3733. This museum has been designed to captivate, and it does. Knowing a bit of the past helps, for Sam Hill was central to the opening of the Columbia River Gorge to farmers and travelers. He was a Mark Twain sort of man, looking for a better way when most of the roads in this country were still held hostage by ruts or mud. Sam Hill was also a renaissance man, traveling the globe, meeting other movers, shakers, and personalities. Loie Fuller, art dancer of the Beaux Arts period and friend of Madame Curie, was close to Sam Hill, as was Queen Marie of Romania. If you know of the *Orient Express* and the Romanovs of Russia, with their royal English relations— or even if you don't—you'll find the displays of nineteenth-century art, culture, and apparel fascinating. The museum was once Sam Hill's unfinished home, and was completed as a museum by Alma Spreckels (yes, the sugar family), another friend of Sam Hill. This place is well worth a visit and, if you wish, a perfect place to picnic, regard the Gorge, and all that brought us to this place, this time.

TRI-CITIES AREA

Hampton Inn → Clover Island Inn → Cabin Suites B&B → Cherry Chalet B&B → Badger Mountain Vineyard and Powers Winery → Bookwalter Winery → Barnard Griffin Winery →

Tagaris Winery and Taverna → Preston Premium Wines →
Country Mercantile → Bin Nº. 20 Wine Bar & Restaurant →
Atomic Ale Brewpub & Eatery → Gloria's La Dolce Vita

Kennewick, Pasco, and Richland comprise a major growth center for Eastern Washington. With more than 150 wineries in the
region, it's a good idea to check in with the Tri-Cities Visitor and
Convention Bureau. Visit www.visittri-cities.com or phone
(509) 735-8486. Graphic-style maps produced by local winegrowers' associations are helpful in locating tasting rooms, but
are not usually drawn to scale. The Three Rivers area map is excellent and will reward you in time saved and traffic avoided.
Request a copy from the Tri-Cities Vistitor and Convention Bureau.

In Richland, **Hampton Inn** at 486 Bradley Boulevard is a
very nice waterfront property on the city's riverfront walk. Use
your browser to call up *Hampton Inn, Richland*. It's faster than
going through the home page, or phone (509) 943-4400. This
inn is focused on touring guests more than commercial traffic.
Service and accommodations are top-rated by travelers, and
they offer a complimentary hot continental breakfast—a buffet,
really—and not the usual donuts and cold cereal. Amenities include laundry facilities, if you've been on the road a few days,
and a fitness room to use while waiting for the dryer to finish up.
If you're a runner or walker, the waterfront walkway leads north
to a lovely park, and south past shorefront condos and a yacht
club. Just the thing for people-watching. Hampton's management also has a sense of humor. The inn acknowledges river
gnats that fly along the shore. A note in each room points out
that the gnats are natural to the area and simply warns: Don't
run with your mouth open. To help remind you, a gnat-shaped

chocolate is thoughtfully provided. It's hard not to enjoy staying in a place like this. A charming restaurant is within walking distance. See the listing on p. 208 for Gloria's.

On an island of its own in Kennewick is **Clover Island Inn** at 435 Clover Island Drive. Visit www.cloverislandinn.com or phone (866) 586-0542. Service and accommodations are very good, with a long list of amenities, and a waterfront resort feel. The Crow's Nest offers dining on the premises. And no doubt about it, the views are striking.

The Tri-Cities area is vibrant, with activities from hydroplane racing on the river to golfing events. So, rooms can fill quickly. And since the cities themselves are relatively new and expanding, few bed-and-breakfasts have been established. Two in Kennewick are Cabin Suites B&B and Cherry Chalet B&B, both with attractive pricing. Close to town and the interchanges that link all three cities is **Cabin Suites B&B** at 115 N. Yelm. Visit www.cabinsuites.com or phone (509) 308-7365. Nicely appointed, this is a comfortable home with three bedrooms and two living rooms available for guests. Complimentary breakfasts are provided with a variety of options. **Cherry Chalet B&B** at 8101 W. Tenth is well out of town on a cherry orchard. Visit www.cherrychalet.com or phone (509) 783-6406. This home, with two guest rooms, is surrounded by waterscapes and well organized for couples or families traveling together. Full kitchen and laundry facilities are just down the hall. Warm-weather breakfasts are a treat on the orchard's edge, near the waterfall.

Just off Exit 109 from I-82, on the edge of Kennewick, is **Badger Mountain Vineyard and Powers Winery** at 1106 S. Jurapa Street. Visit www.badgermtnvineyard.com or phone (509) 627-4986. This is an extraordinary vineyard and winery.

When planting by father and son Bill and Greg Powers began in 1982, the eighty-acre hillside vineyard was surrounded by vacant land. Now an entire residential neighborhood has grown up around it. You might think this could be a source of friction, and with some farming operations it could be. But Badger Mountain began converting to organic viticulture early on. In fact, Badger Mountain was the first vineyard to be certified organic in the state of Washington, and takes deserved pride in its stewardship of the land. Neighbors walk or ride horses along the vineyard roads, and adjoining properties are snapped up at high prices whenever any become available. The vineyard is beautiful to see—and safe. Both Badger Mountain and its affiliated Powers label have been well-recognized by the press, with high ratings. Carrying their organic philosophy even further, the winery adds no sulfites to their wines. See their Web site for a clear discussion of sulfites and labeling. Badger Mountain has also taken a major step in packaging. Their Pure Red Organic Red Wine and Pure White Organic White Wine are packaged in environmentally friendly three-liter containers in which the wine stays fresh for weeks with no preservatives. Don't let the box trouble you. Just recall all those Romans who resisted the idea of corks in bottles. And if you've a yen for even purer organic, taste the Badger Mountain NSA Organic Merlot in the blue bottle. The Powers Cabernet Reserve is striking in its presentation and, with a little time to open up, can surprise you in its smooth, full-mouth presence. An excellent wine, yet moderately priced. But Badger Mountain's Cabernet Merlot can bring you to a pause. This is an outstanding wine. Balanced and complete in every detail, it allows you to slide into the experience of a fine blend.

In Richland, just east of Exit 3 on I-182, are three exceptional wineries located within steps of one another. **Bookwalter Winery** is at 894 Tulip Lane. Visit www.bookwalterwines.com or phone (509) 627-5000. The Bookwalter family is to the soil born, farming in Europe since the eighteenth century. Later generations have been farming in the American West since the 1920s, and producing outstanding white and red wines since the mid-'80s. Today, John Bookwalter represents the tenth American-generation Bookwalter involved in agriculture and by 2000, the winery was capturing gold medals and taking best-of-show awards. *The New York Times* and wine critics were taking notice as well. Bookwalter received top reviews and was designated Winery of the Year. Meanwhile, both the winery and tasting room were evolving. Today, the Bookwalter Wine Lounge features nightly performances from blues to jazz and an excellent bistro-style menu with artisan cheeses and spreads, with gourmet—can there ever be enough?—chocolate. Casual, upholstered chairs as well as table seating make this a comfortable, low-key place for an evening out.

"In a nutshell," John Bookwalter says, "the future is all about these exceptional wines and where they are grown. The next round from us will reflect our efforts on Red Mountain, and will be different but still carry the Bookwalter name."

It's certainly a name and tradition of which to be proud.

Just next door is **Barnard Griffin Winery** at 878 Tulip Lane. Visit www.barnardgriffin.com or phone (509) 627-0266. Rob Griffin was exposed to winemaking at an early age, setting the idea in his mind. After finishing his degree at UC-Davis, he began working as a winemaker in Napa Valley until hired by pioneering Preston Wine Cellars in Pasco. Many vintners focus on vines and terroir, others attend most to processing, a few are taken by an urge to produce a wide range of wines. Rob takes the full measure of each.

"Any favorites?" I asked him.

"I'm most passionate about winemaking," he says with a shrug. "I like to create quality wine and sell it at a good price. When Deborah Barnard and I launched this winery, we were producing fewer than 500 cases a year. Now, we're up to 65,000 cases."

And the winery garners its share of awards: close to fifty in competitions ranging from regional to international. Recently, Barnard Griffin was named Winery of the Year. Yet Barnard Griffin's wines—a dozen or more varietals and blends—are attractively priced.

The Tulip Label Merlot is deep and inviting, well layered, and with enough structure to accept five years or more of aging. Mellow tannins, but more evident than in most Merlots, leading to a fine finish. A top-notch wine, Barnard Griffin's Tulip Label Cabernet Merlot adds a light oak in both aroma and taste to fullness in the fruit. Tannins are well controlled and the finish is long and faithful to each component of the blend. It would be an exceptional wine at twice the price. If sold out at the winery, you might find this in wine outlets throughout Washington. It's well worth the search.

Farther along, **Tagaris Winery and Taverna** is at 844 Tulip Lane. Visit www.tagariswines.com or phone (509) 628-1619 for the winery and (509) 628-0020 for the restaurant. And before all else, let me suggest that there ought to be a saying in the wine business that "The Bottle Stops Here." Tagaris is unique in that respect, for here in the Taverna, wine is served straight from the barrel. Bottled vintages are available for purchase by patrons and wine club members, but these will not exhibit fresh-from-the-barrel flavors—excluding sparkling wines, of course. This is a place where you can experience wine before any bottle shock, recovery, corkage issues, and all the rest. Here, you'll taste what the winemaker and cellar master do. You may sip a vintage almost equal to the current year that is absolutely ready to go. And for those of us accustomed to aging, it can be a little mind-bending.

Except for the furnishings and the marvelous display kitchen, this is the way wine was appreciated in the 1400s—which happens to be when the winery's founding family first began growing grapes in Greece. Today, owner-winemaker Michael Taggares combines the talents of chef Chris Ainsworth and chef de cave Allan Pangborn to produce a first-class experience. Dining areas, public and private, are designed to provide a sense of old-world intimacy, and an upholstered seating area before the fireplace is a perfect place to take a glass of port, an expresso, or mumble over house desserts like the Chocolate Bomb or the Merlot Cheesecake. With someone's hand to hold, it could be heaven. Even without, it's terrific.

Over on the Pasco side of Tri-Cities, **Preston Premium Wines** is just off U.S. 395, about ten minutes north of Exit 14 on I-182 at 502 E. Vineyard Drive. Visit www.prestonwines.com or phone (509) 545-1990. Sometimes it's good to just have a look around, to see the continuity of history. Bill and Joann Preston established the first winery in the Columbia Valley by planting a fifty-acre vineyard in 1972. The nature of viticulture as farming is evident here. Co-owner Cathy Preston-Moncer is my guide through the winery. I asked what her father had in mind.

"Bill Preston had been a farmer for years and he enjoyed good wine. When he realized the potential for a wine industry in Washington, he decided to become a wine-grape farmer, which led to state licensing of Preston as the third winery in Washington State back in 1976. We've been at it ever since. We have 157 acres planted now. It's our thirtieth anniversary. Bill had a guiding philosophy. He believed that everyone should enjoy wine, which meant educating the customer as well as making wine, and not intimidating people. Bill created a self-guided tour with interesting and fun information on wine. When you arrive at the winery, it's clear by the way we're set up. The vineyards are across from the winery, with the crushing equipment below the tasting room for visitors to watch the crush from a bird's-eye view."

As you drive into the winery grounds, you'll find a reminder of how it once was. Adjacent to the lot is a Gulliver-sized piece of steam farm equipment and the quantum leap beyond the horsepower that it represents. Take the stairway up to the tasting-room deck for a view of the vineyards and valley beyond. From there, follow the interior stairs down for the self-guided tour, with stops along the way, each placarded with interesting stuff about winemaking. One of the first overlooks is also a cozy nook for wine and conversation. Just mind your head if you're on the tall side. A low ceiling beam, carpeted against collision, will be right in front of you. Although the tour route now seems perfectly natural—many state-of-the-art wineries today feature overlooks and observation galleries—remember that this was established thirty years ago.

Preston is known for both quality and value. They've won a good share of golds over the years, but they've also been awarded

more than their share of best buys. Since they were first to produce Merlot in Washington, you'd expect that wine to be very
good and it is. Preston's whites range from a fine Chardonnay to
a fun Table Wine under the Long Tail Lizard label. But it's the
Cabernet Sauvignon that draws high praise. If you've been at all
put off by some of the big shotgun Cabs, this is one to curl up
with. Oak is present in aroma and taste as you would expect, but
light in the way it presents. This Cabernet will hold its own with
meats and spicy sauces, yet it is also conversational. Well-
balanced, with enough structure to age well, this Cab is smooth,
with firmly controlled tannins and very attractive pricing. You'll
also be pleased to know that Bill Preston was the first to be selected for induction by the Washington Wine Hall of Fame as a
Legend, a fine grace note for his contributions to wine lovers and
the industry.

Just north of Preston Premium Wines is **Country Mercantile** at 232 Crestloch Road, another legend in these parts. Visit
www.countrymerc.com or phone (509) 545-2192. What began
as a small fruit stand has grown, this way and that, into rooms
filled with produce fresh from the fields next door, gourmet
items of nearly every variety, and homemade ice cream. If it's
pickled, you can probably find it here—along with chocolate
anything—plus gifts and local crafts. It's a popular place with
locals and a great stop for foodies of every kind.

Which brings up thoughts of dinner. On the Pasco side of
Tri-Cities, **Bin N⁰. 20 Wine Bar & Restaurant** at 2525 N.
Twentieth Avenue is in the Red Lion Hotel across from Columbia Basin College. Visit www.bin20.com or phone (509) 544-
3939. It won't hurt to double-check the location on a street
map, since the interchange here can be confusing. The open

dining area off the lobby holds no clue to the restaurant set apart from the hotel scene: Bin N°. 20 is altogether special. Bring yourself, a date, your mate, if you like, but be sure to bring a discerning appetite. From tapas and salads through pastas and entrées, the food is exceptional and well presented. So are the wines—you'll find several favorites here, plus new vintages to sample, in flights if you wish—and the service is both attentive and inconspicuous. Upholstered couches and chairs soften the bistro ambiance. In all, this is a restaurant-lounge that works. If you can get past the quesadilla and artisan toast, go for the polenta strips with tomato chutney or the Thai calamari. The salads really are tossed and not just stirred about. And for a pasta, the capellini with tomatoes, spinach, feta, and fresh basil, tossed in a light garlic white sauce, is a gem. If you've been eyeing platters of elk served in this part of the country, this is a fine place to try it—Bin N°. 20 management has a policy of taking back whatever you don't like. Load up with a big shotgun Cabernet Sauvignon that will stand up to gamy flavors, and you'll be set. Otherwise, the seafood is excellent, along with the chicken dishes. And have you ever wished for a mom's apple pie that novelists write about? I'd begun to believe it was all fiction. But if your server mentions apple-and-caramel pie à la mode, don't hesitate. My, my, Miss American Pie . . .

Okay, we need to shift down a bit here. There's a saying around harvesttime in the vineyards: Good beer makes good wine. If that's so—and who are we to argue with some of the world's top winemakers?—there's a place in Richland. **Atomic Ale Brewpub & Eatery** is at 1015 Lee Boulevard, not far from the Hampton Inn. Ask for directions or phone (509) 946-5465. This pub run by Dave Acton may be even better known for food

than for his handcrafted brews. I'd call it a toss-up. Both are terrific. It's a laid-back and family-style place, with plenty of nonalcoholic choices—this was once an A&W drive-in. As with wine,
it's a good idea to start with a sampler of four or five brews. Discover what calls to you. I love the pale, crisp stuff. You may prefer the dark beers. Either way, it's all brewed on the premises.
Or, if you'd rather stick with wine, Dave has a good list. All the
menu items are made from scratch and there's plenty to choose
from. But it'll be hard to beat the potato soup—no one gets the
recipe, and it's internationally known—or the wood-fired gourmet pizzas. I asked for a sampler model since I'd just had dinner, and devoured the whole thing anyway. They're that good.
Vegetarians don't ride second-class here. The veggie pizzas are
elegant, with a light crust, and garnished as pizza should be.
Dave has a heart for kids, too: red sauce and mozzie with no garlic or other yucky stuff. The place is simply grand.

Gloria's La Dolce Vita at 743 The Parkway is close to the
Hampton Inn as well. Phone (509) 943-7400 for current hours
and seating. Owner, executive chef, baker, and full-time Italian
Gloria Donoso has created a nook—well, double nook because
she's already expanded her place—for diners who want stylish,
nuanced dishes, desserts, and baked goods. Gloria is Sicilian, so
her cuisine would be rustic southern. Think rich, creamy, and
light all at the same time. It's what can come from running a
kitchen your own way. And Gloria does. Her charm and culinary wisdom find their way to each table, no matter what the selection. All this takes dedication. When I was first in graduate
school, my roommate's mom sent Italian food like this back
with him after a weekend at home. I'd never known food like
that before, and feel fortunate to have found the same delicate,
layered tastes here.

LOWDEN AREA

Woodward Canyon Winery → L'Ecole Nº 41

If you're bound for Walla Walla, head south on U.S. 395, which becomes U.S. 12, and continue about 18 miles to the junction with U.S. 730. Turn east, following U.S. 12. Lowden is about 20 miles farther on. It's a slow-down town flanking the highway now, but once known as Frenchtown, settled early by French Canadian trappers. The town's name was changed to Lowden in 1899 to honor the rancher who moved things along in this area, and did not suffer fools gladly. When the Oregon Railway and Navigation Company established a siding here, they misspelled Lowden's name. He took exception to it and let the railroad know that if they couldn't get that much right, the siding would have to go. The sign was repainted forthwith. Lowden is still a farm town, and, with wineries moving in, may reinvent itself.

Woodward Canyon Winery is at 11920 W. Highway 12, on the north side. Visit www.woodwardcanyon.com or phone (509) 525-4129. Watch for the turn into a lot by the winery. The tasting room is in a lovely renovated farmhouse to the east, through a gateway at the end of the walk. Auntie Em might live here instead of Kansas, especially if she knew about the wine. Rick Small and Darcey Fugman-Small established this small winery in the early 1980s and quickly built a reputation for outstanding Cabernet Sauvignon and Merlot. And from its dusky aroma to a full-mouth feeling and luxurious finish, the Walla Walla Valley Cabernet is a delight to drink and pour for others. The wine opens quickly for such a hefty red, with only a touch of Cabernet Franc to help ease it out of the bottle. From first sip to finish, this superb wine can be paired with a wide range of foods and most any conversation. Woodward Canyon Columbia Valley Dry White Riesling is also remarkable. A truly small-lot wine, this is what a Riesling can be, and so rarely is. With lively fruit, plus mineralization not often found south of Washington, this Riesling's forte is subtlety, yet it will dance with seafood, fowl, and Asian spices. Note: it is produced in such small lots and sells out so early that online ordering is recommended when each vintage is released.

Practically next door is **L'Ecole Nº 41** at 41 Lowden School Road. Visit www.lecole.com or phone (509) 525-0940. Turn north on Lower Dry Creek Road and make an immediate left for parking. This period school building, dating from 1915, was part of District 41. Owners Martin and Megan Chubb incorporated that in a name that also memorializes the nineteenth-century French community. The tasting room has so many attractive details that it takes a moment to settle in. A slate surface for jotting your tasting notes, children's artwork, an ornate clock, and a bank stand for sipping away from the bar—it all works together. The tasting-room staff is a delight and the wines are excellent, accumulating high points and new awards with each release.

WALLA WALLA AREA

Inn at Abeja → Green Gables Inn Bed and Breakfast → Dunham Cellars → Seven Hills Winery → Whitehouse-Crawford Restaurant → Spring Valley Vineyard → Basel Cellars Estate Winery → Restaurant 26 Brix

In slumber for nearly fifty years, Walla Walla is just minutes to the east. It developed as an agrarian center in the 1800s and was hot again as an Army Air Force training center during World War II, but as that presence faded, the town returned to its farming roots. Now, as with other areas in the Northwest, the terroir has attracted fine wineries and the area is reshaping itself. Walla Walla is also encouraging storefront and urban wineries, along with top-flight restaurants like 26 Brix. An excellent city-winery map is available from www.wallawalla.org or phone (877) 998-4746.

Inn at Abeja is both a winery and a remarkable inn at 2014 Mill Creek Road. Visit www.abeja.net or phone (509) 526-7400 for reservations. After calling in from the gate, check-in is at the carriage barn straight ahead.

It would be difficult to overstate the charm of this century-old farm, or the care with which it has been restored from the ground up and adapted to new use. As you drive onto this gated property, you'll sense its timelessness. Clark Gable, with his spiffy Lincoln Continental and scruffy jeans, would have fit right in here. Lauren Bacall would, too. So will you. Abeja is one of those rare places to strike a perfect balance. I'd call it casual perfection. However dilapidated the 1903 property might have been when acquired by Ken and Ginger Harrison in 2000, the results of their loving restoration are stunning. It's easier to tear down and build anew, but it takes away from the land and its people. Abeja stands as a keystone in Eastern Washington revival.

Neighboring the Blue Mountains, Inn at Abeja is both charming and uncommon. From the Locust and Carriage House Suites at more than eight hundred square feet with full amenities, to the down-home Bunkhouse—all with kitchens and fridges—accommodations here are top-tier in every regard.

There's plenty of room to swing your arms and have a walk-about, too, down by the creek and across a bridge of hand-laid cobblestones recycled from New York City. Breakfast is served in a well-appointed room by a gracious staff, in what once was the dairy barn. Winery operations are close by; a second-story gallery affords a grand view of all that goes on. It's the passion for extraordinary wine that drives this operation now, under the guidance of winemaker John Abbott and partner Ken Harrison.

"Our wines are produced from estate grapes and fruit sourced from other growers who have a similar passion for quality and the land," John says. "We're fanatics when it comes to combining innovation with traditional methods,"

Production is limited to small quantities of Cabernet Sauvignon, Merlot, Syrah, and Viognier. It is no surprise that these sell out in a hurry. The pale Chardonnay pours lightly, with little of the buttery look and feel of its southern cousins. Aroma and flavors are crisp, with a mineral complement to the fruit. This subtle wine can reshape your notion of Chardonnay. Abeja's Cabernet Sauvignon is a model for Washington reds. Allow it time to relax after uncorking and again in the glass. This is a big wine and needs plenty of oxygen to exhibit its full potential. Deep, dark aromas accented by spice mark this well-balanced Cabernet, and its full-mouth flavors dissolve into a long, exceptional finish. Abeja's Merlot is surprising. So smooth that it seems almost reluctant, the wine soon begins to show greater strength and a very complex character. Tannins are well controlled, though, so it never risks being edgy. Yet there is robustness here, with layered textures uncommon in Merlots. With its memorable finish, this is a wine to keep—if you can.

In town, **Green Gables Inn Bed and Breakfast** at 922 Bonsella Street is within several blocks' walking distance of downtown in a pleasant neighborhood. Visit www.greengablesinn.com or phone (509) 525-5501. Nicely restored, this 1909 Craftsman home makes for an expansive bed-and-breakfast in the traditional style: comfortable rooms, luxury touches, plus electronic amenities. Accommodations are rated tops by travelers. Breakfasts are very good and well presented, with elegant table settings. If you plan to do part of your Walla Walla winetasting on foot, this is a good place to start.

Ready for a little aviation history with your winetasting? **Dunham Cellars** at 150 E. Boeing Avenue, is just off A Street, north of U.S. 12, on airport grounds. Visit www.dunham cellars.com or phone (509) 529-4685. Their winery and tasting room are housed in a huge wooden hangar dating from the mid-1940s. The area is called, with affection, the Wine Ghetto.

Fly Walla Walla

The airport area is a winery hub these days, but the ribs and roof of this place speak of another era. United Airlines began serving Walla Walla in 1937, but the field went big-time as an Army Air Force training center during World War II. The crew of the redoubtable *Memphis Belle* trained here, along with many others. After the war, the government's need for training fields dissolved and a deal was struck with local leaders who saw an industrial park along its sleeping runways.

If only these old hangar walls could speak . . . and they do, in a way, of what has since come to pass. For us, that would be winetasting. And Dunham Cellars wines are outstanding, with annual awards ranging from golds and double platinums, through best of show. Eric and Mike Dunham are very good at what they do. Their Cabernet Sauvignon is light as well as robust, like the hum of a radial engine in the distance. This is a rich, top-notch Cabernet. Very relaxed and approachable, but with excellent aging potential. When swirled, the wine makes nearly perfect Romanesque vaults on the inside of a large Burgundy glass. Balance is impeccable and tannins are bold, but firmly controlled, with oak present, yet quite restrained for a big red. All in all, this is a stunning Cabernet and exemplary of what Washington State can produce. Dunham Cellars Syrah is delicate, yet will leap right out of the bottle for you. Fruit flavors are full, and if you are fairly new to winetasting, this is a Syrah in which you can really taste the chocolate. This spectacular wine will pair well with seafood or white meats, and stand up to spicy dishes as well. Dunham Cellars Trutina is also a delight. Mostly Cabernet Sauvignon, with blendings of Merlot and Cabernet Franc, it would be hard to find a friendlier wine with such sophistication. Bright fruit flavors combine to offer a rich texture blend, with a long, fine finish. In brief: Don't miss these wines from Dunham Cellars. Their Cabernet is exceptional; each wine is marvelous.

In downtown Walla Walla, **Seven Hills Winery** at 212 N. Third Avenue and its companion, the **Whitehouse-Crawford Restaurant** at 55 W. Cherry Street, are located in the same historic building just around the corner from each other—just keep in mind that Third Street is one-way northbound. Visit www.sevenhillswinery.com or phone (509) 529-7198 for the winery and for the restaurant, check in at www.whitehouse crawford.com or (509) 525-2222. Both winery and restaurant are top-tier and further examples of the city's historic assets. The winery is separated from the restaurant by original skylight windows that now form a see-through partition. Diners can watch wine being made and the winery staff can watch diners drinking what they make. There's a definite synergy here—not to mention great food and wine.

The Whitehouse-Crawford structure was built in 1904 by a manufacturer of case goods, and restoring it was a challenge for Seven Hills Winery owner and winemaker, Casey McClellan. Yet there was satisfaction and fulfillment in his voice when I asked about the pitfalls.

"Well, we had to go around with the city to keep the building from being demolished. And there were some other environmental surprises along the way."

Other than how the building seems so well suited to a first-class winery, I asked what pleased Casey the most. He pointed overhead.

"The water tower was a prominent feature of the building. It was in ruin and no longer had any function, but the place didn't look right without it. So we hauled in a huge redwood tank and put it up there. A few twinkly lights for nighttime."

"Do you keep anything in it? Water? Wine . . . ?"

"No, it just holds air. It's our air tower. Looks great, doesn't it?"

It does, and here the building stands in its past and present glory, listed on the National Historic Register.

At the restaurant next door, food-and-wine pairings are of prime importance, with a focus on local farms and Walla Walla Valley wines—a treat when white asparagus is in season. Salads are almost entrées in themselves. Consider the fried duck tenderloin, with new potatoes, sweet onions, and ranch dressing. Or try the warmed polenta terrine with sun-dried tomatoes, olives, mushrooms, Parmesan, and balsamic vinegar. Both are excellent.

Except for occasional single-vineyard releases, Seven Hills wines are blended from several appellations, including the Columbia, Walla Walla Valleys, and Red Mountain. The Riesling is a single varietal, not a blend, yet this wine carries complex aromas and flavors. Well-balanced, it is light but not overly bright, with Washington-style mineralization. Definitely a drink-now wine. Seven Hills Vineyards Cabernet Sauvignon is highly rated and should be. This is a big red, blended to perfection with a touch of Carbenet Franc and Merlot, to bring up depth and complexity without any edginess whatever. You just can't go wrong with Seven Hills.

Just around the corner is the tasting room for **Spring Valley Vineyard** at 7 S. Fourth Street. Visit www.springvalleyvineyard.com or phone (509) 525-1506. There's a frontier quality to the labels, and Spring Valley is proud of its Eastern Washington heritage. Yet the wines are elegant. Try their Uriah Merlot, blended with Cabernet Franc and a bit of Petit Verdot. Full on the palate, it is complex and quite well developed, with fine fruit flavors and a slight smoky quality. Spring Valley's Nina Lee Syrah is just lovely. Not a blend, nor weak-kneed as some Syrahs can be, this is a wine in full blossom. Vigorous yet light, Nina Lee could be paired with all but the most aggressive foods.

Basel Cellars Estate Winery is in the southern part of town at 2901 Old Milton Highway. Visit www.baselcellars.com or phone (509) 522-0200. Plan on visiting this most remarkable estate winery nestled against the Blue Mountains. Its rustic tasting room contrasts with the 22,000-square-foot mansion, which is amazing. Scale and luxury defy comparison, and the grounds and waterscapes are breathtaking, as are the surrounding vineyards. Established in 2001 by Greg and Becky Basel, together with Steve and Jo Marie Hansen, Basel Cellars Estate Winery is this valley's glittering gemstone. Accommodations— pool, spa, cabana, formal and informal kitchens, the works—are reserved for members' use, but it is not difficult to qualify. You'll even receive shipments of wine in the bargain. Check their Web site for details. Basel Cellars and winemaker Trey Busch focus on Bordeaux-style reds, with Sauvignon Blanc and Sémillon also available during summer. The winery limits production to 6,500 cases, however, and their most popular wines sell out soon after release. This resort estate is perfect for celebrations of every kind, as well as reunions with friends and family. It is no surprise that Basel Cellars wins best-destination awards from the travel press.

And the wines are excellent. From its understated label, Basel Cellars Red Wine opens quickly, yet comes on like a full-blooded Cabernet, even though it is a blend of Merlot and Cabernet Franc. Outstanding aroma with spice overtones and a subtle undercurrent of balanced oak and tannins. Rich with a long fruity finish. Basel Cellars Merriment will reward your patience in allowing it to open fully. Another blend of Merlot and Cabernet Sauvignon, with a touch of Cabernet Franc, this wine offers breadth in aroma and widens across the palate. Low-volume production also makes Merriment a good candidate for cellars. The winery's Syrah is superb. With depth in color and aroma, this wine makes it on its own. It is not a blend, and wisely so, for it presents earth and mineral complements to a fruity body that has no edge, yet is intense and full-flavored. This Syrah is lovely just as is. Basel Cellars is that rare combination of splendid surroundings and fine wine. Do make time for a visit.

Walla Walla was for years a steak-and-chops town. No longer. **Restaurant 26 Brix** at 207 W. Main Street is a charming and thoroughly engrossing restaurant in the center of town. Visit www.26brix.com or phone (509) 526-4075. On arrival, you'll find two doors. Go for the one on the left. Working with abandoned space in the Dacres Building, owner and executive chef Mike Davis has worked wonders in creating a restaurant that is a favorite among locals and visitors alike. Half the diners here will know half the other diners here, so with the gorgeous old brick walls and open kitchen, the place can get a little chatty. Still, that's a small price to pay. And on second thought, it may even add to the ambiance. Either way, the food is superb and servers are both attentive and helpful in suggesting food-and-wine pairings.

Mike has been called to the culinary arts since childhood, and it is clear that his heart is in his work. Menus change to reflect seasonal local produce. Our table offered up high praise for the sweet onion soup and the summer corn bisque. The ambrosia salad of Belgian endive, apple, citrus, toasted pine nuts and curdlike mascarpone cheese, with a vanilla vinagrette dressing, was enthusiastically received. Entrées include free-range chicken and lamb, with fine presentations of veal sweetbreads and an Indulgence Plate for seafood fans—a bouillabaisse with Ahi tuna, scallops, and crawfish tails, plus artichoke hearts, in a fennel-saffron broth. For vegetarians, the chanterelle mushroom and herbed risotto, with French herbs, beans and mascarpone cheese, brought raves. This is a don't-miss restaurant for gourmet travelers and is a magnet for farmers and vintners throughout the valley.

BENTON CITY AREA

Terra Blanca Winery and Estate Vineyard → Seth Ryan Winery → Kiona Vineyards and Winery → Tapteil Vineyard → Hightower Cellars

From Walla Walla or Tri-Cities east, you'll be committed to I-82, until the Prosser-Yakima section, and a dodge north to Cave B in Quincy—a beautiful drive in light traffic. Some 15 miles west of Tri-Cities are several excellent vintners.

Exit I-82 and turn north. Turn east onto Highway 224, prior to the bridge, and bear left on 224 as the frontage road continues straight. Turn left for **Terra Blanca Winery and Estate Vineyard** at 34715 N. DeMoss Road and continue a half mile to a right turn up the hill. Visit www.terrablanca.com or phone (509) 588-6082. This winery is one of those magical places that reminds us, just when we think we've seen it all, that we haven't. Owners Keith and ReNae Pilgrim have created an exemplary space in which to sample their wines and their vision for this special place. It is perfectly sited, with gardens and an amphitheater below, and a walkway graced by minimalist arbors. Most winery doors may have seemed little more than that, until you enter this tasting room. The heft and substance of these solid planked doors are large enough to admit a motion-picture crane. Yet they also serve to set the stage for a sweeping two-story tasting room with a thirty-foot bar. Stone facings of slate, marble, and granite are everywhere—Keith was a geologist before becoming a winemaker—but these add to rather than detract from the spaciousness here. The short of it is, from tasting room and special events areas to its amazing wine library, this Red Mountain estate is splendid in its Tuscan styling. One special note: Walk through at least one of the barrel rooms—check on tour times—during your visit. They are remarkable.

Terra Blanca's wines are equal in character to the winery and tasting room. Their Chardonnay is crisp, with light tropical aromas, supported by undertones of oak and spice. And their Syrah is both dusky and balanced with essences of earth, fruit, and spice. It's a robust wine, with firm oaken tones, yet the finish is long and light. The Merlot Estate Reserve deserves special attention. If you've been passing Merlots by, in favor of Pinots or Cabernets, take time to sample this special wine. Velvety, with a robustness about it, Terra Blanca's Merlot presents more than firm tannins to highlight the fruit center, it offers a defined balance. Just a smidge in either direction, and the wine would still be very good. As it is, this Merlot Reserve is outstanding. Fine aromas, with a long, delicate finish. And you can expect it to age well. Terra Blanca's Cabernet Sauvignon is every bit as smooth, yet it has an excitement about it—layered with fruit, chocolate, and spice—the wine presents firm tannins that provide order, from initial aromas to a long, deep finish. Altogether a marvelous wine. A surprise is Terra Blanca's Malbec. Typically used in blends, this varietal is gaining attention. It is more robust than a Merlot and less edgy than the big-red Cabernets—a grand middle choice for pairings with lighter meats and sauces—yet able to stand on its own as a sip-and-chat wine. This Malbec is interesting from the label to the last pour. As with each of Terra Blanca's wines, it is polished and elegant.

Just around a country corner and up the lane are three family-owned boutique wineries. **Seth Ryan Winery** is at 35306 Sunset Road. Visit www.sethryan.com or phone (509) 588-6780. Return to Highway 224 and make a sharp left turn to the east. After Hummingbird Lane, turn north again. Seth Ryan will be on your immediate left. It'll be a change from spaciousness to intimacy as you enter. After that, comparisons will vanish with samplings of excellent wines. Owners are Ron and Jo Brodzinski—Jo is the winemaker—with son Kirk as vineyard manager. Their Chardonnay is a crisp single-varietal, with bright citrus flavors and firmly controlled oak that produce a transparency often missing in a Chardonnay. In reds, consider Jessica's Meritage as an example of how good a blend can be. For Cabernet Sauvignon lovers, Seth Ryan produces a brawny, but not overintense wine, that is well structured and a bit earthy, with light spice notes, and a long, excellent finish. Don't pass these by.

A bit farther up the lane is **Kiona Vineyards and Winery** at 44612 N. Sunset Road. Visit www.kionawine.com or phone (509) 588-6716. If you've been reading winemaker's notes and labels on your travels, you'll recognize Kiona as a vineyard that produces grapes for some of the finest wine blends to be found in the Northwest. Kiona's own wines are no exception. Beginning with a hardscrabble site in 1975, the Williams family had to put in everything from power lines and water wells before planting—all from their faith that the terroir was as good as any in Europe. In 1980, they managed about 500 cases. Now Kiona is shipping more than 25,000 cases and counting. Kiona is found on top wine lists from Washington to New York. Awards have followed. Their wines are both superb and consistent.

Two of Kiona's whites include an Estate Bottled Dry Riesling that would be a best buy anywhere, and Chenin Blanc Ice

Wine. The Riesling is fruity but crisp, with minimal sugars. Very bright, with a languishing finish. The ice wine is a rarity in valley regions, even in the Northwest, and is well turned out, with rich aromas and flavors, but not viscous. Excellent. Kiona's reds are even more impressive. The Estate Bottled Cabernet Sauvignon Reserve aims high and takes the mark. Almost creamy for a Cab, this still maintains a classic structure, with up-front tannins and a richness that covers the whole palate. And Kiona's Estate Bottled Sangiovese Reserve is a wine to write home about to Italy. Robust, without being in the least overbearing, this wine encourages an abundance of food choices that it will complement, from its deep fruit aroma to a very long finish. Sangiovese, when well crafted, deserves a more central place on the U.S. wine stage. Kiona may help place it there.

At the top of Sunset, just as the lane bends west, is **Tapteil Vineyard** at 20206 E. 583 PR NE. Visit www.tapteil.com or phone (509) 588-4460. This is another vineyard name you'll recognize from winemakers' notes and top Northwest labels. A dream ten years in the works, Larry and Jane Pearson wanted to grow super-fine Cabernet Sauvignon grapes, and they have. Their first vines were planted in 1985 and the estate now encompasses twenty-five acres. It is also a small family winery that will grow with its contributions to the industry. Producing about 400 cases at present, Tapteil is the expression of a boutique winery in which each cluster and bottle receive personal as well as professional attention. Biodiversity is the watchword here, and even bottling and labeling are done by hand, when a small army of friends and family drop by to help out. One result is a Cabernet Sauvignon that is at once subtle and spectacular. Don't ask how, just enjoy the way each sip fills the palate. Even the wine's aroma is layered, leading to a complex balance of fruit and tannins. The fine perfumelike fruit center is lustrous and leads to a unique, silky finish. A superb wine in every regard. Don't miss out on this one.

Hightower Cellars is just next door at 19418 E. 583 PR NE. Visit www.hightowercellars.com or phone (509) 588-2867. The tasting room is open most weekends and by appointment. Still, their handcrafted wines are winning such a reputation that this small producer is included along this lane of boutique wineries in the Red Mountain region. Kelly and Tim Hightower are co-winemakers who tend their ten-acre estate vineyard here on Red Mountain. Hightower Cellars also sources fruit from several highly respected vineyards to blend robust red wines that maintain a masculine-feminine balance—a reminder that we haven't mentioned the romance of wine in a while.

Kelly nods. "One night, we were headed for Eastern Washington to check on our grapes and noticed a couple sharing a bottle of wine on their deck. 'Isn't that romantic?' I said to Tim. He smiled and said, 'A bottle of wine is nothing. My love for you is so great, I'm making you two hundred cases.'"

Kelly is right. We tend to forget. But Hightower wines are unforgettable. From their very first release, Tim and Kelly developed a reputation for handcrafting small quantities of unfiltered Cabernet Sauvignons and Merlots, all handpicked and handsorted, with firm but not overbearing tannins. These wines will age nicely and are drinkable now as well. The Merlot is smooth and velvety, with full-mouth flavor that develops quickly after being uncorked. Hightower's Cabernet Sauvignon is both concentrated and full-bodied, yet its fruit qualities and tannins are subtle. Both wines are elegant and a joy to sip and admire. If the Hightowers are not already selling futures, it's likely they will be soon.

ZILLAH AREA

Cherry Wood Bed, Breakfast, and Barn → Maison de Padgett Winery → Silver Lake Winery → Portteus Vineyards and Winery → Windy Point Winery → Sagelands Vineyard → Big John Caudill

If you find yourself feeling rushed along by I-82, there are two other routes to consider between Benton City and Yakima. One is Highway 22, an easy southern run from Exit 82 near Prosser, through Mabton and along the edge of the Yakima Reservation. Another route snakes along I-82, mostly to the north. It's the old road through this part of the country, so there'll be more tourist attractions and peculiar traffic. You can pick up this route at Exit 82 as well. Look for Wine Country Road jogging west and across the Yakima River. Farther along, it resumes its former name: Yakima Valley Highway. Both routes will lead you to Exit 50 for lodging and a Zillah wine loop. A useful map and booklet, *Wine Country,* is available from Wine Yakima Valley. Visit www.wineyakimavalley.org or phone (509) 965-5201. The visitors guide offered by the Yakima Valley Visitors and Convention Bureau is also useful. Stop by their fine new center at 10 N. Eighth Street in Yakima. Visit www.visityakima.com or phone (509) 575-3010 for a copy.

A marvelous—and uncommon—base for fine wineries around Zillah is **Cherry Wood Bed, Breakfast, and Barn** at 3271 Roza Drive. Visit www.cherrywoodbandb.com or phone (509) 829-3500. From Exit 52, drive north on Fifth Street through the intersection with Yakima Valley Highway. Turn right to go east on Gilbert and past Chenye Road, turn left to go north again on Roza. Just before the signed end of the road ahead, turn right and take the next opportunity to the right at the sign marked: TTT Orchards. This is a warm and nurturing place, with opportunities for either conversation or quiet. Cherry Wood is also home to the Chaps and Chardonnay Wine Ride—winetasting on horseback, no less. There's probably no RWI (riding while intoxicated) violation, but the sheriff will be in the lead, so draw your own conclusions. You'll be guided along country lanes to a number of excellent local wineries, with dinner and campfire following. Or chat with innkeeper Pepper Fewel about other ride-and-sip possibilities. A variety of accommodations are available at Cherry Wood. Feeling a little adventuresome? How about a tepee or a classic 1950s Pup trailer? Main house accommodations are tops. Coastal dudes, horse lovers, and vegetarians are all welcome here. Kick your shoes off. Sit a spell and let the road wear off. In a conversation with owners Pepper and Terry Fewel, I asked how this bed-and-breakfast came to be. Terry just smiled. Pepper explained.

"This place is a working orchard and I went out one day to find that a man I'd fired had just been rehired by another man. And I thought, 'Well, that's it. I've been working here in this man's world for most of my life and I'm going to do something where my decisions mean something.' Terry and I talked about it. Cherry Wood is the result."

"Is winetasting on horseback coming along as planned?"

"Better. We now have groups ranging from a few to a whole bunch, next week we have a crowd from Europe joining us. It's great fun and everyone, whether they know horses or not, has a fine time."

A hearty and flexible breakfast is included with an overnight stay. You'll leave refreshed and with a deeper knowledge of how life is lived here.

Close by Cherry Wood are several estate wineries to visit, each colorful in its own way. And another note of caution for the Zillah area: Watch for school zones with 20 m.p.h. limits. These carry double fines on weekdays. That said, let's head for **Maison de Padgett Winery** at 2231 Roza Drive, which is back down the road from Cherry Wood. Visit www.maisonde padgettwinery.com or phone (509) 829-6421. Remember the friendly competition of Sam Sheepdog and Ralph Wolf as a metaphor for winegrowing? Well, labeling is one way of distinguishing wines in the marketplace. And owner David Padgett, formerly of Costco, knows a thing or two about marketing. One result is that Maison de Padgett wines carry startling images as well as attention-getting names such as End of the Road Red, Medusa Muscat, and Singing Toad. The winery itself is striking and produces handcrafted ultrapremium wines. It's a favorite venue for weddings, but individual winetasters are not forgotten. Stop in for a look around the grounds and tasting room, then begin your sampling with a little Risqué Chardonnay.

Silver Lake Winery at Roza Hills is a few minutes east of Maison de Padgett on Highland Drive. Turn north to 1500 Vintage Road. The winery is near the end of the road on the left. Visit www.washingtonwine.com or phone (509) 829-6235. This is a beautiful hilltop tasting room to visit and a fitting recognition of the work of three University of Washington professors and wine lovers who saw the potential in the Rattlesnake Hills. Silver Lake is known for their reds and the Reserve Cabernet Sauvignon has done well in competition. Or, if you're still a little shy about big Washington reds, try the Cabernet-Merlot, with a more round-shouldered taste.

Portteus Vineyards and Winery at 5201 Highland Drive has been winning awards for their wines since the mid-1980s and is recognized by the wine press as a significant producer of Cabernets. Paul Portteus slid into wine from a tour of Bordeaux, Burgundy, and the Rhône Valley aboard a Norton Commando 750—which will have specific meaning for bike fans—and his experience in creating a home brewery aboard his houseboat on Lake Union. All of which led him to purchase the present vineyard in 1980. To their Cabernets, you could add Petite Syrah, Merlot, Zinfandel, and Malbec as well. A Chardonnay is also produced, but this winery's métier is big, smooth reds. With annual sellouts, the winery is being expanded and sons Seth and David will be transitioning into management and winemaking. Visit www.portteus.com or phone (509) 829-6970.

Continuing on Highland Drive, make a left to head west. After a few squiggles, Highland will meet Buena Road at a T-intersection. Turn right and merge onto Yakima Valley Highway. Continue about 5 miles and turn north on W. Parker Heights Road. **Windy Point Winery** is on a ridge less than a half mile farther at 420 Windy Point Drive in Wapato. Visit www.windy pointvineyards.com or phone (509) 877-6824. Mike and Liz Stepniewski built this extraordinary place to frame a magnificent view of the Yakima Valley and make it part of an unforgettable tasting room. With a display kitchen as the centerpiece of such a well-furnished space, it is hard to imagine Windy Point as a boutique winery producing no more than three thousand cases a year. Yet that's how Mike and Liz wish it to remain: warm, inviting, and offering superb wines barreled almost two years. And those wines are award-winners now, drawing attention from the wine press. Windy Point's Merlot holds lovely fruit aromas of deep, dark fruit and the wine exhibits well-balanced tannins and more structure than is usual for a Merlot. Very smooth, with a hint of brightness that keeps it interesting. The Three Points blend of about half Cabernet Sauvignon and Merlot, with a touch of Syrah, carries a full palate of fruit flavors with a light smoky note. Complex structure and firm tannins assure that Three Points will age well. Windy Points Estate Cabernet Franc is just outstanding. Don't dawdle over a purchase, though, the wine is in limited production. This is an elegant wine, full-bodied and rich, creamy almost, with bold, dark fruit and a long, velvety finish—most deserving of your attention. Windy Point is a lovely spot to visit, with superb wines. Make time for this one.

Return to Yakima Valley Highway and turn right to continue west. After about 2 miles the highway becomes Thorp Road. Continue a bit farther and turn north. **Sagelands Vineyard** is at 71 Gangl Road. Visit www.sagelandsvineyard.com or phone (509) 877-2112. Sagelands had a checkered past but is now under solid management and producing very good, affordable wines. The tasting room and grounds are a delight to visit, and the staff is friendly and helpful. Their Merlots and red Cabernets attract the most notice. The Merlot is smooth and well fruited, with a rounded, lingering finish. Sagelands Cabernet Sauvignon is a classic big-red wine, with firm tannins and undertones of spice and smoke. It will stand up to a steak dinner and pour well for conversation. Whether you're traveling west or east, Sagelands makes a good stop.

Here's a gourmet note about a man well known in this area, chef **Big John Caudill,** whom you might otherwise miss. Big John handles special events for some of the top vineyards and wineries in Northwest wine country, and his work is superb in both taste and presentation. If Big John is on the roster somewhere, you'll certainly enjoy his offerings and the light touch he has in pairing food with wine. Visit www .tasting-washington.com or phone (509) 949-7022. Big John crafts excellent cuisine from any standpoint.

YAKIMA AREA

Apple Tree Resort Restaurant → A Touch of Europe Bed & Breakfast → Yakima Cellars

Inns are usually listed first in each section of this book, with restaurants last. This time, however, distance trumps logic and we'll pick them up from east to west. **Apple Tree Resort Restaurant** at 8804 Occidental Avenue is midway between the Zillah winery area and Yakima, in the southeastern exurbs of Yakima. Visit www.appletreeresort.com or phone (509) 966-7140. It's a fine place for lunch or dinner after a round of wine-tasting. And if you have your golf sticks along, Apple Tree—with its signature seventeenth hole on an apple-shaped island—can be a challenging course.

From Exit 34, drive east toward Yakima on Nob Hill Boulevard. At around fifteen minutes, watch for Sixty-fourth Avenue and turn south. After crossing Washington Avenue, turn right on Occidental Avenue and left to the clubhouse. This restaurant offers excellent food, fine service, high-energy ambiance (the nineteenth-hole effect), and panoramic windows overlooking the links and the valley beyond.

Dining is casual here, with no sense of clubbiness, and the menu is filled with both popular and special dishes. Several very good wines are available by the bottle or glass. The Bonair

Chardonnay is excellent, as is the Tefft Merlot. Prices are attractive to moderate. Apple Tree appetizers are very well prepared: onion rings are dry and crispy, the nachos are handcrafted, and the Dungeness crab and artichoke dip in a cream sauce with crostini bread can be habit-forming. Salads are available in half-orders. Just as well, because the entrées are generous, with a wide range of meat dishes and seafood. Either the baked halibut or stuffed salmon will please. The sea scallops, pan-seared with mushrooms in a garlic butter and white-wine reduction are excellent. Pastas are equally good and vegetarians will be taken with the stuffed tortellini adrift in a red sea of artichoke hearts, capers, and mushrooms. The Apple Tree Restaurant is well managed, with neither delays nor any sense of hurry. Enjoy.

Farther west, in the mansion district of Yakima, make **A Touch of Europe Bed & Breakfast** at 220 N. Sixteenth Avenue one of the high points of your winetasting tour. Visit www.winesnw.com/toucheuropeb&b.htm or phone (509) 454-9775. From I-82, take Exit 31 and follow U.S. 12 west. Exit at N. Sixteenth Avenue southbound. After crossing Lincoln, near the hilltop at the end of a rock wall, make a hard right turn into the end of the drive. It's a little like making a short-field landing, so if you miss it as I did, go around at Monroe Avenue, return, and make a left turn into the property.

This graceful inn is surrounded by tree-shaded grounds, and housed in a historic 1889 Victorian mansion. The first floor is appointed with heirlooms and you may dine at a table once owned by the Du Ponts. Even the dining-room windowpanes are original, with the magic of wavy glass from an earlier time. But arresting time is what this marvelous place is about. So much here is at least a century old: furnishings, original fir moldings, lamps converted from gaslights. This inn is what many only aspire to be, yet the price of the air-conditioned accommodations is modest. And owners James and Erika Cenci are masterful at what they do—James, the quintessential host, and Erika, the award-winning European chef and author of *A Touch of Europe Cookbook* (see Connections). Their combined skills are simply astonishing and the inn is drenched in accolades from travel professionals.

Yet this is far more than a bed-and-breakfast. A multicourse candlelit dinner or event may be planned just for you. And it will not only delight, but live on in memory. I hummed-and-yummed my way through grilled portabella mushroom cap topped with goat cheese, accompanied by oven-roasted cauliflower with saffron orzo pasta, and Peruvian purple potato dumplings, while fresh local asparagus and orange bok choy graced the edges of the plate. My dinner companion, even though a dedicated meat person, wondered aloud at the idea of wild boar.

"So, how is it?" I asked.

"Mumph. Wonderful. It tastes like prime rib. . . ."

And that's the way dinner floated along, from appetizers to don't-take-me-yet-lord desserts—goose egg yogurt raisin cake, puff pastry filled with stewed apples. Not to mention the Cascade cloud topped with black currant sauce and Amoretti cream. Wines were perfectly matched to each dish, served by the impeccable James. In her state-of-the-art kitchen—try to seat yourself so you have a view through the door—Erika was in her element.

Morning is filled with more satisfying breakfast morsels. Even an egg over easy becomes a masterpiece in Erika's hands. I've been doing pretty good eggs for years, but this was a revelation.

"How do you do it, Erika?"

"Unsalted butter, the right temperature. All that I learned in culinary school in Berlin."

"They taught you this?" I drew a hand over all that had been set before me.

"No. I learned the beginnings there. All this," she said, "can only come from the heart." And there you have it. If you admire Queen Anne style and value fine food with grand service, A Touch of Europe serves up all three—with heart.

In Yakima, look for **Yakima Cellars** tucked away in the downtown district, at 32 N. Second Street. This is an elegant but easygoing tasting room, with historic charm and a twist.

"We like to greet each visitor, find out where they're from, and what brings them our way," Trisha Franklin says. "I'm proud that our tasting room is elegant but not stuffy, so everyone can relax and enjoy the setting as well as our wines."

Yakima Cellars features a range of regional wines. Three standout offerings begin with their Downtown Red. Take a cue from the name. If you've ever used up a nice Cabernet on meat loaf or tacos, you'll see the need for this wine. It's a fine everyday wine and if you allow a little time after opening, it's just the thing for snacks, American-style cheeses, and refrigerator raids. Yakima Cellars Syrah is a different matter. This wine is robust, with good structure and enough complexity to keep for a while, plus an outstanding finish. But if you sense that I'm saving something here, you're right. It's Coyote Canyon Winery Estate Syrah on fruit from the Horse Heaven region, and it can surprise wine lovers. Big, rounded, and with perfect table manners, this is a stand-alone wine asking little more than quiet appreciation. It is rich, velvety, with full-palate flavors that drift off into a remarkable finish. Don't miss this one. Visit www.yakimacellars.com or phone (509) 469-0621 for hours.

QUINCY AREA

Cave B Winery and Inn at Sagecliffe

If you live in the Northwest, the beauty and reputation of the Gorge Amphitheater will be familiar. It's also a neighbor to **Cave B Winery and Inn at Sagecliffe,** at 344 Silica Road NW. Visit www.caveb.com or phone (509) 785-2283. Take I-82 from Yakima and turn east at the junction with I-90. The route is a sweeping climb up into the high desert—about 60 miles to the Columbia River crossing near Frenchman Hills, with only another 25 miles to Exit 143 and a few minutes on Silica Road to the Cave B entryway. Yet the entire drive seems to last only a few minutes, such is the play of light and shadow across these high-country landforms.

Once reached, you'll find Cave B Inn at Sagecliffe to be one of the most gracious resort wineries to be found anywhere. I know that sounds like a great deal, given the company in this guide. Nevertheless, it's so. Cave B Inn is one of those words-cannot-describe places.

Unexpected, yet once experienced, the overall feeling is that the land, and all who visit, will be the better for what has been created here. Cave B Inn at Sagecliffe seems a form of architectural destiny, like Taliesin West. And that's what its creators, Vince and Carol Bryan, had in mind when they directed architect Tom Kundig to remember that "the land is the client."

For most of us, pulling up to an inn draws our attention to luggage and the rest. Not here. The inn's glass façade—straight through which the gorge can be seen—is compelling, and an attentive valet will take charge of your vehicle. Cave B Inn accommodates cars; it does not cater to them. The panorama of vineyards above and the Gorge below is too sweet to carry the burden of an expanse of blacktop. Each building is sited to complement these stunning views, while curved rooflines reflect the time-blunted hills across the Columbia, and basalt walls on the property appear to be almost natural outcroppings. In short, Sagecliffe is of the land more than it is on the land. And so fine is the whole design, that once seen, it is difficult to imagine this place without these structures.

Such a vision may come in a moment, but its development demands far more time and care. Dr. Vince Bryan, a retired neurosurgeon, together with his wife Carol, acquired this seven-hundred-acre site in 1980 for a winery and a dream.

"We were here largely by ourselves and there were days when the dream seemed obscured. We called this place Mobile Home Vineyards back then," Vince says.

Carol and Vince hold their stewardship of this land with a light touch. Its goals are both physical—horses, golf, hiking—and cultural. One day, guests will be able to engage painters, poets, and scientists in residence at Sagecliffe on a kind of environmental sabbatical.

"People are hungry for this," Carol says, "and for the kind of social inspiration Sagecliffe can offer."

It is a form of magic that the Bryans are talking about, a magic in which all smoke and mirrors are abandoned to allow humans to reconnect with the land and one another.

Dining is already a peak experience at Cave B Inn. At Tendrils Restaurant, just off the two-story lobby, the courses of an evening's meal find harmony in the sunset. Food presentation is exceptional here, without being showy, and the waitstaff is attentive while allowing diners to thoroughly enjoy each serving. Executive chef Fernando Divina's menu is a celebration of aromas, flavors, and textures, regardless of the entrée. Each dish is done to perfection and serves as a reminder that superb food can be healthy as well. From the soup course through a chocolate soufflé, it's an experience not to be missed. Cave B Estate Sémillon Ice Wine put a final shimmer on the meal, with its ripe aromas and flavors of pear, balanced with light oak, and complex textures.

All of which takes us up a slope from the inn to the tasting room and wine cave where winemaker Rusty Figgins works his own special magic.

"We use cane pruning, rather than spur pruning," Rusty explains, "and our Syrah comes from a west-facing slope that is perfect for the fruit."

Perfect is the key word here, for the Cave B Syrah is spectacular. It is not filtered, but egg whites are used to ensure clarity in the bottled wine. The grapes are also handpicked early, which results in the elegant, creamy texture of this Rhônelike Syrah, along with a capacity to age well. Structure is present, yet the tannins embrace the fruit flavors lightly rather than engage them. This Syrah is leggy as well. Give it time to rest after being uncorked and allow it to open further, once in the glass. Your patience will be rewarded. Another stunning wine is the Cuvée du Soleil, a blend of Merlot, Cabernet Sauvignon, and Cabernet Franc in which the Cave B Winery has created an approachable wine structured well enough for a decade or more in the cellar. It is abundant in aromas and flavors, with intense dark fruit and a light earthiness. It is a full-palate blend, but with no hint of edginess. It is simply balanced and secure in itself. Another splendid addition to Cave B wines could be their Sangiovese, a study in boldness refined. Palpable fruit and tannins, but round-shouldered with no gruffness. When released, this wine will pair with both red sauces and unusual spices. Keep watch for it.

WOODINVILLE AREA

Willows Lodge → Barking Frog Restaurant → The Herbfarm → Chateau Ste. Michelle → Columbia Winery → Ross Andrew Winery → Stevens Winery → Mark Ryan Winery → Cuillin Hills Winery → Des Voigne Cellars

Winegrowing and innkeeping in the Pacific Northwest were under way early in the 1800s. So, we'll end our present journey along this West Coast wine trail with a look from that past toward the future—and the idea of wine villages. Woodinville was once the economic hub of a small valley of farms and dairies. That was before Seattle put itself on the map in aerospace and software and the population began pressing north between the Cascade Mountains and Puget Sound.

Still, even before Prohibition, wine was on the collective West Coast mind and soil prospecting was under way. Like California and Oregon, Washington contains major areas of scruffy hillsides, with temperature extremes. No good for the agricultural staples of wheat and vegetables, and not much better for cattle. But a funny thing happened on the thousand-year journey from Tuscany—we learned that grape vines love those rock-scrabble hillsides. Woodinville has since become a gathering place for wineries, community planners, and developers committed to viticulture. The headquarters and wineries of major producers such as Chateau Ste. Michelle were already here.

Extraordinary lodgings and restaurants followed. So a quite natural question arose: What about building on that base and creating a world-class wine village? Mike McClure, who is spearheading the development of wine-related businesses in the southern Woodinville area, believed that concept should be incorporated.

When travelers along the West Coast mention premier inns, **Willows Lodge** at 14580 NE 145th Street in Woodinville brings immediate smiles and nods. Visit www.willowslodge.com or phone (425) 424-3900. Recognized as one of the most desirable getaways, lodge architects made use of salvaged timbers. Its design also gives a nod to the romantic period in which America's great National Park hotels were constructed, yet displays contemporary details that surprise and delight guests. Pacific Northwest arts grace the interior, while fountained gardens border the lodge, just minutes away from two of Washington's best-recognized wineries. The lodge also offers a lovely continental breakfast.

Should you be a little late getting up and about, just walk over to the **Barking Frog Restaurant.** It's right across the entry-drive to Willows Lodge—just step through the hollow tree trunk for the shortest route—and order what you missed, or any of their marvelous breakfasts. And don't overlook the Woodinville Wine Country Package, including personal wine-and-food pairings through several courses. This restaurant is well recognized by the press for its innovative menus and wine lists. For lunch, try the Northwest Kobe beef burger to satisfy a major appetite. Pair it with a big red, like the Sangiovese from Des Voigne Cellars. On the lighter side, try the smoked mozzarella and confit tomato on sourdough, with butternut squash soup, and a Viognier from Cuillin Hills Winery. Make Barking Frog reservations through Willows Lodge by phone.

Right next door is another top-tier restaurant, **The Herb-farm** at 14590 NE 145th Street. Packed with charm, an amazing wine list, and prizewinning menu items, this place can leave you breathless. The Herbfarm Romantic Suites are also available through Willows Lodge—a blessing, since The Herbfarm enjoys four- and five-star ratings. Dinner begins with a tour at four in the afternoon and continues as a unique experience in food theater—even the staff is introduced—through nine courses, with six carefully paired wines. Visit www.theherbfarm.com or phone (425) 485-5300. Reservations well in advance are advised.

Chateau Ste. Michelle, just a minute or two west of Willows Lodge, is at 14111 NE 145th Street and without doubt is a must for wine lovers. Visit www.ste-michelle.com or phone (425) 488-1133. Chateau Ste. Michelle is generally credited with establishing a commercially viable vineyard in 1934 under an earlier name, the National Wine Company. After several mergers, vineyards across Eastern Washington were brought together, and wines were launched under an earlier Ste. Michelle label in the late 1960s. By the mid-'70s, Chateau Ste. Michelle was receiving top awards and reviews at the national level, and the winery was considered not only a top-tier producer, but inspiring as well. In the wake of Ste. Michelle's marketing ability, the Washington wine industry, planting a full ten years after Oregon, literally took off. Today, it is often easier to find Washington wines in top New York restaurants than on the wine lists of their own state.

The Chateau in Woodinville, located on what had been Hollywood Dairy land dating from 1912, was soon listed on the National Register, and opened for tours. As the umbrella company, Ste. Michelle Wines Estates now ships at least four million cases a year, of which one million cases are produced by Chateau Ste. Michelle—whites at the Woodinville facility, and reds at the Canoe Ridge Estates winery on Highway 14, just above the Columbia River. A frequent question is: How do they do it? A more revealing question would be: How can they do it so well?

Keith Love of Chateau Ste. Michelle acknowledges that the company is big. "Regardless of volume," he says, "our overriding emphasis remains on quality."

In fact, more than thirty of the company's wines have made *Wine Spectator*'s annual list of the world's top one hundred wines, which certainly speaks to quality.

In 2006, Ste. Michelle Wine Estates arranged a partnership with Antonini Wines, a world-class Italian winemaker, built a new winery on Red Mountain for part of that joint venture, and acquired Erath Winery in the Willamette Valley. All this has been accomplished with care and integrity, and wines from the Chateau Ste. Michelle family underscore the point.

We haven't spoken much about the moods of wine, yet two whites from Horse Heaven Hills convey special qualities and a connection to life's cycles. The Chardonnay from Canoe Ridge Estate is full and rich and velvety, with complex fruit and structure, while the Sauvignon Blanc from Horse Heaven Vineyard presents much of the same character. But consider, as you sample them, the seasons they suggest. The Chardonnay is filled with petals unfolding in the straw-colored light of spring, while the Sauvignon Blanc speaks of Indian summer: elegant and knowing, with the pale light of autumn yet to come. Drink both on the patio—the Chard when flowers bloom, the Blanc as early leaves signal renewal. Can wine be symphonic as well? Beethoven's "Eroica" is a complex, finely structured celebration, and so is Dr. Loosen's Eroica Riesling. Give it a moment to open and this top-rated wine will reward you with traditional fruit and crispness, with a touch of sweetness, and a lingering finish that calls for Asian dishes or shrimp from the grill. Now to a trio of Columbia Valley red wines from Chateau Ste. Michelle. Canoe Ridge Estate Merlot is an elegant yet expressive wine, with fruit slightly forward and firmly controlled tannins forming a base for background spice and oak—all very structured, yet not at all contrived. The Cabernet Sauvignon from Indian Wells comes from the bottle like an old friend. Tannins are present but not obtrusive in this conversational wine, with well-expressed fruit and a down-to-earthiness that rounds out the palate and a lingering finish. Cold Creek Vineyard Cabernet Sauvignon expresses the balance and concentration and flavors that have come to characterize Washington wines: bold, well mannered, sensuous, and velvety, from aroma through a luxurious finish. The wine opens with ease and should also age well to give pleasure some time from now.

Pioneering **Columbia Winery** is just across from Chateau Ste. Michelle and a short walk from Willows Lodge, at 14030 NE 145th Street. Visit www.columbiawinery.com or phone (425) 488-2776. Whatever else the University of Washington may be up to, individual faculty members have been involved with winemaking from early on. Even as the oenological reputation of UC Davis grew, faculty members at UW [yew-dub to locals] founded a number of outstanding Washington wineries, often with little but intuition, heart, and a garage. Columbia—originally Associated Vintners—is one of those wineries and a leading label in the state. Columbia, under the guidance of winemaker David Lake, was also a leader in bringing such diverse wines as Syrah and Viognier together in fermentation. It takes vision to create and manage such crossovers, and Columbia Winery is known for the quality of wine that follows its vision.

From Columbia, continue east across the river on 145th Street and turn left (north) at the signal onto 140th Place NE / Highway 202. This route will take you from landmark wineries to an area where you'll find the boutique tasting rooms of owner-winemakers who specialize in artisan wines, often in handcrafted lots of 600 or fewer cases per year.

Turn right (east) on 190th and watch for an early turn right (south) onto 142nd Avenue. **Ross Andrew Winery** is at 18512 142nd Avenue NE. Visit www.rossandrewwinery.com or phone (206) 369-3615. Drawing from specific blocks of vines in Red Mountain, Horse Heaven, and Yakima Valley areas, owner-winemaker Ross Andrew Mickel handcrafts high-scoring Cabernet Sauvignon that is, true to its own fashion, breathtaking. Color and aroma are consistently deep, inviting, and textured. Tannins are well controlled, yet the structure is present and well-balanced. Blending, with softer wines such as Merlot and Cabernet Franc, keeps the wine approachable, yet this Cabernet should cellar well for some time.

A few steps away is **Stevens Winery** at 18510 142nd Avenue NE, where Tim and Paige Stevens produce small lots of outstanding wines. Their Yakima Valley Syrah is full and rich, with a strong sense of place, and that same wine-terroir connection is evident in their other wines, which frequently sell out early. Visit www.stevenswinery.com or phone (425) 424-9463.

Continue south, around a loop that becomes 144th Avenue NE and will carry you north to three more exceptional boutique wineries. If Walla Walla was surprised at the success of its airport Wine Ghetto, Woodinville will soon favor its Warehouse Wineries gang.

For a lighthearted tasting experience—and exceptional wines—include **Mark Ryan Winery** at 19501 144th Avenue

NE, F-900. Visit www.markryanwinery.com or phone (206) 910-7967. Owner-winemaker Mark Ryan McNeilly is serious in his commitment to handcrafted wines that draw on flavors carrying the signature of a particular terroir. His high-scoring blend of Cabernet Sauvignon, Merlot, Cabernet Franc, and Petit Verdot is from a Red Mountain vineyard, Ciel du Cheval. Since that translates from the French into Horse Heaven, Mark named his blend Dead Horse—a plum-deep wine, with firm tannins and notable texture. Give this one enough time to open and it will reward you with broad shoulders and fine table manners. Another red blend, Long Haul, comes all the way from the Columbia Valley region. This wine presents bright fruit highlights, with smoky tannins and an elegant finish. If you like big reds, these are both winners.

Cuillin Hills Winery is at 19501 144th Avenue NE, Suite C-200. Visit www.cuillinhills.com or phone (206) 459-2689. From the label—a lone piper in the half-light—it's easy to see the balance between masculinity and romance presented by Cuillin [pronounced kooh-lin] Winery and owner-winemaker Derek Des Voigne. Almost an endangered species, Viognier has found a new following thanks to work by Derek's handcrafted wines—and vineslingers like the Rhône Rangers. Cuillin Viognier is earthy and rich, but takes a different path than Chardonnay or Gewürztraminer. It is relatively dry, yet blossomy, without going overboard. And it holds a rich color and aroma. When done well, as with Cuillin, it will stand up to most light meats and sauces. Derek's Sangiovese is nearly the inverse. With deep color and aroma, this wine is truly a big red with fewer qualities to forgive. It is well-rounded, approachable, and willing to be paired with foods with rich, red sauces to Texas-style meat right off the grill. It's a winner.

It's no accident that **Des Voigne Cellars** is also located at 19501 144th Avenue NE, Suite C-200, for owners-winemakers Darren Des Voigne and Derek Des Voigne are brothers, both devoted to the joys of handcrafted wine. Visit www.desvoigne cellars.com or phone (425) 415-8466. A glance at the Des Voigne Cellars label design further announces the resemblance. Here, the romance is Tuscan with a socially elegant male presence. And that retro-Deco view carries over into Darren's wines. His Merlot is stalwart, yet easygoing and sophisticated. Imagine yourself at dinner by moonlight, overlooking a lovely bay. Wouldn't a fine Merlot be just the thing? Darren's Merlot could be just the wine—easygoing in its aroma and flavors, yet distinctive in structure. It will open quickly, a fine quality in dinner wines, and can grace pairings with most meats and light spices. In short, it can bring flowers to your table.

In **Woodinville,** established properties, as well as the warehouse crowd, are now emerging as part of an overall design. Woodinville intends to become not only a prime destination for travelers west of the Cascade Mountains, but a true wine village, with planned residential areas, shops and boutiques, fine wineries, top restaurants, and inns of international stature.

Mike McClure, a partner in MJR Development, is taking me on a brief tour. He points out a grassy area with soccer fields and a baseball diamond.

"That's part of our theme, being sure to include families and kids. The wine village we're creating is not about wine or shops, it's about community. What I've come to appreciate about wine is that it is a great facilitator. It brings couples together, along with neighborhoods and businesses that become part of a greater mainstream, rather than merely coexisting. One of the newer wineries is owned by a man from France who reminds us that what he wants to accomplish is to bring friends and families back to the dinner table. Here in Woodinville, we think that's a pretty good idea."

The West is filled with towns that are in the process of using wine to reinvent themselves. And most will agree that it's not about the wine or what happens on the taste buds. It's about the companionship upon which any sense of renewal is founded. It's what the Etruscans knew and what they left, with great trust, in our care.

PARTING NOTE

These are difficult times, but what era cannot claim the same? Wine is no antidote, but it can enrich life, love, conversation, and even the simplest meal. It has been my pleasure to have your company on this tour of happy discovery. I wish you many sweet two-lane miles, with encounters of good fortune.

And I leave you with this thought:

> *Wine is the most civilized thing in the world.*
> —Ernest Hemingway

Connections

Books

At Home in the Vineyard: Cultivating a Winery, an Industry, and a Life, Susan Sokol Blosser. Berkeley: University of California Press, 2006. It's not easy to be young and out in front, on the edge of a whole new viticultural movement in Oregon. As the author would likely tell you, though, establishing any vineyard isn't easy, so you might as well be among the leaders. Susan is also one of the first women to head a winery—and raise a family while doing it—in the West. This book is a personal record of what it takes to be a professional success. The book holds much of the exuberance of *The Boys Up North,* yet there is some melancholy here as well, with sober reflections on the responsibility we all share for stewardship of the land.

The Boys Up North: Dick Erath and the Early Oregon Winemakers, Paul Pintarich. Portland, Oregon: The Wyatt Group, 1997. The Willamette Valley has seen two pioneer immigrations: one in the 1800s and another in the 1970s, when the wine pioneers dedicated to wine grapes settled in. To read this unpretentious book is to appreciate the growth—and legacy—of Oregon winemaking.

Decantations: Reflections on Wine, Frank J. Prial, wine critic for *The New York Times.* New York: St. Martin's Griffin, 2002. This delightful collection of stories and commentary is what many publications in the wine world fail to embody. Wine is part of life's celebration, not merely a product to evaluate. Indeed, viticulture is often the antithesis of competition. In this charming and urbane book, you'll find wisdom, history, and humor ready to be uncorked.

The Grail: A Year Ambling & Shambling Through an Oregon Vineyard in Pursuit of the Best Pinot Noir in the Whole Wild World, Brian Doyle and Mary Miller Doyle. Corvallis: Oregon State University Press, 2006. If you've ever wanted to hang out in a vineyard and never found the time or rainy-day muscle to do so, this delightful book is just the thing. Open and joyful in its writing. The author might dislike the idea that this book is a must-have. Nonetheless, it is.

The Merlot Murders: A Wine Country Mystery, Ellen Crosby. New York: Scribner, 2006. When solitude strikes, few things pair better with a just-for-me wine than a comfy chair before the fire and a good mystery. Whether your reading palate runs to tea cozies or gothic mayhem, this book is a treasure. Ellen is an established journalist, and her experience infuses the story's fabric with a rare and subtle credibility. Characters are well wrought, as is the plot, and with action taking place in a Virginia vineyard, there are winemaking tidbits on nearly every page. Altogether a well-told tale. Also, watch for *The Chardonnay Charade,* second in her series.

The Northwest Wine Guide: A Buyer's Handbook, Andy Perdue. Seattle: Sasquatch Books, 2003. A handy guide to wines in Washington, Oregon, British Columbia, and Idaho, with brief notations on each winery covered, together with wine-buying tips. Several newer wineries are not included. Look for a later release, if available. Otherwise, pick up this edition.

Red, White, and Drunk All Over, Natalie MacLean. New York: Bloomsbury USA, 2006. This is a book to remind us that maternal terroir, bottled captivity, and eventual freedom become part of us when we drink wine. Few writers speak to the song our senses sing in harmony with a wine's melodic strain as does Natalie. The perfumed scent of a wine may suggest to her the feeling of slithering into that little black dress, while its aroma of leather reminds me of my time-worn flight jacket. It's different, yet the same. The author understands that part of wine's magic is its capacity to mirror past and present pleasures—in a single glass.

The Simple & Savvy Wine Guide: Buying, Pairing, and Sharing for All, Leslie Sbrocco. New York: HarperCollins/William Morrow, 2006. So you're getting into wine and are eager to know: What wine should I choose for the Chinese takeout I'm having tonight? Leslie can tell you. Or you're out on the town and have decided on sharing a Kobe steak. Probably a red wine, right? But which one will stand up to the entrée and not overpower the caramelized onions? Trust the author and things will work out. This gem of a book puts some fun back into selecting and enjoying wine, and even includes a guide to bathtub wines for day's end.

The New Sotheby's Wine Encyclopedia, Fourth Edition, Tom Stevenson. London and New York: Penguin Group/Dorling Kindersley, 2005. Sometimes knowledge really does come by the pound. Stevenson's reference work weighs in at more than six hundred pages and covers virtually every aspect of wine appreciation, growing, and serving. The book encompasses viticulture worldwide, with lavish illustrations—including images of French châteaux that will awaken your wanderlust. Stevenson's book is reader-friendly as well. A wondrous personal resource— and a terrific gift for either novice or experienced wine enthusiasts.

Timberline Lodge Cookbook, Leif Eric Benson. Portland, Oregon: Graphic Arts Center Publishing Company, 1991. Whether you're searching for dinner or inspiration, this book is marvelous to take from the shelf and thumb through. Recipes are often uncomplicated, though the end result seen on these pages is the work of a master chef and a photographer who really knows lighting. Altogether, a beautiful book to regard.

A Touch of Europe Cookbook, Erika G. Cenci. Victoria, British Columbia: Trafford Publishing, 2005. A collaboration between chef Erika and book-designer husband James, this book is filled with sensible ideas we never knew or have long since forgotten. Wisdom, as well as European-style recipes, turns up on nearly every page. For those who have lived too long from the freezer bin, Erika's gentle but quick-witted advice arrives as a blessing. Keep it handy.

DVDs

Mondovino (Diaphana Films, 2004) is a documentary from award-winning director Jonathan Nossiter. This film highlights worldwide forces and major wine players as these affect smaller estate wineries; it can be an eye-opener. The director wisely lets personalities speak for themselves on camera. At first, the handheld camera techniques can be bothersome, but the overall story makes up for it. Consider viewing the bonus feature beforehand for a clearer grounding during the film.

Rick Steves' Europe is an outstanding public television series featuring European wines and cuisine as part of travel to extraordinary destinations. Rick walks viewers through old-vine estates where wine grapes have been grown for 2,500 years, visits Etruscan wine caves still in use, and shares classic Italian dishes and wine with innkeepers, vintners, and their families. Episodes on "Siena and Assisi: Italy's Grand Hill Towns," "Tuscany's Dolce Vita," and "Italy's Great Hill Towns" offer a fascinating look at wine regions where traces of the Etruscan period blend into the rural Italy of today—with a visceral connection to the coastal valleys of America's West Coast. Rick's crew maintains high production values and the writing is both clever and charming. Visit www.ricksteves.com and select the Travel DVDs tab or check Rick's television schedule. If you are not already in love with Italy, these shows could do the trick.

Magazines

Touring and Tasting is first-class. With outstanding photography and layout, this publication will help keep you up-to-date and salivating over your next visit to wine country. Articles range from wine touring to cuisine and collecting. Primary focus is on Central and Northern California. Published semiannually by Vantage Communications, Santa Barbara, California. Visit www.touringandtasting.com or phone (800) 850-4370.

Wine Press Northwest covers wine country throughout the Pacific Northwest (including British Columbia and Idaho), and is both professional and charming in reviews of wine, events, and the industry at large. Articles are straightforward and well illustrated. After spending time in Oregon and Washington, you'll find many acquaintances represented in these pages. Top-notch Web site as well. Published quarterly in Tri-Cities, Washington. Visit www.winepressnw.com or phone (800) 538-5619.